MAKING
CABINETS
& BUILT-INS
Techniques & Plans

MAKING
CABINETS
& BUILT-INS
Techniques & Plans

By Sam Allen

Sterling Publishing Co., Inc.   New York

ACKNOWLEDGMENTS

I would like to thank my wife, Virginia, for her help in preparing this book. Without her help and encouragement, this book would not have been possible. I also want to thank my mother, Betty Allen, for her help in preparing the manuscript and some of the photos used in the book. My brother, John Allen, has always encouraged me, and I want to thank him also.

This book is based largely on practical experience I have gained during 20 years of woodworking, so I would like to thank the experienced cabinetmakers with whom I have worked for generously sharing their knowledge with me.

Edited by Laurel Ornitz

Library of Congress Cataloging in Publication Data

Allen, Sam.
  Making cabinets & built-ins.

  Includes index.
    1. Cabinet-work—Amateurs' manuals. 2. Built-in
  furniture—Amateurs' manuals. I. Title. II. Title:
  Making cabinets and built-ins.
  TT197.A45   1986   684.1'6   86-5997
  ISBN 0-8069-6330-1 (pbk.)

Copyright © 1986 by Sterling Publishing Co., Inc.
Two Park Avenue, New York, N.Y. 10016
Distributed in Canada by Oak Tree Press Ltd.
% Canadian Manda Group, P.O. Box 920, Station U
Toronto, Ontario, Canada M8Z 5P9
Distributed in the United Kingdom by Blandford Press
Link House, West Street, Poole, Dorset BH15 1LL, England
Distributed in Australia by Capricorn Ltd.
P.O. Box 665, Lane Cove, NSW 2066
Manufactured in the United States of America
All rights reserved

CONTENTS

INTRODUCTION

This book is designed to lead you step by step through the fundamentals of making cabinets and built-ins. Beginning with selecting materials, reading plans, and laying out the cuts on the wood, the book progresses through joinery and assembly techniques, plus all the other basic components of cabinetmaking to a complete set of plans and directions for an entire system of cabinets. Then, in a separate Appendix, you'll find a built-in planner, which will help you visualize the completed installation and give you the chance to try various layouts on paper.

The term "cabinetmaking" is sometimes used in reference to making all kinds of fine furniture; but in this book, it is used in its strictest sense. It simply means making cabinets, both freestanding and built-in.

Recent technology has added many new materials and techniques to the craft of cabinetmaking. Although commercial cabinetmakers use these new products extensively, traditional materials and practices are still important to today's cabinetmaker. This book will give you a firm foundation in traditional methods, as well as introduce you to some of the most recent technological developments in the field.

Tools

Some people have the impression that you must invest a large amount of money into tools before you can build cabinets, but this is not true. With a few basic tools, you can build all but the most complex cabinets; however, additional tools, especially power equipment, will make the job faster, and less physical labor will be involved.

Here is a bare-minimum list of tools to get you started in cabinet-making:

One 12′ tape measure with ¾″ blade
One combination square
One 16 oz. finishing hammer
One set of screwdrivers
One 26″ 10-point crosscut-panel saw
One set of butt chisels (¼″, ½″, ¾″, 1″)

One set of twist drills (¹⁄₁₆″–¼″)
One set of spade bits (⁵⁄₁₆″–1″)
One ¼″-chuck electric drill
One block plane
One jack plane
One sharpening stone
One four-in-hand file
Two 4″ C-clamps
Three 4′ bar clamps

You can do most of the procedures described in this book with this basic set of tools.

ADDITIONAL EQUIPMENT

Once you have a basic set of tools, there are a few portable power tools that you may want to consider for your next purchase. The first is a router. This tool makes joinery much easier and allows you to create decorative edges for doors and drawer fronts. It is also very useful when you are working with plastic laminates. You may also want to consider a portable circular saw, which makes cutting out the parts easier, especially when you're working with 4′ × 8′ sheets. If you are making cabinets with a lot of curved cuts, a saber saw can be a very useful tool.

When you are ready to make some larger investments in tools, consider some stationary power equipment. Probably the first piece of stationary power equipment you should buy is a table saw or a radial-arm saw. A jointer should probably be your next large investment. After you have those two pieces of equipment, the rest depends on the type of work you are doing. A bandsaw is useful for making curved cuts. A lathe will enable you to make legs, spindles, and other turnings. With a shaper you can make decorative edges on doors and drawer fronts faster than if you made them with a router. You may want to consider one of the multipurpose machines, but keep in mind that these large pieces of equipment are not essential for you to get started in cabinetmaking. You can accomplish a great deal with the basic set of tools, so don't let the high cost of extra equipment keep you from enjoying the craft of cabinetmaking.

Safety

It is absolutely crucial that you keep your tools sharp and in good working order. A dull tool makes you exert too much force for maintaining good control. When you work with a chisel, clamp the work down and keep your hands behind the blade. Wear eye protection whenever you are doing any operation that sends dust or chips flying. When you are using power equipment, don't wear loose clothing, such as a necktie or a shirt with floppy sleeves, and remove jewelry, such as necklaces and rings. If you have long hair, tie it back when you work. You don't want your clothing, jewelry, or hair to get caught in a piece of equipment.

Always keep your fingers well clear of the cutting part of any piece of power equipment. Use push sticks when necessary. Use the guards provided with power equipment. *If you keep safety in mind while you work, your enjoyment of cabinetmaking won't be marred by an accident.*

1
MATERIALS

Wood is the basic material of the cabinetmaker. There are many varieties of wood and several man-made wood composite products that are used in cabinetmaking. Before you begin building cabinets and built-ins, you should have a basic understanding of these materials so that you can buy your materials intelligently and use them correctly.

Wood Properties

The dry, cut, and surfaced boards you buy at the lumberyard began as part of a living tree (Illus. 1). The way that trees grow and the arrangement of their cells give wood its unique properties.

Tree cells are long, thin cylinders; some may be 100 times longer than they are wide (Illus. 2). Ninety percent of these cells run vertically in the standing tree; they are called longitudinal cells. It is the direction, density, and structure of these cells that give wood most of the properties that affect cabinetmaking. In addition to the longitudinal cells, all woods have horizontal cells, called ray cells. They radiate from just below the bark towards the middle of the tree. In most wood species, these cells are so small that they are not noticed. However, oak and a few other types of wood have very prominent ray cells. Ray cells can affect the way wood shrinks as it dries. The effect this has on cabinetmaking will be discussed later in more detail.

As it grows, a tree adds an additional layer of cells around the outside of the trunk in a layer just below the bark called the cam-

Illus. 1. Tree rings appear as parallel lines in the section of the trunk that has been cut lengthwise. Where the trunk has been cut crosswise, the rings show their true circular outline. The thin dark line between the outer bark and the inner wood is called the cambium; it is the area where all growth occurs. The small removed block shows the size of the enlarged sections in Illus. 2.

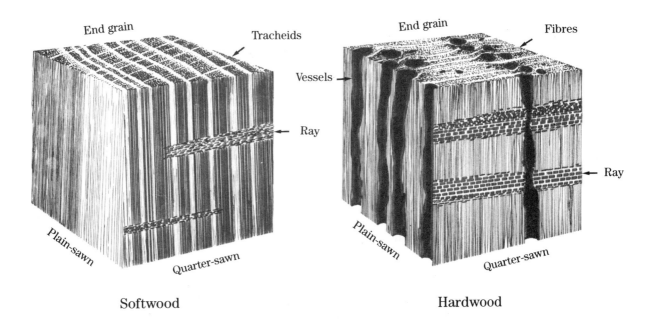

Illus. 2. These enlarged cubes of wood show how the cell structure varies between softwood and hardwood. Notice that softwood is fairly uniform in its structure, whereas hardwood contains specialized vessel and fibre cells.

bium. This process adds both height and width to the tree. Periods of rapid growth in the spring create cells that are larger and less dense than the cells produced during the slower growth of the summer. The wood produced in the spring is called earlywood, and the wood produced in the summer is called latewood. Together these two layers produce one annual ring. The annual rings are very important to the cabinetmaker because they produce the grain pattern that gives wood its character and affects how well the wood can be worked.

Most of the living processes take place in a narrow band around the outside of the tree. This area is composed of the last few annual rings and is called the sapwood. The older wood in the middle of the tree is called the heartwood. The heartwood no longer conducts sap to various parts of the tree as the sapwood does; it is inactive and essentially dead. A variety of materials, collectively called extractives, collect in the heartwood. These extractives vary from one species to another, and they give the heartwood properties that are different from the sapwood. In some species, such as walnut, the extractives contain pigments that give the heartwood a darker color than the sapwood. In species such as redwood, they contain natural preservatives and toxins that make the heartwood resistant to fungus, decay, and insect damage. Resinous extractives in the heartwood make it more durable than the sapwood in some species.

SOFTWOODS AND HARDWOODS

There are two major classifications of wood: softwood and hardwood (Illus. 3 and 4). These classifications do not actually refer to the hardness of the wood; rather, they refer to the wood's cell structure.

Softwoods come from trees that bear needles, such as pines and firs. The cell structure of softwoods is very uniform; almost all of the wood is made from a single type of cell, called a tracheid (Illus. 2). Tracheids are hollow cells that are filled with fluids while the tree is alive. When the tree is cut, the fluids evaporate, leaving the hollow outer shell of the cell.

In some species of softwood, there is little difference between the tracheids in the earlywood and those in the latewood. These species are highly prized for their easy-working qualities. A few such species are eastern white pine, western white pine, and sugar pine.

In other softwood species, the earlywood tracheids are thin-walled and the latewood tracheids are thick-walled. The resulting

 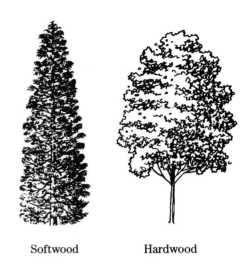

Softwood   Hardwood

Illus. 3 (left). Trees with needles are classified as softwoods and trees with broad leaves are classified as hardwoods. Illus. 4 (right). Softwoods usually have a large central trunk that extends their entire height; small branches are arranged radially around the trunk. This structure makes them ideal for producing the large boards necessary for building construction. Hardwoods have a trunk that may branch off in several directions as the tree grows.

wood tends to have an uneven grain. Uneven-grained woods are usually stronger than even-grained woods, but they are more difficult to shape and have a greater tendency to split when nailed. Two examples of uneven-grained woods are Douglas fir and southern yellow pine.

Hardwoods come from trees that have broad leaves. Their cell structure is more complex than that of softwoods. Instead of a single predominant type of cell, the hardwoods have several specialized cells that perform different functions (Illus. 2). The strength of a hardwood comes from its thick-walled cells, called fibres. They have practically no interior cavity and do not help the tree conduct fluids from one part to another. The other main type of cell in a hardwood is the vessel cell. Vessel cells perform the fluid-transfer function necessary for the tree to maintain itself. These cells are large, thin-walled, and hollow.

When boards are cut from a tree, some of the vessel cells are sliced through. These openings in the surface of the board are known as pores. Some species, such as oak, have very prominent pores. These species are called open-grained woods. Species, such as maple, that have small, less noticeable pores are called closed-grain woods.

Hardwoods are also classified as either ring porous or diffuse porous. In ring-porous woods—such as oak, ash, and elm—most of the vessel cells are concentrated in the earlywood. This gives these woods a distinctive grain pattern, but it also tends to make them uneven grained and therefore more difficult to work. Diffuse-porous woods—such as birch, alder, and basswood—have their vessel cells distributed evenly throughout the annual ring. They are very even grained and easy to work. Some woods—black walnut, for example—fall between these two classifications. They are called semiring porous. In these woods, the earlywood has large pores that gradually diminish in size as they reach the latewood (Illus. 5).

Illus. 5. Hardwoods are divided into three smaller classifications according to the arrangement of their vessel cells. The birch, on the left, is an example of a diffuse-porous wood. The vessel cells are evenly distributed throughout the wood and are not very discernible. The walnut, in the middle, is an example of semiring-porous wood. The vessel cells are more prominent in the earlywood, and diminish in size throughout the latewood. The oak, on the right, is an example of a ring-porous wood. The very prominent vessel cells are concentrated in the earlywood part of the ring.

DENSITY

The actual measure of a wood's hardness is its density. Wood density is measured by specific gravity, which is the ratio of the weight of a substance to the weight of an equal volume of another substance—

that of water. Specific gravity numbers of less than one indicate that a material will float in water. The harder the wood, the higher its specific gravity.

You can see by looking at Illus. 6 that the terms "hardwood" and "softwood" are misleading. The least dense wood on the table is balsa, and balsa is a hardwood. Southern yellow pine, which is a softwood, is almost as dense as black walnut, which is a hardwood, and considerably denser than several other hardwoods, such as basswood, cottonwood, and alder.

Most of the popular cabinet woods have specific gravities of between 0.4 and 0.7. Wood in this density range is hard enough to withstand physical abuse, yet soft enough to be worked with ordinary tools.

Wood with a specific gravity of 0.5 to 0.6 is ideal for cabinet-making. Black walnut, black cherry, and mahogany fall into this range. Although softer woods, such as pine, dent too easily to be used for desks or table tops, they are frequently used for cabinets where denting isn't a problem. Harder woods, such as oak and maple, are used for cabinets that will receive a lot of abuse.

MOISTURE CONTENT

Green wood freshly cut from a tree is almost 30 percent water. As this water evaporates, the wood shrinks. Because of variations in cell structure, some parts of the wood shrink more than others. This sets up internal stresses that cause boards to twist, warp, and split. Before using a board, you want it to be dimensionally stable. A dimensionally stable board has a moisture content of about 6 to 9 percent.

Moisture is removed from lumber in two ways: by air drying or kiln drying. Air drying relies solely on natural evaporation. The wood is stacked so that air can circulate freely around it. This process can take up to several years and usually won't lower the moisture content below 12 percent. Most cabinet-grade lumber is kiln dried. With kiln drying, large ovens bake out the moisture. Kiln-dried lumber has a moisture content of 6 to 9 percent.

Even kiln-dried lumber shrinks or swells slightly with changes in humidity. Usually woods with higher specific gravities shrink and swell more than the less-dense woods. If you don't account for this shrinking and swelling when you build a cabinet from solid lumber, cracks and loose joints will result.

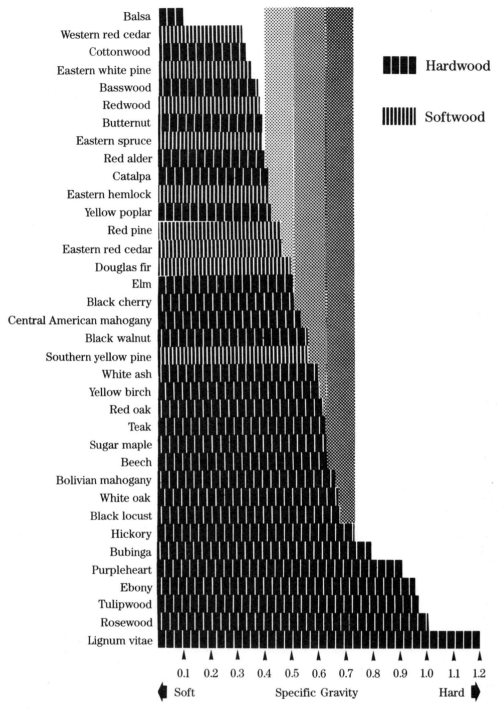

Illus. 6. Specific gravity is a measure of wood density. Density affects the working properties and wearing qualities of the wood. In this chart, any wood represented by a band that touches a grey area is considered a cabinet wood. The medium-grey area represents those woods that combine good-working properties with good-wearing properties. The light-grey band represents woods that are very easy to work, but may not be hard enough to withstand heavy use. The darkest grey band represents woods that are a little more difficult to work, but will withstand heavy wear. Woods outside of the grey area can be used in cabinetmaking; however, they are not considered primarily cabinet woods.

The problem of wood movement is exaggerated by modern central heating. An antique that has survived for hundreds of years in a drafty old house may crack and loosen when moved to a centrally heated, modern setting. For this reason, it may be necessary to modify the design of an antique reproduction to allow for wood movement. For example, some Shaker furniture isn't designed to allow for much wood movement since the humidity was fairly constant in the old Shaker buildings. If you follow an old Shaker design exactly, you may have problems with the piece in a modern building. Solutions to this problem are covered in Chapters 4 and 6.

KNOTS

A knot is actually the joint between the main trunk of a tree and its limb. A tight knot forms at the base of the limb, where its fluid channels connect to the fluid network of the tree. A tight knot in a board will not fall out since it is firmly attached to the surrounding wood. This type of knot presents some problems in working with the wood because the growth pattern changes abruptly around the knot, making operations such as planing and surfacing more difficult.

As long as the branch is alive, new connections will be made to the fluid channels and the knot will remain tight. However, if the limb dies due to damage or lack of light, a loose knot will form as the tree increases in diameter past the point where the limb is attached. The trunk will grow around the limb, but the wood of the limb will be separated from the wood of the trunk by the limb's bark. This will produce a knot that will eventually fall out of a cut board, leaving a hole.

On selected trees in commercially managed forests, all side branches are removed from the first 16 feet of the trunk. This pruned section produces clear lumber with no knots. The added labor of pruning accounts in part for the higher price of clear lumber.

How Wood Is Cut

The way wood is cut into boards can affect the grain pattern and the dimensional stability of the board. The basic grain pattern of a log is a set of concentric rings. Cutting through these rings at various angles produces a variety of grain patterns. Solid lumber is cut in basically two ways: plain sawn and quarter sawn (Illus. 7).

Cabinetmakers use two words—grain and figure—to describe what most people simply refer to as grain. To a cabinetmaker, grain

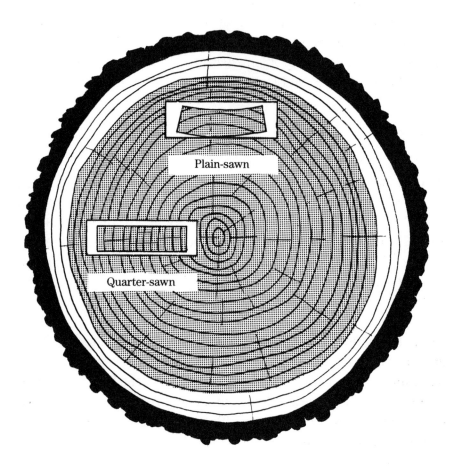

Plain-sawn

Quarter-sawn

Illus. 7. Plain-sawn lumber is cut so that the faces of the board are tangent to the rings. This produces a pleasing figure on the face, but boards cut this way are more apt to cup and change dimension across their width. Quarter-sawn lumber is cut so that the face forms a 90° angle with the rings. The figure of most quarter-sawn wood is a series of parallel lines unless the wood has prominent medullary rays, in which case the most distinguishing characteristic will be wild ray marks. Quarter-sawn wood is more dimensionally stable than plain-sawn wood; its width does not vary as much with moisture change and it has less tendency to cup.

refers to the direction of the tracheid or fibre cells in the wood. The way the board is cut creates a grain direction in the board. The fibres may intersect the surface at an angle, as shown in Illus. 8. Figure is the design created by cutting through the concentric rings at an angle. In practice, grain and figure are frequently interchanged and, in casual conversation, many cabinetmakers refer to both properties as grain. However, when clarity is essential, cabinetmakers will distinguish between the two words.

Plain-sawn boards are cut from the log with the saw blade tangent to the annual rings. With this method, the blade cuts through relatively few rings and the board contains a larger segment of each ring than quarter-sawn lumber. The plain-sawn method produces a

Illus. 8. Grain direction is important when using tools such as chisels or planes. The chisel, on the left, is cutting with the grain. Notice how the chip tends to break off above the cutting line, leaving a smooth, even cut. The chisel, on the right, is cutting against the grain. The wood tends to tear ahead of the chisel, causing chipping, gouges, tear-outs, and a rough cut.

figure pattern on the surface of the board that consists of parabolas (U- or V-shapes) and ellipses (ovals). When softwoods are cut in this manner, they are usually called flat-sawn boards or flat-grained boards.

Quarter-sawn lumber is cut so that the saw blade passes at a right angle to the rings. This means that many rings are cut through, but the board contains only a small segment of each ring. The face of the board shows only the edge of the rings, so the figure is a series of closely spaced parallel lines. Woods, such as oak, that have large ray cells produce an interesting effect when they are quarter sawn.

Since the ray cells run at right angles to the rings, the saw blade may slice through them lengthwise. This produces interesting, irregularly shaped marks on the surface of the board. Softwoods cut this way are frequently referred to as edge grained or vertical grained.

In practice, many boards are cut at angles ranging between tangent to the rings and 90° to the rings. For the purpose of classification then, an arbitrary division has been set at 45°. A board that has been cut so that its rings form an angle that's between 45° and 90° with its surface is called quarter sawn, whereas a board with rings that form an angle of less than 45° is called plain sawn. A board that falls in the midrange at about 45° exhibits characteristics of both types of cutting.

When wood is tangent to the rings, it shrinks and swells about twice as much as it does when it's perpendicular to the rings. This means that in a plain-sawn board, most of the shrinkage and swelling takes place across its width; whereas in a quarter-sawn board, most of the dimensional change takes place across its thickness. Since the width of a board is greater than its thickness, any change in width will be more critical than a change in thickness. For this reason, quarter-sawn boards are considered more dimensionally stable than plain-sawed boards. Plain-sawn lumber has a tendency to cup in the direction shown in Illus. 7, whereas quarter-sawn lumber usually remains flat as it dries.

When uneven-grained wood, such as fir, is plain sawn, it is difficult to get a truly flat surface because the softer sections of the grain tend to wear down faster during sanding operations. It is easier to get a flat surface on quarter-sawn lumber because the soft sections of the wood are less exposed.

Because of its greater stability, quarter-sawn lumber has been the cabinetmaker's choice for hundreds of years; recently, however, tastes have changed, and the figure of plain-sawn lumber has become more popular. The choice then boils down to a trade-off between figure and dimensional stability. Each project is different, so you should make your choice based on the function of the cabinet and the way you want it to look.

Lumber Grades

There are two grading systems for lumber, one for hardwoods and one for softwoods.

HARDWOOD GRADES

There are five grades of hardwood in the system used by the National Hardwood Lumber Association. The grading system is based on a principle called clear-face cuttings. Illus. 9 demonstrates this concept. There is also a minimum size for each grade (see Illus. 10).

First and Seconds (FAS) This is the highest grade. These boards are almost completely free from knots or defects. They are 6″ or wider and 8′ or longer. The boards yield 83⅓ percent clear-face cuttings that are 4″ or wider by 5′ or longer, or 3″ or wider by 7′ or longer.

Selects This grade has one side that is equal to FAS and one side that is No. 1 common. This grade is useful when you only need one good side. The boards are 4″ and wider by 6′ and longer. They yield 83⅓ percent clear-face cuttings.

No. 1 Common (Thrift) This grade is more economical for small projects when long, wide boards aren't necessary and you can cut parts from clear sections between defects. The boards are 3″ or wider by 4′ or longer. They yield 66⅔ percent clear-face cuttings that are 4″ or wider by 2′ or longer, or 3″ or wider by 3′ or longer.

Two additional grades are also available, but they are usually not used in cabinetmaking; they are No. 2 common and No. 3 common.

SOFTWOOD GRADES

The Western Wood Products Association has designated six grades of softwood.

C Select and Better This is the best grade; it has only minor imperfections. It can be very expensive.

D Select This is still a very high quality grade. It will contain a few sound defects.

3rd Clear This is the grade most suited to general cabinetmaking. It is priced lower than the first two grades, but still allows for a large percentage of clear cuts.

No. 1 Shop This grade has more knots and defects than 3rd clear, but it is still useful for making the smaller cabinets since you can cut around the defects.

No. 2   This is also called shelving grade. It has quite a few knots and it is only useful for cabinets when you want a knotty effect.

No. 3   This is the lowest softwood grade. It is usually unsuitable for cabinet work.

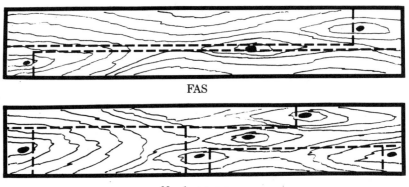

FAS

No. 1 common

Illus. 9. The placement of knots or other defects in a board determines the largest board that can be cut that would miss all the defects. When the defects are placed in a manner that allows a few large clear boards to be cut from the original board, the board receives a higher grade than a board that would have to be cut into several smaller boards to avoid all the defects. Clear-face cuttings are purely imaginary; its the principle of clear-face cuttings that gives the cabinetmaker an idea of the size of usable boards that can be cut from a board of a particular grade. You can cut the first and seconds (FAS) board, on the top, into two large pieces with almost no waste. You would have to cut the No. 1 common board, on the bottom, into three smaller boards with a considerable amount of waste to obtain clear-face cuttings.

Minimum Sizes for Hardwood Grades

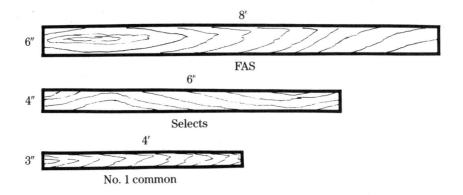

Illus. 10. In addition to the placement of defects, hardwoods are graded according to size. This illustration shows the smallest board for each grade.

Surfacing

When a board is first sawed from a log, it has a rough surface and may vary in thickness and width, and the edges are not square with the face of the board. You can buy this rough-cut lumber just as it left the saw, but you need a jointer and a surface planer to work with it. That's what most commercial cabinet shops do. Most do-it-your-selfers, on the other hand, don't have the equipment for dealing with rough-cut lumber; so they pay a little more to get lumber that has been surfaced at the mill. There are several different types of surfacing available. For most beginners, the best is S4S, which means surfaced four sides. An S4S board has smooth and parallel faces as well as smooth edges that are square with the face.

If you own a jointer, you may want to buy S2S (surfaced two sides). This type of board has smooth and parallel faces, but the edges are still rough and uneven. There are two other types of surfacing, but they are not frequently stocked by most dealers. They are S1S1E (surfaced one side one edge) and S1S2E (surfaced one side two edges).

Lumber Sizes

You can purchase lumber in random widths and lengths or by standard dimensional lumber sizes. Rough-cut lumber and most S2S boards are only sold in random widths and lengths. Large cabinet shops buy lumber in large units. These large units of random widths and lengths provide a variety of sizes that will meet most shop needs with little waste.

People usually only want to buy enough lumber for one project at a time and they need specific sizes. You have two choices: You can buy standard-sized dimensional lumber or you can go to a lumber dealer that lets you sort through various random sizes to find what you want. Buy lumber in the smallest pieces that will work for your project. There's no sense in buying a large board and cutting it up into small pieces because large boards are priced higher in most cases.

STANDARD SIZES

The nomenclature used for designating standard sizes can be a little confusing to the beginner. The actual size of a board is always smaller than the nominal size used for designating the board. The sizes refer to the rough-cut size of the board. Planing and smoothing operations reduce the thickness. This means that a board with a nominal thickness of 1″ is actually about ¾ of an inch thick when surfaced. For thicknesses greater than 1″, there is a difference in the actual thickness between hardwoods and softwoods. The thickness of a board can also be designated by a system called the quarter designation. In this system, the nominal thickness is designated in quarters of an inch. Therefore, 1″ nominal (¾″ actual) boards are called 4/4's.

PRICING

Since dimensional lumber is commonly priced by the piece, it is easy to tell how much it will cost. If it is not priced by the piece, it will usually be priced by the linear foot, so you simply multiply the cost per foot by the length. Rough-cut lumber is sold by the board foot. One board foot is 144 cubic inches. A board that is 1″ thick and 12″ × 12″ is one board foot, so is a 1″-thick board that is 6″ × 24″. Any combination of width, length, and thickness that equals 144 cubic inches is one board foot. Anything less than 1″ thick is still calculated as 1″ thick; so up to 1″, you can figure board feet the same way as square feet: Simply multiply the length times the width. If the measurements are in feet, then you have board feet. When the measurements are in inches, you need to divide the total by 144. Anything thicker than 1″ is figured in increments of ¼″. Thus, a board that measures 1¹⁄₁₆″ thick would be figured at its nominal size of 1¼″. For calculations, this translates into 1.25″. To get board feet in this instance, figure the square feet and then multiply your answer by 1.25.

Most lumberyards have a chart that gives board feet equivalents for most sizes of boards, so calculations are usually unnecessary. Simply find the section of the chart for the correct thickness; then find the point where the length and width line up on the chart. Once you have the board feet, you can figure the total price by multiplying the board feet by the price per board foot.

Veneers

Solid wood that is less than ¼″ thick is referred to as veneer. Usually made from expensive wood, veneer is used for covering the face of a less expensive wood. The log or piece of log from which veneers are cut is called a flitch. Veneers are usually sliced from the flitch with a large mechanical knife, but they can also be sawed.

Veneers are sliced in three ways. Flat-sliced veneers are the equivalent of plain-sawn lumber. Quarter-sliced veneers are the equivalent of quarter-sawn lumber. The third method is rotary slicing and it has no equivalent in solid lumber.

With rotary slicing, the log is mounted in a large lathe and rotated. A knife slices a thin sheet of veneer from the log as it rotates. The cut is made almost parallel to the rings. This method produces a large sheet of veneer without any seams. The figure produced by rotary cutting is quite different from that produced by the other two methods. The narrow annual ring is exaggerated in width because the cut is so close to parallel with the ring. Some species, such as fir, produce a wild figure when rotary cut. Other species, such as oak and birch, produce a pleasant figure that is very suitable for use on fine cabinetry.

You can purchase quarter-sliced and flat-sliced veneers by the flitch. Each sheet is stacked in the order it was sliced. The figure on adjacent pieces will almost be identical. You can put these pieces together in patterns.

Plywood

Plywood is a man-made product produced by laminating veneers together (Illus. 11). Wood has been laminated for hundreds of years, but early laminates had all of the grain running in the same direction. Plywood, on the other hand, has every other sheet of veneer running with the grain direction at a 90° angle to the previous sheet. Plywood always has an odd number of laminations so that both face veneers will have their grain running in the same direction.

A major advantage of plywood is its dimensional stability. Because the grain is running in two different directions, the effect of changes in moisture content is minimized. Plywood simplifies construction practices because special precautions to account for dimensional change are not needed. Another advantage of plywood is that it is available in 4′ × 8′ sheets, so you can make large cabinet parts from a single piece instead of from several boards glued together.

Plywood is available with a softwood-face veneer, usually fir, or with a variety of hardwood-face veneers. There are various grading systems for softwood and hardwood plywoods.

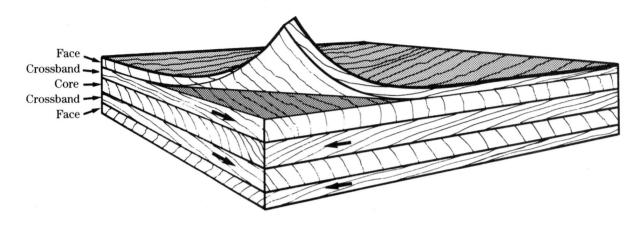

Face
Crossband
Core
Crossband
Face

Illus. 11. Plywood is composed of veneers called plies that are laminated together. The outside plies are called faces. The middle ply is called the core. Plies that have a grain direction opposite the grain direction of the face plies are called crossbands.

SOFTWOOD PLYWOOD GRADES

Softwood plywood is graded according to the type of wood used, the type of glue used for laminating the plies together, and according to the quality of the face veneers.

Although fir is the most commonly used wood for softwood plywood, there are about 30 species of softwood used in plywood manufacturing. These species are classified into four groups, according to their structural stiffness.

Group 1 consists of Douglas fir that originates in the American Northwest, western larch, tanoak, and several varieties of pine.

Group 2 includes Douglas fir that originates in the southwestern United States, several other varieties of fir, Port Orford cedar, western hemlock, lauan, western white pine, and Sitka spruce.

Group 3 includes lodge pole pine, ponderosa pine, redwood, Alaska yellow cedar, and red alder.

Group 4 includes subalpine fir, sugar pine, western poplar, Engelman spruce, incense cedar, and western red cedar.

You may have noticed that a couple of hardwoods, such as lauan and alder, are included here. Even though they are technically hardwoods, they are included in the list of softwood species used by the American Plywood Association.

Two types of glues are used: interior, which is moisture resistant but not waterproof, and exterior, which is fully waterproof.

The quality of the face veneer is designated by a letter. The highest quality is N, which means natural or that the face veneer is suitable for a natural finish. However, this veneer is not commonly stocked by most dealers. The highest grade commonly available is A. This grade is smooth with only slight repairs. Grade B is a solid-surface veneer that permits circular plug repairs and tight knots. With a grade-C face veneer, knot holes to 1″ diameter are permitted and small splits are also allowed. The lowest grade available is D, which permits knot holes to 2½″ along with some splits.

Different combinations of face veneers are available, with one side that is a higher grade than the other.

As previously mentioned, N-grade face veneers are the highest quality available. They are usually only available as a special-order item and are very expensive. N-N has N veneers on both sides; N-A has an A veneer on the back; N-B has a B veneer on the back. N-N, N-A, and N-B are only available in a ¾″ thickness. N-D has a D-back veneer and it's only available in a ¼″ thickness.

A-A is the highest quality that is commonly available. It is used when both sides of the sheet will be visible.

A-B is the type that is usually used for cabinet work. It has one good face with a back that is almost as good.

A-C is only available with exterior glue. This is a good choice for cabinets that will be subjected to a great deal of moisture.

A-D is frequently used for the bottom or back of a cabinet, where the back of the plywood will not be visible.

B-C is only available with exterior glue. It is not commonly used for cabinetmaking.

C-D (commonly called CDX) is available with exterior glue, and has two rough faces. Intended for building construction, it is not generally used for cabinetmaking. This type of plywood is supposed to be used in large sheets. When it is cut into smaller pieces, it frequently has separated plies.

Fir plywood is often available in the following thicknesses: ⁵⁄₁₆″, ⅜″, ½″, ⅝″, ¾″, and ⅞″. Thicker plywood is available for structural applications, but it is not commonly used for cabinetmaking.

HARDWOOD PLYWOOD GRADES

The grading system for plywood with a hardwood-face veneer is different from the grading system for softwood plywood. There are five grades of face veneer used on hardwood plywood.

A (also called premium) is the highest grade. The veneers used are almost totally free from defects. When more than one piece is used for covering the sheet, the figure and color are carefully matched.

1 (also called good) is the second grade. The veneers are almost the same quality as A, but they aren't as carefully figure matched. They are color matched.

2 (also called sound) uses veneers that are very high quality, but they aren't matched for color or figure.

3 (also called utility) allows for some small defects in the veneer.

4 (also known as backing grade) allows for large defects such as 3"-diameter knot holes. This grade is only used as a backing for a sheet that has a higher grade on its face.

The first three grades—A through 2—are acceptable as face veneers for cabinetmaking. They are equally smooth and free from defects. The major difference is in the amount of care taken in figure matching.

The best way of buying hardwood plywood is selecting the individual sheets yourself. You may find that you prefer the pattern of the unmatched veneers on a particular sheet of a lower grade over the matched veneers of a higher grade. A-grade veneers are uniform, and this is appropriate for many uses; but some of the lower grades that allow for more color variation have more individual character, so select your plywood on the basis of what you want your finished project to look like.

There is one additional grade called SP or specialty. Veneers in this grade may have certain defects such as knots or worm holes that, under the normal grading system, would allow them only to be used as backings. However, since their specific defects give beauty or character to the wood, these veneers are used as face veneers and are graded SP. In some instances, SP veneers may be more expensive than A veneers, and they are only available in limited quantities.

As with softwood plywood, different combinations of face and back veneers are available in hardwood plywood. One of the most popular combinations for cabinetmaking is A-2. This combination actually gives you two good sides. Some of the more expensive varieties—walnut, for example—are available with birch backs. It's best to use them when only one side of the plywood will show. Most of the ¾" hardwood plywood readily available do not have backs any lower than grade 2; however, ¼" plywood is often available with a grade-4 back.

There are more than 150 species of wood available as face veneers for hardwood plywood, but most of them are only available as special-order items. The most common species that you will find at most dealers are birch, lauan, oak, walnut, mahogany, basswood, and cherry. These are roughly listed according to their availability. Almost every lumberyard carries birch plywood because it is widely used in the building trades. Lauan, which is commonly called Philippine mahogany, is available at many home-center-type outlets that cater to do-it-yourselfers. Oak is also available at some home centers, although it is not as widely available as lauan. The other varieties listed are usually only available at the largest outlets, or by special-order from local lumberyards or mail-order lumber outlets. The mail-order outlets sell hardwood plywood in small parts of a sheet, which is an advantage with the more expensive species. If you special-order them locally, you will probably have to purchase a full sheet.

You can cut the veneers used for hardwood plywood in one of three ways: plain sliced, quarter sliced, or rotary cut. Oak and birch produce a pleasing figure when they are rotary cut, so rotary-cut veneers from these species are frequently used for plywood. Most other species are only readily available plain sliced. Quarter-sliced veneers are used only on special-order plywood.

Almost all of the hardwood plywood readily available is interior plywood, which uses a water-resistant glue. The exterior type of hardwood plywood uses a very waterproof glue. Hardwood plywood is also available with a lumber core (Illus. 12). This type is frequently

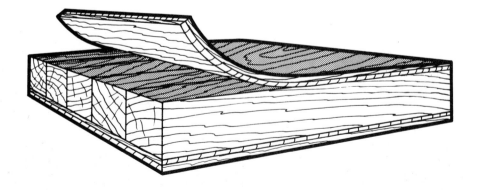

Illus. 12. Lumber core plywood is a good substitute for solid lumber. Strips that are glued together into a panel form the core ply of a plywood sheet. The core is much thicker than the core of standard plywood and the crossbands are thinner.

used in cabinetmaking. It has a face veneer, a thin crossband on each side, and a thick core of solid lumber.

Plywood edges that are visible from the exterior of the cabinet usually must be covered in some way to make them visually acceptable. Several types of edge treatments that can be used with plywood cabinetry are discussed in detail towards the end of this chapter.

Reconstituted Wood Products

There are a number of wood products that are made of wood chips, particles, or fibres. These products are all made by combining the small pieces of wood with glue and then bonding them with heat and pressure (Illus. 13).

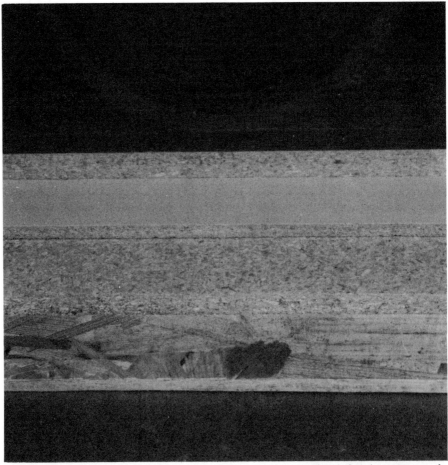

Illus. 13. Reconstituted wood products, from top to bottom: plastic laminate-covered particle board, vinyl-covered particle board, standard particle board, oriented strand board, and hardboard.

PARTICLE BOARD

Particle board is probably the most widely used reconstituted wood product for cabinetmaking. It is made from very small particles of wood bonded with a large percentage of glue. The high glue-to-wood density makes particle board very hard and heavy. A sheet of particle board weighs more than a sheet of plywood. Two types of particle board are available: underlayment and industrial grade. Underlayment is meant to be used as a flooring material under carpet or vinyl. It doesn't have the density or surface finish needed for most cabinet work. Cabinetmakers use industrial grade particle board. It has a very smooth, dense surface. Particle board is generally available in ½″, ⅝″, and ¾″ thicknesses.

Because particle board has no figure on its surface, it is not decorative enough to be used on the exterior of cabinets. Its use is therefore limited to interior parts and shelves, except in utility cabinets. To make particle board more useful as a cabinetmaking material, manufacturers have developed two particle board products that have decorative surfaces on their faces. One type is similar to hardwood plywood. It is called composite plywood. It has face veneers of hardwood, thin crossbands, and a thick particle board core. The other type has a thin plastic laminate veneer that has imitation wood grain, solid color, or some other decoration imprinted on it. Plastic laminate-covered particle board is very popular among commercial cabinetmakers because it eliminates all finishing steps and the plastic laminate surface is durable and easy to clean. A similar product is vinyl-covered particle board. As the name indicates, the surface is covered with a thin sheet of vinyl. This product is frequently used for drawer construction or for cabinet backs.

Particle board can produce durable cabinets when used correctly, but some deviations in standard design practices are necessary. The span of particle board is not as great as the span of plywood or solid lumber, so additional supports for shelves and tops may be necessary. Because ordinary screws don't hold very well in particle board, you should use special fasteners, as described in Chapter 5. You should not attach hinges and other hardware to a particle board edge; you need to use special hardware that attaches to a face. Particle board is not very water resistant and loses strength quickly when exposed to water. (Plastic laminate on the face can help to alleviate this problem.) Some joints are not suitable for use with particle board (see Chapter 4).

Because of its high percentage of glue, particle board dulls cutting tools rapidly. If you will be using particle board extensively, you should use carbide-tipped cutting tools.

As with plywood, the exposed edges of particle board need to be covered in some manner. Various types of edge treatments are discussed later.

HARDBOARD

After particle board, hardboard is the next most frequently used reconstituted wood product. It is most often used in ⅛″ or ¼″ thicknesses for cabinet backs and drawer bottoms.

Hardboard is made from wood fibres that are combined into a mat and compressed by rollers into sheets. It is available with either one smooth side or two smooth sides.

Three grades of hardboard are available: service, standard, and tempered.

Service grade is a low-density panel that you should use when high strength is not required.

Standard grade is the type most frequently used in cabinets. It has high strength and a dense surface that finishes well.

Tempered hardboard has resins added to the fibres, and it is heated during manufacturing to improve its stiffness and water resistance.

WAFER BOARD

Wafer board is made from larger chips of wood, instead of from the fine particles used in particle board. It is similar to particle board in most respects, but not quite as heavy. Some people find the pattern of chips on the face very attractive and like to use wafer board as the finished surface on their cabinetry.

ORIENTED STRAND BOARD

Oriented strand board (OSB) is similar to wafer board in appearance; but since its strands are oriented in layers as with plywood, OSB has much more strength than wafer board or particle board.

Edge Treatments for Plywood and Particle Board

When raw edges of plywood or particle board are visible from the outside of a cabinet, you will usually want to cover them.

VENEER TAPE

One of the most popular types of edge treatments for plywood is veneer tape, which is a very thin piece of wood bonded to a paper backing. The paper reinforces the veneer so that it is more flexible and can be made thinner than unreinforced veneer.

Veneer tape is available in most of the popular wood species. It comes in rolls 8′ long or longer. It is usually available in two widths: $^{13}/_{16}″$ and 2″. The $^{13}/_{16}″$ width is the most widely used; it will fit standard ¾″ plywood. This size is also used for thinner plywood with the overhang trimmed off. The tape is available with a heat-sensitive adhesive back or without adhesive. Both types are applied in basically the same manner; the only difference is that the heat-sensitive type is attached by passing a hot iron over the tape, whereas the plain type is applied with contact cement.

In most cases, the tape is applied after the cabinet has been assembled. Usually simple butt and mitre joints are used where pieces of tape meet, so even though a bookcase may have dado joints for the shelves, the tape is applied in a continuous strip along the side; the tape on the shelves butts into the side tape. The corners are usually mitred. The same bookcase may have a rabbet at the top corner, but the tape will be mitred.

Applying Veneer Tape You should carefully think through the order in which you will apply the tape to make the application easier. Joints are made during application.

Cut the pieces of tape slightly long at first; if you are using the plain type, apply contact cement to both the back of the tape and the edge of the plywood. When the glue has dried, place the tape on the edge so that it overhangs at both ends and on both sides (Illus. 14). Lightly rub the tape down with your fingers and then use a pair of scissors to trim the overhang at the ends close to the wood. If you look at a pair of scissors, you will see that if you cut in one direction, the flat inside of one blade will rest against the end of the board; try to cut this way because it will trim closer than it would if you held the scissors in the other direction (Illus. 15).

Next, use a small wallpaper seam roller to roll down the tape to get a firm bond (Illus. 16). The reason for trimming the ends first is that if the roller slips off the end with some tape overhanging, the tape will break and tear out fibres from the good part of the tape. When the tape has been thoroughly rolled down, use a razor knife to trim the excess from the sides. Press the side of the knife against the plywood so that it will follow the edge (Illus. 17). If the grain direction of the tape starts to pull the knife into the good portion of the tape, stop cutting and cut from the opposite direction.

After the edges have been trimmed with a knife, wrap a piece of

Illus. 14. You need to apply veneer tape with a slight overhang on the sides and at the ends.

Illus. 15. You can use scissors to trim veneer tape. Notice how the scissors are positioned so that the flat-inside edge of the lower blade is resting against the wood.

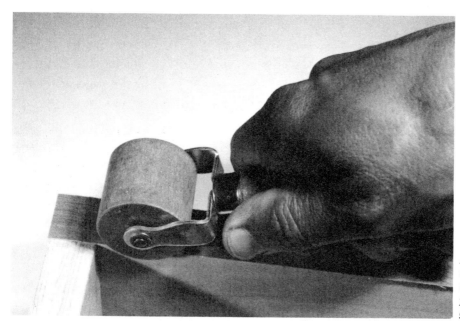

Illus. 16. When you use contact cement to apply the
tape, use a small roller to
press the tape down for a
good bond.

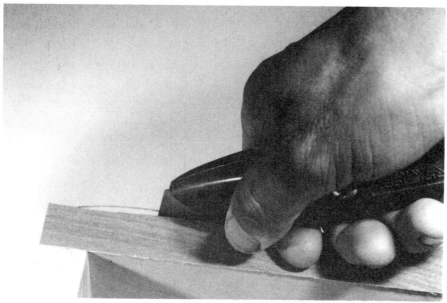

Illus. 17. Use a razor knife
to trim the edges of the tape
flush with the sides of the
board.

150-grit sandpaper over a small block of wood and sand off the last
of the overhang. Sand with the folded edge of the sandpaper facing
forward (Illus. 18). If you hold the block so that a cut edge of the
sandpaper is forward, the edge may catch on the grain of the tape
and tear the tape. Hold the block on a slight angle so that it touches
only the edge until the tape is even with the edge; then flatten out
the block a little. The edge of the tape should be slightly bevelled to
prevent it from catching and being torn off later. At this point, the

joint between the tape and the face veneer of the plywood will be almost invisible. Next, sand the ends. Use only a downwards stroke to sand the ends; any upwards movement of the sandpaper will tend to tear up the tape. Don't attempt to apply all of the tape at once; each edge should be applied and trimmed separately.

Next, cut the joints. Use a combination square for guiding a razor knife. Butt joints need to be trimmed back so that the extra width of the tape is removed and the edge of the butt is even with the edge of the plywood. To do this, place the square against the side of the cabinet and line up the edge of the blade with the edge of the plywood; now use the edge of the square as a guide for the knife to trim the tape. To make a mitre joint, place the 45° face of the square against a side of the cabinet and line up the edge of the blade with the corner of the joint. Use the knife to make a 45° cut (Illus. 19). Use the point of the knife to lift the corner of the scrap piece and then remove it.

Now apply the glue to the adjoining edge, being careful not to get any glue on the tape that has already been applied. When the glue has dried, apply the next piece of tape. At this point, don't worry about the joints; simply let the tape overhang the ends as before. When the edges have been trimmed and sanded, cut the joints. Place the square in exactly the same position as when you cut the joint on the previous piece. When you remove the scrap, the joint

Illus. 18. Bevel the edges of the tape with sandpaper. Notice how the sandpaper is held on the block; the fold is facing forward to prevent the edge from catching on the tape and tearing out a sliver.

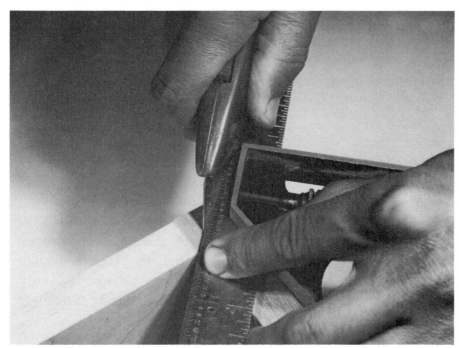

Illus. 19. Use a combination square and a razor knife to cut a mitre at the corner where two pieces of tape meet.

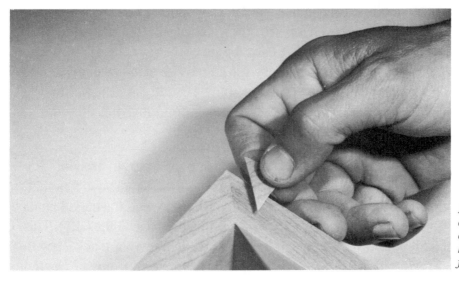

Illus. 20. When you apply and trim the second piece of tape with the square and knife, you'll get a perfect-fitting mitre joint.

should match perfectly (Illus. 20). Use the roller to press the joint down and then continue on to the next piece of tape.

You apply the heat-sensitive tape in the same manner, except you don't need any glue. Instead, you use a hot iron to press the tape in place and melt the glue, in one operation. When making joints, don't pass the iron over the piece of tape that overlaps the first one applied; stop just before you get to the joint. After you've trimmed the joint, iron it down.

Making Your Own Veneer Tape   You can make your own veneer tape; but since it won't have the paper backing, it won't be as flexible and it will need to be a little thicker. To make your own tape, use a piece of solid lumber of the same species as the face veneer of the plywood. The board should be slightly thicker than the plywood if possible.

Joint an edge of the board. Set the table-saw fence so that the distance between the far side of the blade and the fence is ¹⁄₁₆″ less than the width of the board. Run the board through the saw with the freshly jointed edge on the outside of the blade. This should produce a ¹⁄₁₆″-thick strip. Joint the edge of the board again to remove the saw marks and then move the fence ¹⁄₁₆″ closer to the blade and make another cut. Continue in this manner until you have enough strips. As the fence gets closer to the blade, be sure to use a push stick. Don't try to use every last piece of the board; discard it when it becomes too small to be handled safely.

If you would like the strips to be a little thinner, you can sand the back side with a belt sander. Clamp one end of the strip to the bench, and hold the sander so that the motion of the belt pulls the strip away from the clamp. If you try to sand in the other direction, the strip will simply curl up and break.

This type of edging is applied in much the same manner as the commercial type, but the joints must be cut differently. Cut the joints with a backsaw and a mitre box before applying the tape.

PLASTIC T MOULDING

You can also use veneer tape on particle board, but probably the most popular edge treatment for particle board is plastic T moulding. This is a plastic moulding that has a cross section shaped like a "T." The tail of the "T" is barbed with small ridges (Illus. 21). This moulding is available in solid colors, such as brown or black, or with a wood-grain pattern in colors that match several types of plastic-veneered particle board.

Applying Plastic T Moulding   You apply moulding by cutting a narrow kerf in the middle of the particle board edge. The barbed tail of the moulding fits into the kerf and the barbs keep it in place. You can cut the kerf with a table saw, but the blade must be thinner than usual or the moulding will not fit tightly. A special router bit is available to make the kerf; it has a ball-bearing pilot to keep the bit in position even around curves.

Place the moulding in the kerf and then drive it home with a

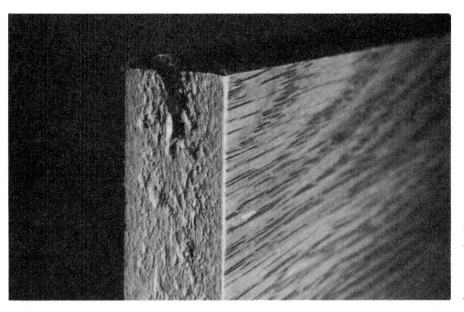

Illus. 21. You should apply plastic T moulding in a kerf cut in the edge of the board. Barbs on the tail of the moulding hold it in place.

rubber mallet or a hammer and a block of wood to protect the moulding. If the moulding is a little too wide, you can trim it with a razor knife after it is in place.

You can bend moulding around corners, but you must trim the tail away from the bend. Cut a V-shaped notch at the point of the bend. Make the cuts at 45° angles (Illus. 22). Commercial shops use a special nipper to make the cut in a single operation. Slightly round the corners of the board where the T moulding must be bent. When trimming parts, such as doors or drawer fronts that will have mould-

Illus. 22. To bend T moulding around a corner, cut a V-shaped notch in the tail. Notice that the corner of the board has been rounded.

ing on all four edges, apply the moulding in one piece. Notch the moulding to bend at the corners. Plan the position of the notches so that the two ends of the moulding will join in the middle of the least visible edge.

OTHER METHODS

There are several other methods for hiding the raw edges of plywood or particle board (Illus. 23). When the cabinets are made of fir plywood, pine screen mould is often used. Screen mould was originally designed to hide the edges of the screen in screen doors and windows; but because it is ¾″ wide and ¼″ thick, it makes a

Illus. 23. Left to right: screen mould, self-edge using a strip of plywood cut at a 45° angle, V-shaped solid wood insert, and flat solid wood insert.

perfect edge covering. The corners are slightly rounded, but the face is flat. You can apply the moulding with glue and small brads, or with glue alone. You can use contact cement, in which case no clamping is needed. If you use a glue that also requires clamping, pieces of masking tape placed at close intervals will be sufficient.

If only one face of the plywood will show, you can use the second method in Illus. 2 . Cut the edge at a 45° angle, as if you were making a mitre joint. Take the piece that was cut off the edge, reverse it, and glue it back onto the edge so that the face veneer is on the front edge. You can also use a wedge of solid wood that has been cut to a 45° angle.

A similar method employs a V-shaped groove. This method is a little more difficult, but it looks good from both sides. Set the table-saw blade to a 45° angle and then cut the groove in two passes. Make a wedge of solid wood to fit into the groove and then glue it in place. After the glue has dried, sand the corners until they are flush with the faces.

Another method for edging plywood involves cutting a ⅛"-deep groove in the edge with a dado blade. Set up the saw so that only the face veneer is left on either side of the groove and then cut a solid wood strip to fit into the groove.

Plastic Laminates

Plastic laminates are often used for covering counter tops or entire cabinets. They are made from layers of Kraft paper, which are impregnated with phenolic plastic resin. The top surface of the laminate is made of rayon paper impregnated with melamine plastic resin. It can be imprinted with an imitation wood grain, a solid color, or another pattern. High heat and pressure bond the paper and resin into a tough, durable material.

Plastic laminate is available in two thicknesses: ¹⁄₁₆" for counter tops and ¹⁄₃₂" for other parts of the cabinet. It is commonly available in sheets up to 5′ × 12′. When you buy plastic laminate, always get a piece larger than you need to allow for fitting and trimming. If you will be using a self-edge, be sure to add the width of the edge to the size when you buy the material.

Plastic laminate is quite flexible, but it is also brittle. Handle it carefully to avoid cracking it, and don't try to bend it around too sharp a corner.

Plastic laminate can be cut with ordinary woodworking tools, but it will dull them quickly. If you will be cutting a lot of plastic laminate, you should use carbide-tipped tools that will last longer.

You can cut plastic laminate on the table saw. *The sharp chips that fly off of the laminate as it is being cut can be dangerous, so wear eye protection, preferably a full-face shield.* If there is a gap between the bottom of the fence and the saw table, the plastic laminate will slip under the fence and the cut will be off. To avoid this, clamp an auxiliary wood fence to the rip fence and make sure that it is tight against the table. The flexibility of the laminate makes it difficult to handle by yourself on the saw. Large pieces may require three people—one to guide and support the front, another to support the side, and another to support the rear. It is easier to handle a large piece if you bend it across the width. Keep it flat against the table near the blade and fence, but lift the far side off of the table. This will make the piece more rigid and give you more control.

Instead of cutting the laminate with a saw, you can cut it the same way as you cut glass. For this, you will need a special carbide-tipped knife. Use a straightedge to guide the knife and scratch a line on the face side of the laminate. Go over the line several times to make sure it's deep enough. Place the piece on a bench with the line barely overhanging the corner. Apply downwards pressure to the overhang and the plastic laminate will break along the line.

WORKING WITH PLASTIC LAMINATES

To apply plastic laminates, you need to follow special procedures. The first step is cutting off the self-edge strip, if you will be using one. For counter tops the edge is usually 1½″, but the strip should be cut 2″ wide to allow for trimming.

Next, cut the main piece, allowing for about a ½ inch overlap on all edges.

The self-edge is a narrow band of plastic laminate used for covering the edges of a counter top. If the counter has rounded corners, you can bend the self-edge around the corners. Test a scrap to see how sharp a bend the laminate can make before it breaks. If you need to make a sharper bend, try heating the laminate with a hot air gun or use a belt sander on the back surface of the laminate to decrease its thickness in the area that must bend.

Glue the self-edge in place with contact cement. Apply the cement to both surfaces with a brush or roller, and let them dry for the amount of time specified on the cement container. The contact cement will grab as soon as the two surfaces touch, so position the edging carefully. Bend the laminate away from the edge, except at one end. Line up that end and then slowly bring the rest of the strip into contact with the edge. Use a roller to press the laminate firmly in place.

Now trim off the overhang. You can use a router or a special carbide-tipped hand-cutting tool. A special router bit is required for trimming plastic laminate. It has a pilot that rides against the surface of the work (Illus. 24). Always clean off any glue that accumulates on the pilot before making another cut or the bit won't cut accurately. There are two types of trimming bits.One makes a square cut; the other makes a bevel cut. To trim the self-edge, you need to use the square-cutting bit.

After trimming the laminate with the router or hand cutter, use a file to make the top edge of the laminate exactly flush with the wood. Hold the file flat against the wood to guide it. Don't rock the file or the edge will be rounded and a gap will show when you apply the next piece.

Before applying glue to the main piece, make sure it fits correctly. If any of its edges must butt against a wall or another part of the cabinet, it may be necessary to fit the edges by scribing (see Chapter 10). You can use a block plane or a file for trimming to the line. *The edge can become very sharp while you are planing, so use care when you're trimming with a block plane. Try to position your fingers so that they won't hit the edge of the laminate should the plane slip off the edge.*

Illus. 24. A router equipped with a laminate-trimming bit is one of the most efficient ways of trimming the overhanging edges of the plastic laminate. The bit has a pilot that rides against the side of the board to guide it. The pilot will follow curved surfaces as well as flat ones. It will also follow irregularities in the surface of the board, so you should fill them in or sand them out before you apply the laminate.

When the edge is completely trimmed, apply contact cement with a brush or roller to the back of the plastic laminate and the surface where you are applying it.

If the piece of plastic laminate is large, it will be difficult to position accurately. If you can get help, have someone else hold one end high above the work, while you position the other end; then gradually lower the laminate and press it in place as you go.

Another method that is very useful when the pieces are difficult to handle involves covering the wood with strips of scrap wood or plastic laminate. Then put the piece of plastic laminate on top of the strips and slide it into position. Pull one of the strips out at one end, and press that end down. Work from that end to the other, pulling out one strip at a time and pressing the laminate in place.

Some people think that paper should be used for this purpose, but it seldom works very well. Even when completely dry, contact cement is somewhat tacky. The paper often sticks to the cement and rips, making a mess that is very difficult to remedy.

If you use scraps of plastic laminate, use only pieces that have never had contact cement applied to them or else they will stick to the surface. Use a roller to firmly press the laminate to the wood. You can also use a block of wood and a hammer to press it down, but the bond won't be as good. Hammering on the wood block only creates a small bond area directly below the block, whereas rolling bonds the entire surface.

Now trim the excess laminate from the edges. You can use the bevel type of router bit for this operation. When a counter butts against a wall, it is difficult to trim all the way to the wall because the router base hits the wall before the cut is complete. In this case, trim as close as you can and then use a pair of tin snips to cut off the remaining part (Illus. 25). The tin snips will leave a rough edge, so don't cut right next to the edge. Leave a little overhang and file it off. Finally, smooth the edge with a file.

When covering an entire cabinet with plastic laminate, very simple joints are usually used in the cabinet construction since the plastic laminate will cover them completely. You can drive nails and screws in the face of the board if you set them and putty them over before applying the laminate. The laminate is usually applied in this order: first the sides, then the front, and finally the top.

There are two ways to apply the laminate to a face frame. The first method is easy, but wastes some of the laminate. Apply a single piece of laminate to the entire front. Drill an entrance hole into each opening and use the router to trim the laminate out of the openings. Finally, use a file to square up the corners. The second method conserves material, but is more difficult. Cut the laminate into strips and apply them individually to each stile or rail. When a stile meets a rail, cut the laminate to make a mitre or a butt joint. A mitre is easier in this case because it allows you to let the strips overhang. If you make a butt joint, you have to line up the edge of the strip with the edge of the board as you apply it.

Illus. 25. You can use tin snips to trim areas that can't be reached with a router. They will leave a rough edge, so don't trim right to the edge; leave some overhang and remove it with a file.

2
READING PLANS

Your first projects will probably be easier and turn out better if you use a prepared set of plans. Several magazines specialize in woodworking plans, and most of the popular do-it-yourself magazines contain one or two woodworking projects per issue. There are also many books of plans in print. In addition, you can purchase plans from many of the mail-order woodworking-supply houses. Once you have selected a set of plans to work from, you need to know how to read the plans before they will do you any good.

Types of Lines

All drawings are made of lines. Just as different letters of the alphabet are put together into words, different types of lines are put together to make a drawing. Different types of lines have different meanings (Illus. 26).

VISIBLE LINES

A thick, solid line is called a visible line. It is used to represent the visible outline of an object. This type of line is used only to represent what you could actually see if you viewed the object from the exact angle that the drawing shows.

HIDDEN LINES

Any part of the object that is hidden from view is represented by a dashed line of medium thickness. The dashes are equal in length and equally spaced. In woodworking, one of the most important functions of hidden lines is to show how a joint is constructed. Parts of an object may show up as hidden lines when drawn from one viewpoint and as solid lines when drawn from another.

DIMENSION LINES

To actually build the object portrayed in a plan, you need to know the size of each part. Two thin lines, called extension lines, project from the part to be measured. Another thin line, called a dimension line, connects the extension lines. Where the dimension line touches the extension line, there is frequently an arrowhead or a dot. Somewhere along the dimension line, there is a space where the actual measurement of the part is written in.

For cabinet work, dimensions are usually given in inches, and the symbol for inches (″) is omitted. However, when both feet and inches are used on the same drawing, feet are indicated by a single mark (′) and inches are indicated by two marks (″). When there isn't enough room on the drawing to write in the measurement between the extension lines, the measurement is written close by and an arrow called a leader line connects the measurement to the correct part. The leader line may be straight or S-curved (Illus. 27).

CENTER LINES

A center line is a type of extension line. It is used for indicating the middle of a hole (Illus. 28). A center line is the same thickness as an extension line, but there is a small dash where the line crosses the middle of the hole. It takes two center lines crossing at right angles to indicate the middle of a hole. Dimension lines are drawn from a good reference point, such as the edge of a board, to the center line.

Center lines make it easy to position a hole. When you are building a project, you simply measure from the reference point shown in the drawing and make a cross that indicates the point where you will place the middle of the drill bit. The diameter of the hole is given either by a dimension line running diagonally across the hole or by a leader line. The measurement given will be followed by *DIA*—indicating diameter, which is the distance from edge to edge—or by *R*—indicating radius, which is the distance from the middle to the edge.

Most simple drawings will contain only the lines mentioned here. Complex drawings, on the other hand, may also include some of the other lines shown in Illus. 26.

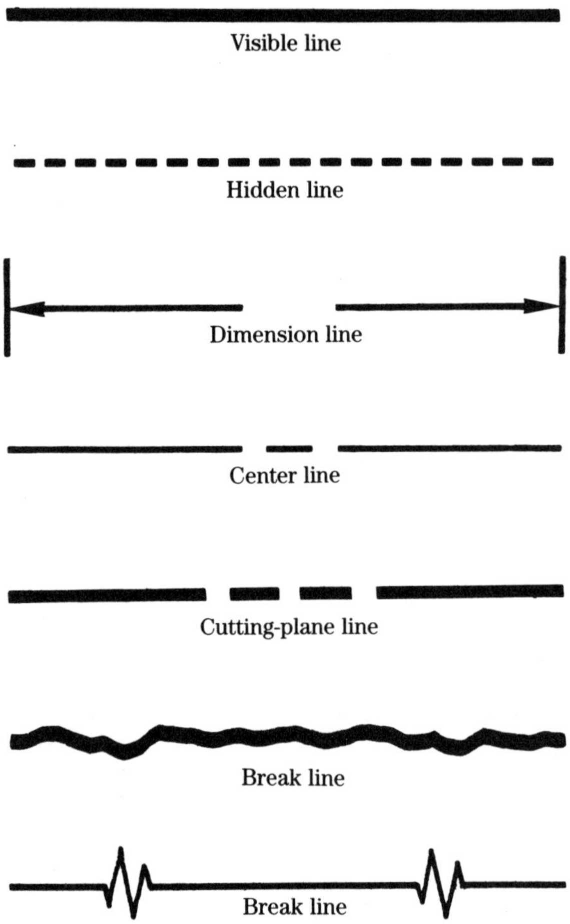

Visible line

Hidden line

Dimension line

Center line

Cutting-plane line

Break line

Break line

Illus. 26. Types of lines.

Dimension lines with arrows—inch marks omitted.

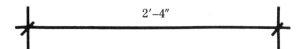

Dimension lines with dots—inch marks included.

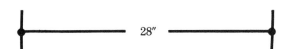

Dimension line used in architectural drawings—length expressed in feet and inches.

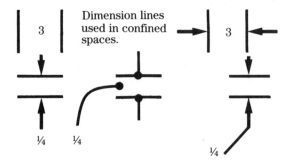

Dimension lines used in confined spaces.

¼   ¼   ¼

Illus. 27. Types of dimension lines.

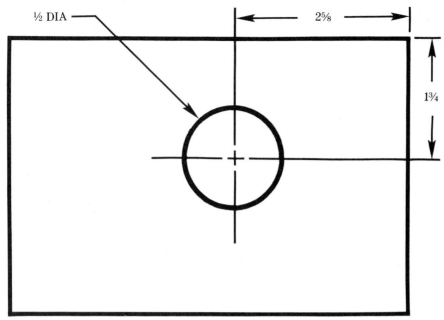

½ DIA

2⅝

1¾

Illus. 28. You can use center lines to find the placement of a hole.

Types of Drawings

There are several types of drawings used in woodworking plans; some are more difficult for the draftsman to draw than others, and some are better suited than others for a particular project. You will find all of the following types of drawings used in plans, so you need to be familiar with them all. Generally, the drawings that are the most difficult for the draftsman to draw are the easiest to understand. Plans in magazines and books that are intended for the beginning woodworker generally use some of the most sophisticated types of drawings so that all the aspects of construction are clearly shown. On the other hand, plans intended for professional use generally use simple drawings because it is assumed that the reader is familiar with the construction techniques and skilled at reading plans.

MULTIVIEW DRAWINGS

The multiview drawing is the most fundamental type of drawing used in cabinet plans; but for the beginner, it has a couple of drawbacks. It is difficult to visualize an object from a multiview drawing unless you are experienced at reading plans, and many details appear as hidden lines, making the drawing confusing. The advantage of a multiview drawing, however, is that all parts of the plan are the same scale and appear in their true shape. Other types of drawings distort scale and shape in order to show perspective. Because of this, a multiview drawing is ideal for dimensioning. Usually a set of plans includes a multiview drawing to show the dimensions and other drawings to clarify the details.

A multiview drawing is based on the fact that a cube has six sides. This means that there are six possible ways of viewing any three-dimensional object. A multiview drawing of a child's block with a different letter on each side appears in Illus. 29. You can see that each side is drawn independently of the others. Only what you can see by looking directly at one face of the block appears in each view. In most cases, only three views of an object are needed to define its shape: the top, the front, and the right side. For this reason, multiview drawings are frequently called three-view drawings. The views

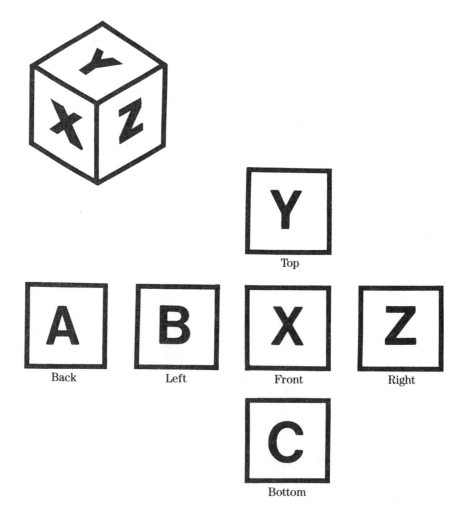

Illus. 29. A child's block illustrates how the six views of a multiview drawing are placed on the page.

are usually placed in the same relationship on the page, so they are not normally labelled. Illus. 30 shows the conventional placement of the standard three views. In some cases, a nonstandard view gives more information than the standard three views. Sometimes the bottom is shown instead of the top, or the left side is substituted for the right side. If the views aren't labelled, you can tell what view is used by its placement on the page, as shown in Illus. 29. If non-standard placement is used, the views will be labelled.

In some cases, when one view is not important, only two views are shown. For example, the top view in Illus. 30 doesn't add much information other than the shape of the glue blocks. If a set of plans covered the base construction with other detail drawings, the top view of this drawing would probably be omitted. Notice that the top view is omitted in Illus. 31.

To determine all of the dimensions of any one piece of a project, you need to refer to more than one view. For example, in Illus. 30, you can get the width of the back from the front view, but the side view shows the height and thickness.

One aspect of three-view drawings that often confuses people is the way parts on different planes are depicted. For example, in the multiview drawing of a breakfront in Illus. 31, the top section is recessed back from the lower section; but in the front view, the top and bottom appear to be on the same plane. The offset only appears in the side view. Anything you can see from the front is drawn in the front view whether or not it is on the same plane. In multiview drawings, you always need to look at more than one view to deter-mine the shape of the object.

Visible lines take precedence over hidden lines; so in some views, the visible lines hide details that would otherwise be shown by hidden lines. Usually you need to look at two views to understand what a particular hidden line means. In the top view in Illus. 30, there are diagonal hidden lines in the corners. The part that these lines represent may be positioned anywhere from the top to the bottom of the cabinet. To find out where they are, look at the side view. The only line that matches the diagonal lines in the top view is a short hidden line in the base of the cabinet. Together, these lines describe two triangular glue blocks in the corners of the base. An-other example is the hidden lines in the middle of the front edges of the top and sides on the front view in Illus. 30. By looking at the side view, you can see that this indicates the ¼"-plywood back and the rabbet into which it fits.

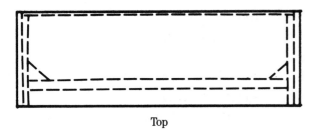

Top

Note: All boards ¾ thick unless dimensioned.

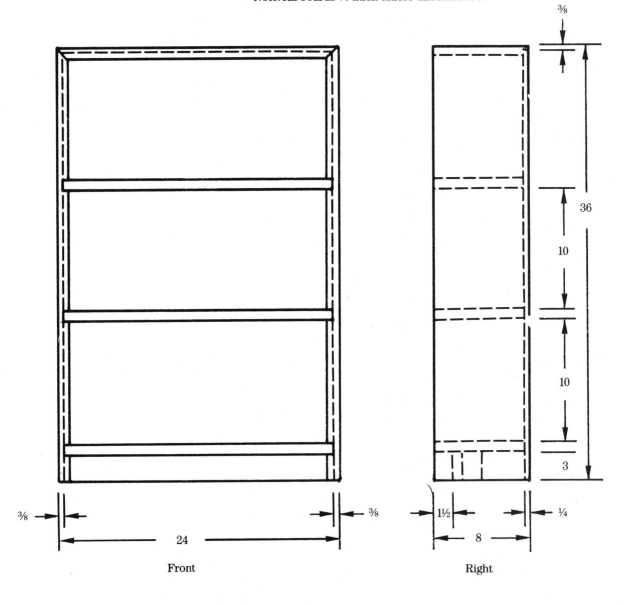

Front

Right

Illus. 30. This three-view drawing of a bookcase shows the standard placement for top, front, and right-side views.

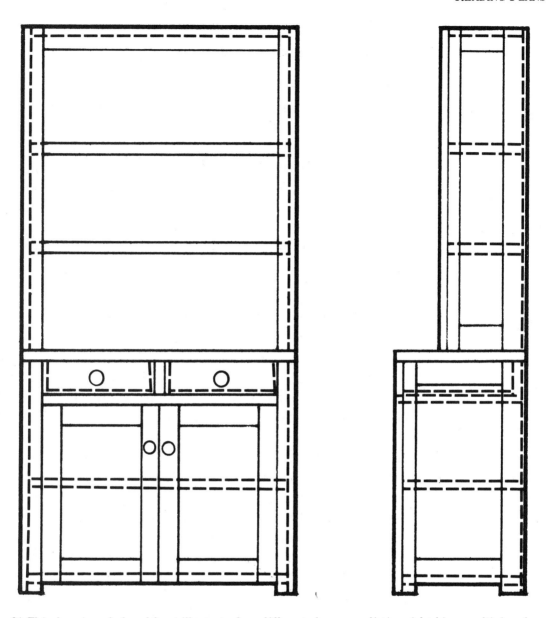

Illus. 31. This drawing of a breakfront illustrates how different planes are distinguished in a multiview drawing. There's no apparent difference between the top section and the bottom section in the front view. The side view shows that the top section is not as wide as the bottom section.

To keep multiview drawings from looking cluttered, only essential dimensions are shown. When parts are the same size, dimensions may be given for just one part. And some dimensions must be calculated from other dimensions that are given. For example, the length of the shelves in the bookcase is not given, but an overall width is given, and the distance from the outside to the end of the shelf is given. To get the shelf length, you have to subtract the distance from both sides from the overall length.

PICTORIAL DRAWINGS

It's difficult to visualize an object from multiview drawings because they lack a three-dimensional quality; therefore, pictorial drawings are used to give a clearer idea of the shape of an object. Pictorials are usually supplementary drawings used in conjunction with a multiview drawing. Most of the dimensions are usually shown on the multiview drawing. Hidden lines are omitted from pictorial drawings unless they are needed for clarity. Pictorials may use wood-grain patterns or shading to add to the illusion of depth and to distinguish solid areas from open areas.

Oblique Projections In an oblique projection, all three of the standard views in a multiview drawing are combined into a single view. The front view appears just as it would in a three-view drawing. The top and the right-side views are attached to the front view with their receding lines drawn at an angle. Any angle may be used, but a 45° angle is the most common. This type of drawing presents all three views in a single image. While not exactly the same as photographic realism, an oblique projection does give a three-dimensional effect, making it much easier to interpret than a multiview drawing.

When its receding lines are drawn the same length as they would be in a three-view drawing, the drawing is called a cavalier projection (Illus. 32). However, normally receding lines are foreshortened by the eye. The cabinet projection (Illus. 33) has a more true-to-life appearance since its receding lines are drawn one-half the length that they would be in a three-view drawing.

All dimensions that can be placed on a three-view drawing can also be placed on an oblique drawing. Dimensions on the front view appear the same as they would on a three-view drawing. Dimension lines for the side and top views follow the angle of the receding lines, but otherwise they appear the same as they would on a three-view drawing.

Isometric Drawings An isometric drawing is similar to an oblique drawing, but the object appears to have been rotated so that you are looking directly at one corner (Illus. 34). As with an oblique drawing, all three views are presented in a single image; the difference is that all of the lines appear to be receding lines. This type of drawing is slightly more realistic looking than the oblique projec-

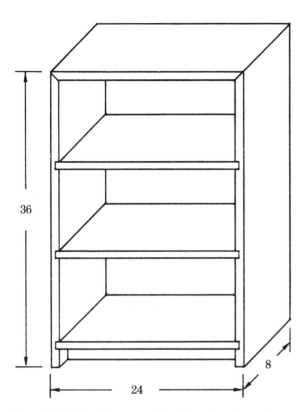

Illus. 32. This oblique cavalier drawing shows how dimensions can be placed on an oblique drawing. Notice that the shelves appear deceptively deep. Cavalier drawings tend to distort depth perception.

Illus. 33. This cabinet drawing gives a more accurate idea of the depth of the shelves. All the receding lines are drawn one-half scale. The wood grain and shading add to the realism of the drawing, but the wood graining isn't only decorative; it shows you how to orient the grain direction on each part.

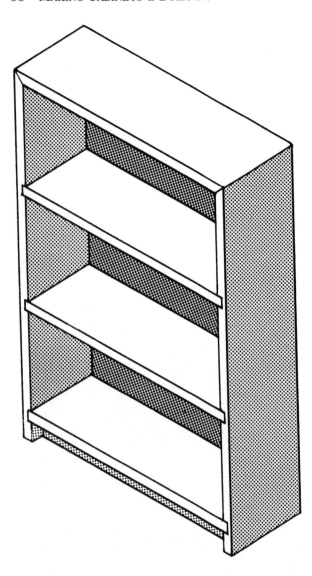

Illus. 34. This isometric drawing of the bookcase in Illus. 33 has more realism. Dimension lines can be included on isometric drawings in the way that is shown in Illus. 32.

Detail A

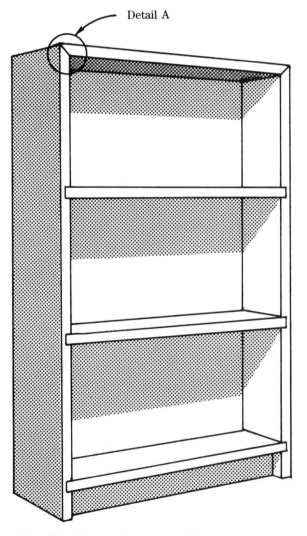

Illus. 35. Of the various types of drawings, perspective drawings look the most natural. The area labelled Detail A *is enlarged and cut away in Illus. 37.*

tion, but both are about as easy to read. If dimension lines are used, they are placed parallel to the lines they refer to; but frequently, isometric drawings are used for clarifying the shape of the object, and dimensions are given on another drawing.

Perspective Drawings Perspective drawings are complex to draw, but objects drawn this way are some of the easiest to visualize because the drawing clearly shows what the completed project should look like (Illus. 35).

Dimensions can be placed directly on a perspective drawing, but frequently a perspective drawing is used to give you an overall idea of a project with a multiview drawing giving you the actual dimensions.

Exploded Views An exploded view is a good way to show how all of the parts of a project fit together. In an exploded view, each part of the project is drawn separately but in proper relationship to the rest of the parts in the project. When it is unclear where a particular part goes, dashed lines are used to indicate where the part is attached. Exploded views do not usually have dimensions, but the parts may be keyed to other drawings with letters (Illus. 36).

Details

Anything that needs to be enlarged or otherwise clarified in the main drawing is circled and labelled *Detail*, followed by a letter. The cutaway in Illus. 37 is a detail of the bookcase in Illus. 35. There are several types of details. Some details are simply enlargements of small areas on the main drawing; others may be cutaways or cross sections.

CUTAWAYS

In a cutaway drawing, part of the exterior surface of the project is removed to make hidden details more clear. A thick, irregular line, called a break line, indicates the section that has been removed. Solid areas under the broken out section are indicated with section lines, which may appear as a wood-grain pattern or simply as equally spaced diagonal lines (Illus. 38). The detail shown in Illus. 37 is a cutaway. When thin materials, such as ¼″ plywood, are drawn in a cutaway, a gentle curving line is frequently used as a break line (Illus. 39).

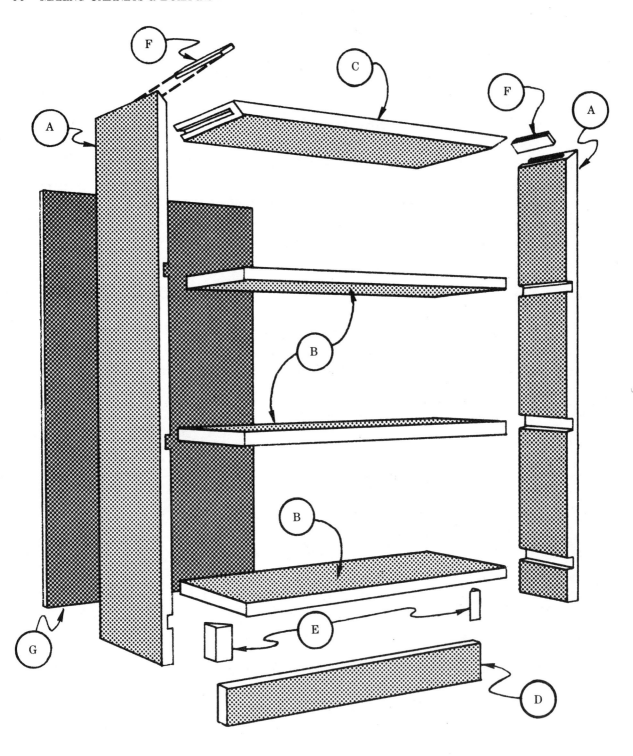

Illus. 36. Exploded views show how the various parts are assembled. The letters refer to the parts in the instructions and on the bill of materials. The dashed line connecting part A to part F clarifies where part F fits.

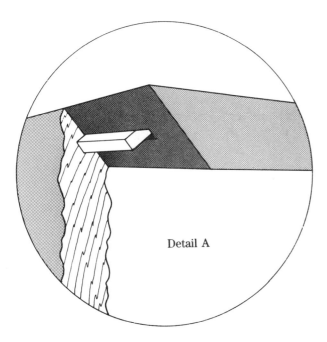

Detail A

Illus. 37. This detail is an enlarged corner of the bookcase shown in Illus. 35. Part of the side is cut away to reveal the spline that joins the two parts.

Universal

End grain

Edge grain

Face grain

Plywood

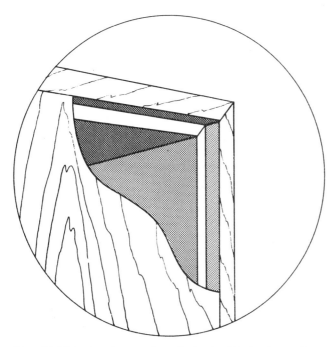

Illus. 39. This detail shows how the back of the bookcase fits into the sides and top. This gentle, curving type of break line is used when the material being represented is thin— that is, ¼" thick or less.

Illus. 38. Types of section lines.

CROSS SECTIONS

Another type of detail is the cross section. In a cross section, you can see what a part would look like from the end if you were to saw through the part at the point indicated by a cutting-plane line. A cutting-plane line is a thick dashed line. Its ends extend past the

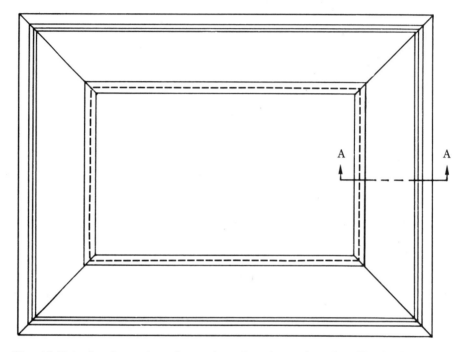

Illus. 40. This plan for a mirror frame shows how the cutting-plane line is placed on a drawing.

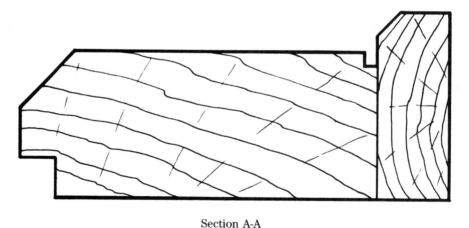

Section A-A

Illus. 41. This sectional view shows the cross section of the mirror frame at the point indicated by the cutting-plane line in Illus. 40.

end of the object, and are bent at a right angle to the main part of the line. Each end has an arrowhead drawn on it. The arrows point in the direction of view. Therefore, if the arrows point to the right of an object, the cross section is drawn as if you were standing to the left of the object looking at the right half after having cut away the left (Illus. 40).

When the cutting plane passes through a solid part of the object, the area on the cross-sectional view is covered with section lines (Illus. 41).

REVOLVED SECTIONS

Sometimes a cross section is simply drawn on top of the place where a cutting plane would be drawn. This is called a revolved section because it is as if you cut a small slice out of the part and revolved it 90°. The table leg in Illus. 42 shows how revolved sections can clarify the shape of a part.

LONG BREAKS

Another form of break line is used for shortening long details in a drawing. A table leg is an example (Illus. 43 and 44). This type of break line indicates that a section of the line is missing to make the drawing fit on the paper. When long breaks appear, you can assume that the broken out section is identical to the rest of the part shown in the drawing.

CENTER LINES

Center lines can be used as break lines on symmetrical objects (Illus. 45 and 46).

Full-Size Patterns

Some sets of plans that you can purchase include full-size patterns. A full-size pattern is one view from a three-view drawing that is drawn the exact size of the completed part. It is especially useful for irregularly shaped parts, such as gingerbread trim or carved legs. Since you can transfer a full-size pattern directly to the wood, chances for error in measurement are minimized.

Architectural Drawings

Architectural drawings, such as house plans, include drawings for the cabinet work that will be included in the project. However, the

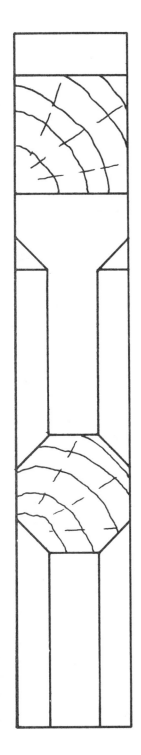 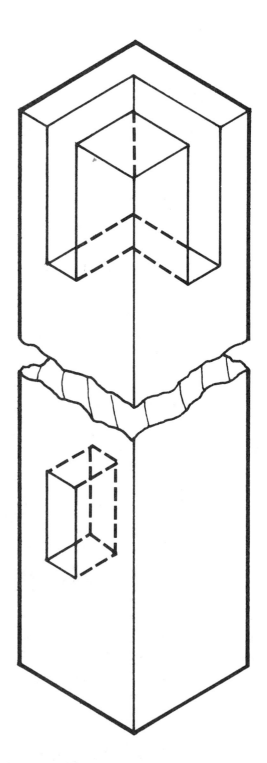

Illus. 42 (left). Revolved sections show the cross section of a part without separate details drawn in. The cross section is drawn in the position where the cutting-plane line would appear. Illus. 43 (right). Break lines shorten a long object so that you can use a larger scale for the drawing. You can assume that the broken out section is similar to the areas that are drawn in.

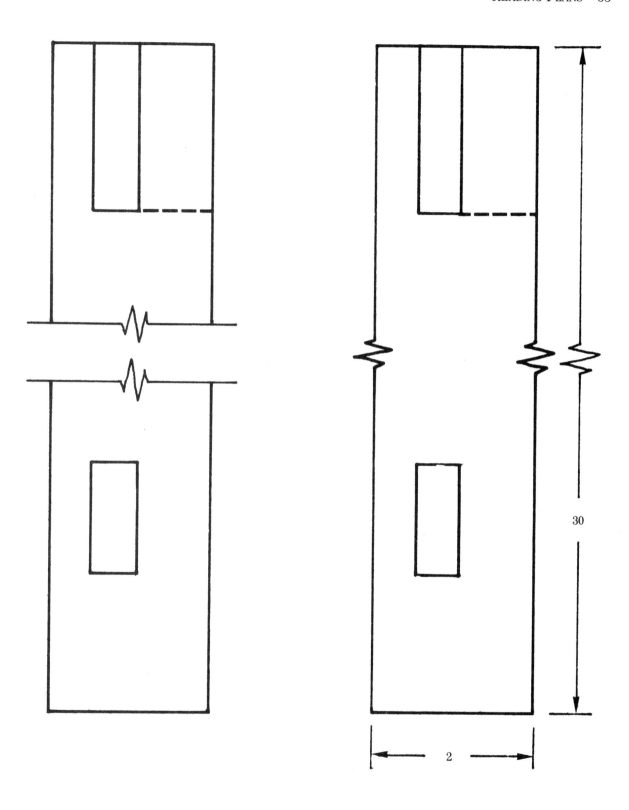

Illus. 44. Here is another form of break line that is used for shortening long objects on the drawing.

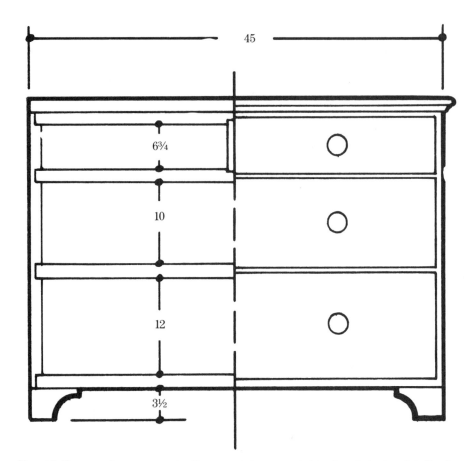

Illus. 46. You can also use a center line as a cutaway point to show interior details of the object.

architect assumes the cabinetmaker knows all about standard construction practices, so the cabinet plans included in architectural drawings usually only indicate the outside dimensions and placement of the cabinets (Illus. 47).

The cabinetmaker is expected to furnish a set of shop drawings, showing the construction details of the cabinets. Cabinets in architectural drawings are shown in elevations that are equivalent to the front view of a three-view drawing. Shop drawings are usually three-view drawings. Generally, shop drawings don't show every joint; several details of typical joints are shown, and it is left up to the cabinetmaker to use these typical joints in their proper applications.

Choosing a Set of Plans

When choosing a set of plans, there are several things to look for. First, the drawings should be clear and appropriate for the project.

Illus. 45. When an object is symmetrical, as is this lathe-turned leg, it is common practice to draw only half of the outline, stopping at a center line.

A simple project may only require a single three-view drawing, whereas a complex project may require several types of drawings with details, exploded views, and cutaways. Make sure that there is a detail for anything that isn't clear on the main plan.

Generally, for your first projects, it's a good idea to choose simple projects that have very detailed plans. The plans found in magazines are some of the best. They often include step-by-step instructions and detailed photos that help to clarify the construction process. They also usually include a bill of materials that lists all the lumber and hardware that's required so that you can purchase the right amount of materials. Plans that can be purchased by mail vary in quality. Some mail-order full-size plans are little more than giant

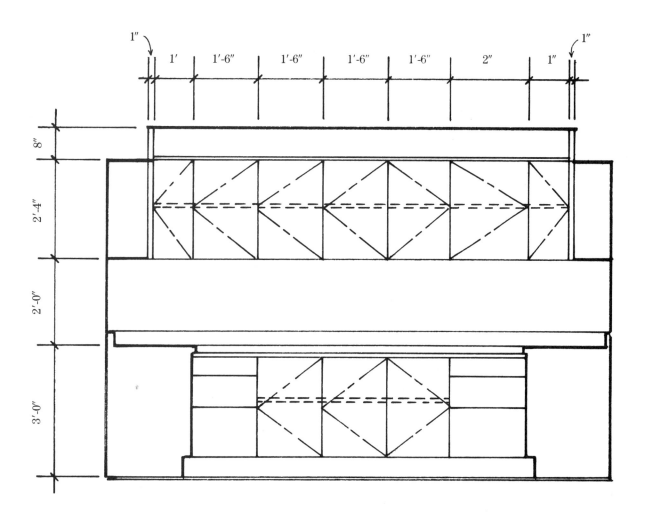

Illus. 47. Architectural drawings are not as detailed as drawings intended for less experienced cabinetmakers. In this drawing, the diagonal lines with dashes in the middle point to the hinge side of each door.

three-view drawings with no instructions or details, whereas others include detailed directions and all of the necessary drawings.

Scaling

When you lay out the parts of a project on the wood, you need to know every dimension of each part. If the dimension is not given on the drawing, it is still possible to get the dimension if the drawing is drawn to scale.

On a scale drawing, each measurement is a fraction of the actual measurement. The scale of the drawing is noted somewhere on the drawing, usually in the right-hand lower corner. On cabinet drawings, the scale is usually given in relationship to 1 foot, such as $1'' = 1'$, or as half size, eighth size, etc. However, not all drawings are to scale. If no scale is given or if the words *not to scale* appear, you can't get measurements directly from the drawing unless they appear in dimension lines.

By measuring the length of a line on a scaled drawing and multiplying the measurement as indicated by the scale, you can find any measurement. For example, if a drawing is half-scale and you measure a line as ⅜″, the actual measurement is ¾″. With some scales, such as half-scale, it's easy to convert the measurements, and you can use an ordinary tape measure or ruler to scale from the drawings. But since most standard measuring devices are divided into 16 divisions per inch, some scales are difficult to convert.

A measuring tool that eliminates having to calculate the scale is the architect's scale. This is a special ruler that has a standard scale plus 10 reduced-size scales (Illus. 48). Using an architect's scale, it is possible to read the measurement directly without any calculation. To conserve space on the scale, each line contains two different scales, except for the full-size scale, which has only one. Each scale is designated by a number at the end of the scale. The full-size scale is designated by 16, which means the scale is divided into sixteenths of an inch. The reduced-size scales are designated by the number of inches equal to 1 foot; therefore, the scale marked ½ means that ½″ = 1′. This is not the same as half-scale, which means 6″ = 1′. There are two scales per line; so ¼ and ⅛ share the same line, but they start at opposite ends of the scale. Thus, reading left to right produces ⅛, whereas reading right to left produces ¼. The divisions on the scale equal 1 foot, except for a 1-foot section between zero and the end of the scale that is divided into smaller increments. To measure distances less than 1 foot, use this section of the scale. To measure distances more than 1 foot, place the scale so that one end of the line to be measured falls on an even foot mark and the other end falls in the section past zero that is divided into smaller increments. The total length of the line is the number of feet shown on the scale plus the inches and fractions of an inch shown in the section past zero.

Remember, when scaling from oblique cabinet drawings, that the receding lines are drawn at one-half the scale of the rest of the drawing. Generally, perspective drawings cannot be scaled.

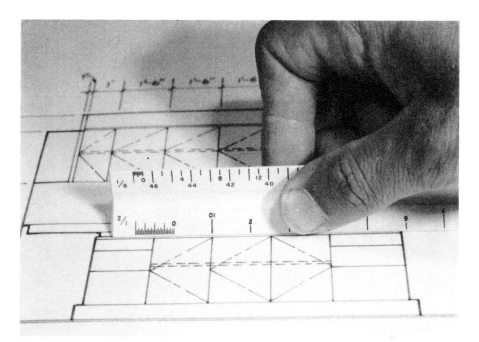

Illus. 48. The architect's scale allows you to take direct measurements from a scaled drawing. In this case, a scale of ½″ = 1′ is being used. Since two scales overlap on each side of the scale, every other number refers to a different scale. The 10 refers to the 1″ scale that starts at the other end; it is also 1 on the ½″ scale. The 2 is the 2′ mark on the ½″ scale. Inches are read in the section between 0 and the end of the scale.

Transferring Full-Size Patterns

There are two methods for transferring full-size patterns to the wood; with one method you use carbon paper, and with the other you use a tool called a pounce wheel.

With the first method, you thumb-tack the plan to the wood so that it can't move and then you slide a piece of carbon paper under the plan. The type of carbon paper specifically made to be used with a pencil works better than the type made for a typewriter. Now trace over the lines on the plan to transfer them onto the wood. You can use a pencil or you can make a stylus by sharpening a dowel in a pencil sharpener. The stylus won't leave pencil marks on the plan, making the plan easier to use again. When you have finished tracing over one section, slide the carbon paper to a new section and trace it. When all the tracing is done, remove two of the thumb tacks, but leave the other two in place and lift the plan to see if all the lines transferred onto the wood. By leaving two thumb tacks in place, you can lay the plan back down in the proper position if it is necessary to retrace a line that didn't show up.

With the second method, you thumb-tack the plan in place and roll the pounce wheel over the lines. The pounce wheel has many small points around its edge that make small dents in the wood. If the dents are not visible enough, you can rub a little bit of powdered chalk from a chalk line over them to make them stand out. Although some woodworking dealers sell pounce wheels, you can also find them at fabric stores because they are used for transferring sewing patterns onto fabric as well. The pounce wheel can also be used with a special type of carbon paper sold at fabric stores. This carbon paper is available in several colors, which is an advantage on dark-colored wood, where the standard blue carbon paper is sometimes hard to see.

Transferring Grid Patterns

Plans that come from magazines and books don't usually include full-size patterns. To get a full-size pattern for a complex shape, you must enlarge a grid pattern, which they usually provide. The grid pattern is covered with grid lines that are similar to those on graph paper (Illus. 49). Somewhere on the drawing, the scale of the grid, such as 1 square = 1 inch, is noted. To enlarge the pattern to the correct size, draw a grid on a large sheet of paper, spacing the lines the distance specified in the note—in this case, 1 inch. Now draw in the lines that appear in the small grid into the large grid freehand. This is fairly easy to do because the grid lines give you a point of reference.

Don't worry about the overall shape; just concentrate on the square where you are working. For example, if the line in one of the small squares goes from the lower right corner of the square to the upper left corner of the square, draw a line in the corresponding large square from the lower right corner to the upper left corner. If the squares in the small grid are spaced closely enough, you won't have to worry too much about curves. Most details can be broken

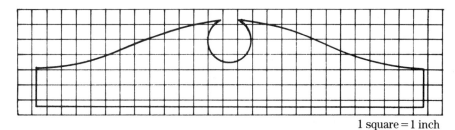

1 square = 1 inch

Illus. 49. When a complex shape is drawn less than full-scale, it's common to draw grid lines over the area. The grid lines are used to enlarge the pattern to full size.

down into fairly straight lines within the square, but the overall effect of many squares will create the correct curve.

The pantograph is a machine that can enlarge or reduce drawings. It has levers with variable pivot points that control the amount of reduction or enlargement. A stylus on one lever is traced over the plan, and a pencil attached to another lever redraws the plan at the desired size. You can purchase a pantograph from one of the many mail-order woodworking companies.

There are other ways of enlarging a pattern, thanks to modern technology. One of the best is by using a photocopy machine that is capable of enlargement. Photocopy machines usually can't enlarge more than 200 percent at one time, so you may have to place the first enlargement back in the machine and enlarge again to get the size you need. Keep enlarging in this manner until the grid lines are the correct size. You will need to enlarge very large patterns in sections using this method.

Another machine you can use for enlarging plans is the opaque projector. Many libraries have opaque projectors available for loan. With this method, you place the pattern in the machine and project the image on a wall. Adjust the projector's distance from the wall until the grid lines are the proper size, and then tape a piece of paper on the wall and trace the pattern onto it. When you are using this method, be sure that the projector is square with the wall and is not tilted up or down; otherwise, you will get distortions.

You can achieve a similar result by taking a photograph of the plan using slide film and then projecting the slide in a projector. When you take the photograph, be sure that the camera is perfectly square with the plan so that there won't be any distortion.

There is one other method for projecting the plan. Many libraries have machines that make overhead transparencies from printed materials. Take the plan in and have a transparency made and then use an overhead projector to enlarge the plan.

Bill of Materials

Many better-quality plans include a bill of materials. This is a list of all the parts in the project, including the sizes and materials that are used. The parts are usually keyed to one of the drawings with letters. If the bill of materials includes a note saying *All Dimensions Actual*, then board widths are given exactly as they will measure when cut. If this note is not included, the width and thickness may be nominal sizes that will vary from the actual size. Here is an example of a bill of materials for the bookcase in Illus. 36.

Bookcase

BILL OF MATERIALS
(All Dimensions Actual)

Part	Description	Material	Size	No. Req'd
A	sides	¾″ plywood	36 × 8	2
B	shelves	¾″ plywood	23¼ × 7¾	3
C	top	¾″ plywood	24 × 8	1
D	toe kick	¾″ plywood	22½ × 3	1
E	glue blocks	pine	1¼ × 1¼ × 3	2
F	spline	¼″ hardboard	7½ × ¾	2
G	back	¼″ hardboard	33 × 23¼	1

3
LAYOUT, SQUARING, AND CUTTING

When you begin a project, you first need to lay out the sizes of the pieces onto the wood. The parts of the project must be square and flat. If the boards you are using are not square, then you need to square them up. Next, the parts should be cut to size. These first three steps are critical to the entire cabinetmaking process. Inaccuracy in any one of them will affect all of the operations that follow.

Layout

It is often said that woodworking only needs to be accurate to $\frac{1}{16}$ of an inch, but a $\frac{1}{16}''$ gap in a joint looks pretty bad on a piece of cabinetry. Obviously, cabinetmakers need to measure much more accurately than plus or minus $\frac{1}{16}$ of an inch. Accurate layout, therefore, is essential to quality work.

It is not necessary or even desirable to lay out all the parts at once. It's very difficult to account for losses in size that result from saw kerfs (the widths of the cuts made by the saw) or from jointing boards between cuts. It is much better to lay out the parts individually when you are ready to cut each part, but you need to plan ahead and have a firm idea of how you will cut out the parts if you want to make the best use of your material.

Some plans include a cutting plan that shows you how to fit the parts onto the stock. This is especially important when you are using material, such as plywood or particle board, that comes in large sheets. If your plans don't include a cutting plan, sketch one for yourself before cutting out the parts (Illus. 50). In making a cutting plan, you have to keep two things in mind: ease of cutting and making the most efficient use of your materials. Where grain direction is important, you need to keep that in mind as well. It is difficult to stop a cut part way through a large sheet. Lay out the parts so that pieces of the same width line up; that way, you can cut all the way through a sheet without stopping. This may involve some waste, but it makes cutting much easier. Also, keep in mind that you will lose about $\frac{1}{16}$ of an inch for each saw kerf, so you can't get four 12″-wide shelves from a 4′ sheet of plywood. You either have to split the difference between each shelf or settle for three shelves from that sheet.

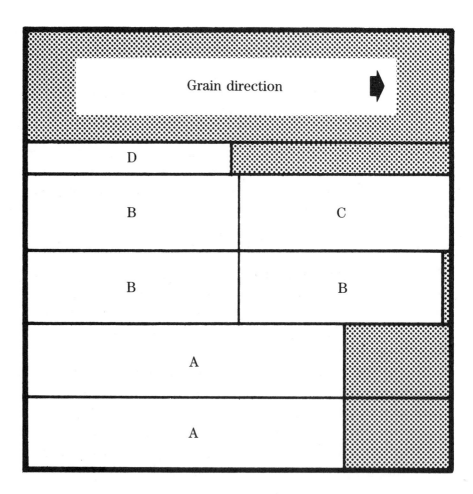

Illus. 50. A cutting plan helps to minimize waste and make cutting easier. The shaded areas are un-used.

THE STORY STICK

One of the cabinetmaker's secret ways of measuring more accurately than plus or minus $\frac{1}{16}$ of an inch is by using the story stick. A story stick is simply a scrap of wood that is 1 or 2 inches wide and a little longer than the length of the board being measured. You should use the story stick when you need to make multiple joints in several boards. Lay out the position of the joints on a story stick and then transfer the marks to the boards from the stick; this way, you minimize the chance for error by only measuring once. Another advantage of the story stick is that you can use it for setting up machines to make joints or holes. You can make a test cut on the story stick to make sure that the setup is right; and if the setup is wrong, you haven't ruined the actual board.

Another way cabinetmakers measure very accurately is by taking measurements directly from the work whenever possible. Once you have one part cut, use it as a reference for parts that have to match it. If you are using a table saw for cutting out the parts, make all the cuts that are the same size before moving the fence or stop.

You shouldn't lay out or cut certain parts, however, until you've begun the actual assembly of the cabinet. For example, a flush door needs to be custom-fit to the opening after the cabinet has been assembled. Some parts, such as face-frame stiles and rails, can be marked for length directly from the boards where they are attached. To do this, hold the part in place and mark its length directly from the side of the adjoining board.

This method totally eliminates the need for using a tape measure and the tendency to round off to the nearest $\frac{1}{16}''$. One caution when using this method: Don't tilt the board by putting one end inside the opening and letting the long end hang over the end, or you will end up with an error. The board must be held square with the front. On larger projects, it is difficult to hold the actual board in place, so you should use a story stick to transfer the measurement. With the story stick, you also have the added advantage of being able to cut it to length and test-fit it before you cut the actual part.

Of course, you can't use these methods in every case, so you also need to learn how to accurately read a tape measure.

USING A TAPE MEASURE

The tape measure is one of the fundamental tools of the cabinetmaker. Most cabinetmakers use a 12′ tape with a $\frac{3}{4}''$-wide blade. The accuracy of the tape depends on the end hook on the blade. Good-quality tapes have a hook that is either loosely attached to the blade or swings out of the way for inside measurements. The loosely attached type is the most convenient because it automatically compensates for inside measurement. There is exactly the right amount of play in the attachment holes so that the hook pulls out slightly when it is hooked over the end of a board and it pushes in when it is pressed against something for an inside measure. This way, the end of the tape is in the same position in both cases. Most tape measures are divided into sixteenths of an inch, but some are divided into thirty-seconds for the first foot and sixteenths thereafter.

When you use a tape measure, you must keep it flat and straight. Line up the tape with an edge of the board. If you place it at a slight diagonal, you will get an incorrect measurement. Also, keep the tape flat against the board all along its surface. If the board has a slight bow in it, and you let the tape span the bow, the measurement will be incorrect. When measuring a board with a bow, put the tape on crown side (the side that is high in the middle); this makes it easier to keep the tape flat against the surface.

To read the tape, look squarely at the edge you want to measure. Viewing the tape from an angle leads to inaccuracies.

Since most tapes are marked in sixteenths of an inch, there is a tendency to subconsciously round off the reading to the nearest sixteenth. To avoid this, cabinetmakers think in terms of fat sixteenths and thin sixteenths. If the measurement is exactly at a sixteenth mark, they call it *dead on* or *on the money*. If a board measures a little longer than $11^{7}/_{16}$″, but it's closer to $^{7}/_{16}$″ than $^{1}/_{2}$″, you would call it *11 and a fat $^{7}/_{16}$″*. If the board is really closer to $^{1}/_{2}$″ but not dead on, call it *11 and a thin $^{1}/_{2}$″*. When measuring this way, try to immediately transfer the measurement to the work so that you can keep the visual image in your mind of exactly where the mark should fall between the sixteenth marks on the tape. When you are laying out a project from the plans, always make your measurements dead on. Only use fat and thin measurements when you are fitting a part to another part that has already been cut.

There are two ways of making inside measurements. Most tapes have a note on the case, such as: *add $2^{1}/_{2}$″ for inside measure*. This means that if you butt the hook against one side and the back of the tape case against the other and then take a reading at the point where the tape exits the case, you can get the actual inside measurement by adding $2^{1}/_{2}$″. Although this method tends to be awkward, it is probably the best way for a beginner to take inside measurements. However, many experienced cabinetmakers prefer bending the tape up the opposite side and reading the dimension directly, but this takes experience because the tape is bent right at the point where you need to read. To learn this method, take readings both ways and notice where the actual measurement falls on the curve. Although this method may seem inaccurate, someone who is experienced with it can usually get an accurate reading.

MAKING MARKS

A sharp pencil is the usual marking tool for most cabinetmakers; but when very accurate marks are required, a sharp knife or an awl will make a finer line. When you make a mark, draw a small arrowhead with its point at the exact measurement. It's difficult to line up exactly on a single line because the line is seldom perfectly square and you are often left wondering whether it was the low side or the high side of the mark you meant to use. An arrowhead, on the other hand, leaves no room for doubt. Make an X on waste areas to avoid confusion later on.

USING A SQUARE

Once you have a measurement marked on the board, use a square to draw a cutting line. A try square or a combination square works well on boards up to about 10 inches. For larger boards, it's best to use a framing square. Place the square against the best edge; a factory edge or a jointed edge is preferable.

Occasionally check your square for accuracy by performing this test: Choose a scrap board with a good straight edge, and then place the square against the edge and draw a line. Next, flip the square over so that it is still against the same edge but on the opposite side of the line, and then align the square with the line you just drew. It should line up perfectly; if it doesn't, your square has lost its accuracy. Dropping the square or other rough treatment can account for the inaccuracy.

Truing and Squaring

The boards you use for building a cabinet must be flat and square. Both faces should be parallel to each other, and the edges should be square (exactly 90°) with the face and parallel to each other. For your initial projects, it's a good idea to use plywood, particle board, or high-grade S4S lumber. Plywood and other man-made sheet material are very dimensionally stable and resist warping; they are surfaced at the mill to be smooth and flat. Sheet material also comes with four factory edges that are square and true, so you have a good square reference point for all other cuts. High-grade S4S lumber is also surfaced at the mill to be flat and have true, square edges.

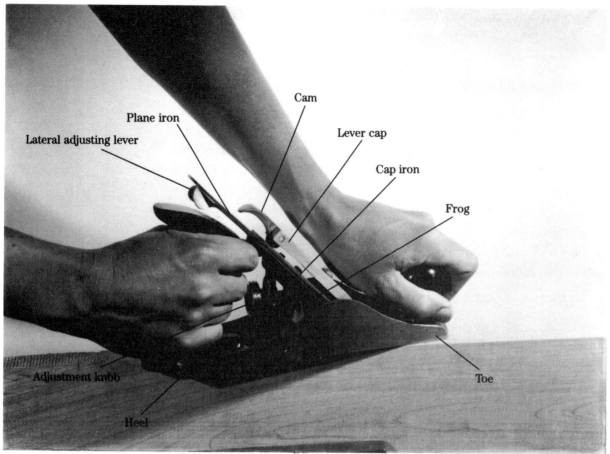

Illus. 51. The parts of a plane.

If you choose your lumber carefully, you won't need to do any initial surfacing or squaring; however, a time will come when you will need to know how to true and square a board. Sometimes a board may warp after you buy it. Some boards have internal stresses; when you cut into the board, you upset the balance of stresses, and the two pieces will curve off in different directions. If you want to work with rough lumber, you definitely need to know how to true and square a board.

The plane is the hand tool that is most useful for truing and squaring lumber. In terms of power equipment, the jointer and the surface planer are the most useful.

USING A PLANE

You should have a block plane and a jack plane in your basic set of tools. The block plane is used mostly for fitting and trimming. For truing and squaring, the longer jack plane is especially useful. An even larger plane, called a jointer plane, can also be used for truing and squaring.

Illus. 51 shows the parts of a plane. For rough cuts, turn the adjustment knob to expose more blade; then pull the blade in some for fine-finishing cuts. The cap iron should be set at about $\frac{3}{32}$ of an inch away from the cutting edge for rough cutting; for finish work, move the cap iron closer. For most work, $\frac{1}{16}$ of an inch is a good distance; but for very hard wood, move the cap iron even closer to the cutting edge. The lateral adjustment lever keeps the blade straight in the throat. Grasp the plane, as shown in Illus. 51. Apply forward pressure on the rear handle and downwards pressure on the front handle. At the end of the cut, release the pressure on the toe of the plane.

When you set a plane down, put it on its side. This protects the blade and the surface you are setting it on. When you put a plane away, retract the blade. This will protect the blade from getting nicked by some other tool.

CORRECTING DEFECTS

The four most common problems you will run into are cupping, bowing, twisting, and edges that aren't true.

Cupping   This usually occurs in plain-sawn boards. The board curves or cups in the direction that is opposite to the annual rings. To test for cupping, place the blade of a square on the board, as shown in Illus. 52. If you can see light between the blade and the

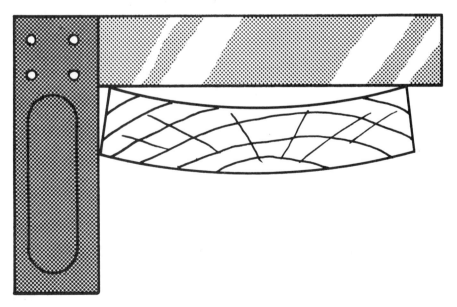

Illus. 52. Using a square to test for cupping.

board at the edges on one side of the board and in the middle on the other side, the board is cupped.

To correct cupping with a plane, clamp the board to a workbench so that the high edges are up. Plane-down the high edges. Take a medium cut with the plane and hold the plane at about a 10° angle to the grain direction. Push the plane parallel to the grain direction. If the blade catches or tears out chips of wood, plane in the opposite direction. Periodically check the surface with a square, and stop planing when the blade of the square rests flat all across the surface. Now turn the board over and repeat the process, only plane-down the high point in the middle of the board. When both sides are flat, set the plane for a shallow cut and dress up both sides to get a smooth surface.

To correct a cupped board with power equipment, you need a jointer and a surface planer. First run the side with the high edges over the jointer until the blade is cutting all the way across the face, and then place the board with the jointed side against the table of a surface planer and run the board through the planer until the high middle of the board has been cut off. Simply running a cupped board through the surface planer without jointing it first won't correct most cupped boards. This is because the feed rollers will press the board flat against the table during the cutting, but the board will spring back to a cupped shape after it leaves the outfeed rollers.

Correcting a cupped board decreases the thickness of the board. Extremely cupped boards may become so thin that they are useless for their intended applications. If a board is too cupped to salvage by planing, save it for a time when you need some thin strips. However, if you rip a cupped board into several smaller boards, the cupping in each of the smaller boards will be minimal. You can then use these smaller boards the way they are or you can correct them with some minor planing.

Bowing   This is a curvature along the length of a board. Although you can usually see bowing by sighting along the board, you can also test for it by placing a straightedge along the board. You can usually use slightly bowed boards without correcting them. This is because clamping the bowed board during assembly will frequently take the bow out and other parts of the cabinet where the board is attached will hold it straight once the glue sets or fasteners are installed.

If a board is badly bowed, use it for shorter parts. Cutting it into smaller lengths will usually bring the bowing into acceptable limits.

If you have no other alternatives, you can use a plane to remove the bow. Place the board on a bench with the crown (the side that is high in the middle) up. Clamp or nail a small board to the bench at one end of the board that will act as a bench stop. This prevents the board from moving as you plane. Plane-down the crown, pushing the plane in the direction of the bench stop. Check your progress by placing a long straightedge on the face of the board; when it lies flat on the face of the board, stop planing and turn the board over. Repeat the process, but remove wood from the high ends of the board instead of from the middle. This process will make the board thinner than its original thickness; if that is unacceptable on the cabinet you are building, your only alternative is using another board.

It is difficult to remove a bow using power equipment because both the jointer and the surface planer tend to follow the bow. One method that works, however, is using the jointer to remove wood from the high ends by placing the board over the blade past its middle and pushing it through, and then turning the board end for end and repeating the process. When the ends are cut down to the level of the middle, put the jointed side down on the surface-planer table and take a cut off the top. Set the cutting depth very shallow because the board gets thicker towards the middle.

Twisting   Boards tend to twist along their length due to internal stresses set up as the cells dry out. A board that is cut from a part of the tree that has an uneven cell structure will likely twist as it dries. Slightly twisted boards can be clamped flat during assembly, but a badly twisted board may pull the rest of the cabinet out of square.

The best solution for a twisted board is cutting the board into smaller parts. You can plane diagonally from one high corner to the other on both sides of short boards to remove the twist.

Edges That Aren't True   The edges of a board must be straight (without high spots or dips) and square with the face of the board. This is especially important when two boards will be edge-joined together to form a larger part. To see if the edge is straight, place a straightedge on the edge or sight along the edge (Illus. 53). Use a square to see if the edge is square with the face (Illus. 54).

If you find high spots on the edge, make a mark on the face of the board where they begin and end. Marking on the face is better than marking on the edge because marks on the edge are liable to get planed off. Clamp the board in a vise with the edge up and plane

Plane down high spots.

Straightedge

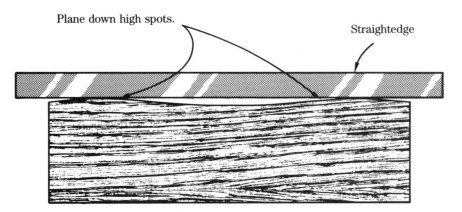

Illus. 53. Checking for high spots with a straightedge.

down the high spots, checking your progress with a straightedge. When the edge is straight, set the plane for fine cut and take one long continuous pass along the entire edge of the board.

If the edges are not square with the face, clamp the board edge up in a vise, hold the plane square with the face, and plane along the entire edge. If you have difficulty holding the plane square with the face, try using a shooting board (Illus. 55). The shooting board

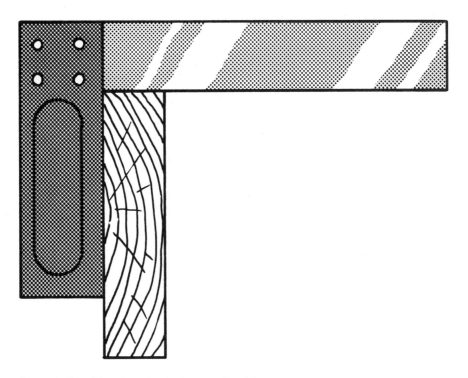

Illus. 54. Checking the edge-to-face angle with a square.

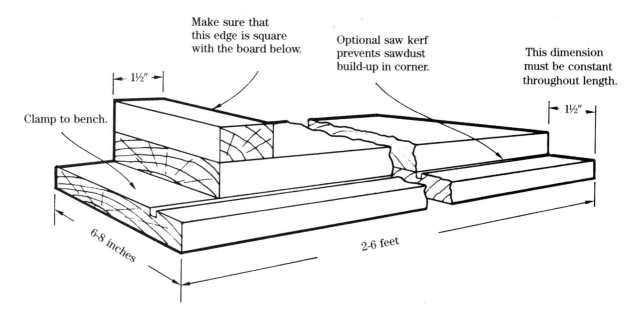

Make sure that this edge is square with the board below.

Optional saw kerf prevents sawdust build-up in corner.

This dimension must be constant throughout length.

1½"

1½"

Clamp to bench.

6-8 inches

2-6 feet

Illus. 55. A shooting board helps to guide the plane when truing an edge. You should place the board with its end against the stop on the shooting board and the edge to be trued slightly overhanging the lipped section of the shooting board. The plane needs to be placed on its side on the lipped part of the shooting board. Keeping the side of the plane against the shooting board ensures a square edge on the board being planed.

guides the plane and keeps it square. Rub some paraffin on the part that the side of the plane rides on to lubricate it. Place the board to be planed on the shooting board with the edge projecting about ⅛ of an inch past the lip of the shooting board. Place the plane on its side and rest it against the shooting board. Now plane along the entire edge of the board, making sure that the side of the plane is always resting on the shooting board.

Truing an edge—or jointing, as it is commonly called—is the primary job of the jointer. If you have a jointer, use it for jointing the edges of your boards. The main thing to remember is to keep the face of the board against the fence at all times to ensure that the edge will be square.

SURFACING AND SQUARING ROUGH LUMBER

When you are working with lumber that has been surfaced at the mill, you have at least one flat surface to use as a reference point for squaring the other edges. With rough lumber, on the other hand, you don't have any flat surfaces to begin with. Thus, your first task is getting one flat surface.

Examine both faces and choose the one that appears to be the flattest. If the face isn't cupped and contains only minor irregularities, you can place that face on the table of the surface planer and surface the other side until it is flat, and then you can turn the board over and surface the first side. If neither side is flat enough to be placed directly on the planer table, you will have to run one side over the jointer first. You'll need a large jointer if you plan on surfacing wide boards. Run one face over the jointer until it is flat, and then place that face against the table of the surface planer and surface the other face.

When you have both faces flat, choose the best edge and run it over the jointer. When that edge is square, you need to cut the other edge so that it is parallel to the jointed edge. The easiest way of doing this is setting the rip fence of a table saw to the width of the narrowest part of the board (or to a specific width if you are cutting the board to width at this time). Place the jointed edge against the fence and run the board through the saw.

Finally, square the ends by placing a square against the jointed edge and marking a square cut across the face.

You can also square and surface rough lumber by hand. If you plan on doing very much hand planing of rough lumber, it would be a good idea to invest in a jointer plane. This plane is about 23 inches long. The long sole spans low spots and allows the blade to cut down high spots, making it easier to get a flat surface.

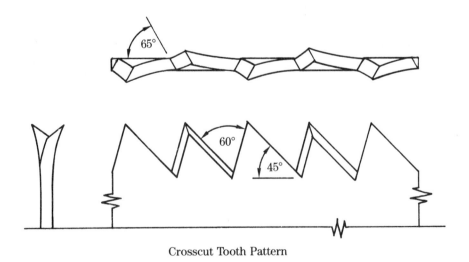

Crosscut Tooth Pattern

Illus. 56. The teeth of a crosscut saw resemble a knife blade. This type of saw cleanly shears off the wood fibres.

Begin by planing one face flat. Set the plane for a deep cut and plane diagonally across the surface. When the surface is fairly flat, reduce the thickness of the cut and plane with the grain. When you have finished one face, turn the board over and plane the other side. The trick is keeping the two faces parallel. Measure the thickness of the board at several points along both edges. Take more wood off the thick areas so that the board is uniformly thick throughout.

When you have finished the faces, use a shooting board to joint one edge. Now measuring from the jointed edge, mark a line parallel to the jointed edge on the other edge of the board. If there isn't a large variation from parallel on the rough edge, simply plane to the line to bring the edges parallel. When a lot of wood needs to be removed to make the edges parallel, saw along the line with a rip saw and then dress up the cut with a plane set for taking a thin shaving.

Cutting

When you have a flat and true board and you have laid out the cuts, the next step is cutting the parts to size. For smaller projects, a good handsaw can be as fast and accurate as a power saw; but for larger projects, a power saw will be more accurate and will make the job easier.

USING A CROSSCUT SAW

A crosscut saw has specially sharpened teeth that cut the longitudinal fibres in a board (Illus. 56). You should use the crosscut saw for making cuts across the grain. The easiest way of cutting small boards is by firmly clamping them to a workbench. It's easy to cut larger boards if you hold them down with your knee on a sawhorse. Place the board with the good side up because the crosscut saw tends to tear small splinters from the bottom side of the board.

Position the saw blade so that the entire cut will be made on the waste side of the line. Hold the saw at about a 30° angle to the edge and square with the surface. Hold the saw in your dominant hand (right or left) and place your other hand on the board with your thumb resting against the smooth steel of the blade, just behind the teeth. Your thumb acts as a stop, preventing the blade from wandering past the line until it gets started.

To start the cut, pull up on the saw without exerting much pressure to get a small kerf started; then push downwards, exerting a little pressure and using a short stroke. As the blade enters the wood, lengthen your stroke and exert more pressure. The saw cuts on the downwards stroke, so don't exert any pressure on the return stroke. When the blade is about 1 inch into the wood, begin taking long strokes that travel almost the full length of the blade and continue sawing in a steady, moderate rhythm. Short, fast strokes only wear you out and aren't as productive as long, rhythmic strokes. When you get near the end of the cut, support the waste end of the board with your free hand and revert back to short, gentle strokes to avoid breaking the waste off before finishing the cut. If the waste is not supported, it will break off prematurely, tearing a splinter out of the face of the board.

You can cut plywood the same way as solid lumber, but the face veneer will tend to chip and splinter along the cut. One way of minimizing this is by placing masking tape on both faces of the plywood so that it covers the area of the cut. Make your cutting line on top of the tape so that you can see it. Press the tape down firmly so that it adheres to the wood. After you make the cut, remove the tape. The tape should prevent most of the chipping, but some types of plywood will chip even when you use the tape. If this happens, place a straightedge along the cut line and cut through the face veneer with a sharp knife before making the cut with the saw. This should eliminate all chipping, as long as the saw doesn't stray past the knife cut. Usually it is only necessary to make the knife cut on the bottom face of the board; but in severe cases, you may need to make a knife cut on both faces.

USING A RIP SAW

You should use the rip saw for making cuts parallel to the grain. The rip saw has teeth shaped like small chisels, which shave away the wood parallel to the grain (Illus. 57). When you cut with the rip saw, you follow the same basic procedures you used with the crosscut saw, except you hold the saw at a steeper angle—at about 45°. And since rip cuts are usually longer, you need to use a different method for supporting the board.

For short boards, simply hang one end of the board a few inches off the bench and begin cutting. When the saw gets near the edge of the bench, stop cutting and move the board farther out past the edge. Continue in this manner until there is too much of the board hanging off the bench for you to handle. At this point, it will be easier if someone else supports the end of the board for you. If you

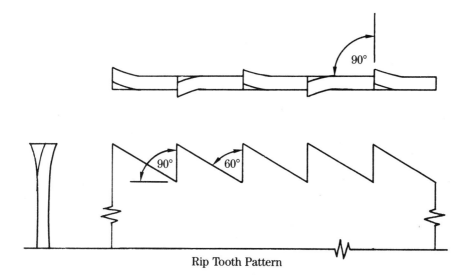

Rip Tooth Pattern

Illus. 57. Rather than shearing off the fibres, the rip saw actually planes away small shavings from the saw kerf.

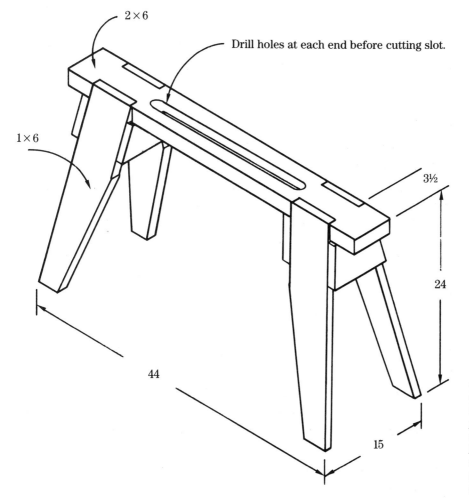

2 × 6

Drill holes at each end before cutting slot.

1 × 6

3½

24

44

15

Illus. 58. A ripping saw horse makes ripping by hand easier. The board is positioned over the slot so that the saw is in the slot. For long cuts, the board is moved forward each time the saw reaches the end of the slot.

can't get help, turn the board around so that the cut portion is on the bench and finish the cut working away from the bench. Keep the saw as close to the bench as you can to minimize up-and-down movement of the board.

For longer boards, support the board with two sawhorses. A handy accessory for making rip cuts is the ripping horse (Illus. 58). This is a sawhorse that has an extra-wide top and a slot running down the middle. Simply place the board to be ripped on the horse, leaving enough room between the end of the board and the end of the slot for the saw, and then begin ripping.

USING POWER SAWS

Three types of power saws are usually used for cutting parts to size: the portable circular saw, the table saw, and the radial-arm saw. The portable circular saw is the least expensive of the three and the one most frequently used by do-it-yourselfers. Large cabinet shops usually have table saws and radial-arm saws, which are especially suited for specific jobs even though they are both multipurpose machines. The radial-arm saw works well for crosscutting and, in a large shop, is usually set up for that job alone. The table saw is especially good for ripping, but it can handle crosscutting as well.

Whenever you use power equipment, follow all of the manufacturer's directions and safety precautions, keep all parts of your body away from the blade, and use the guards that are provided.

If chipping occurs when you are cutting plywood with a power saw, use the same techniques of applying tape or making a knife cut that were described for cutting with a handsaw.

Portable Circular Saw   Before cutting with a portable circular saw, set the depth adjustment so that only about ¼″ of the blade will protrude from below the board. Place the board with the good side down (the opposite of handsawing). Lay out the cut with a square, as you would for a handsaw. The saw base will keep the cut square, so you only need to worry about following the line. There is a mark at the front of the shoe that indicates the blade position; place the tip of the table on the board and line up the mark with the cutting line. Look at the manufacturer's directions to find out how to position the mark so that the cutting line is left on the good side of the cut.

Make sure that the blade is not touching the wood, and then start the saw. *Keep your fingers away from the cutting path, both in front of and behind the saw.* Advance the saw into the board at a speed that doesn't lug down the motor. Follow the cutting line with the mark at the tip of the shoe.

The easiest way of supporting a board for ripping with a portable circular saw is by placing it on a piece of scrap the same length and allowing the blade to cut slightly into the scrap.

You can make rip cuts up to about 8 inches by using an auxiliary fence that attaches to the saw. The fence should ride against a jointed edge. You can also use a straight board as a cutting guide. Measure the distance from the side of the shoe to the blade, and then clamp the board that distance from the cutting line. Make sure that the board is the same distance away from the line, all along its length. To keep the cut straight, let the side of the shoe rub along the board as you cut.

Radial-Arm Saw   To crosscut with a radial-arm saw, place the board on the table with the good side up. Put the best edge against the fence. To lay out a board for cutting on the radial-arm saw, it is only necessary to make a small mark on the edge of the board at the correct length. The saw will make a square cut automatically. With the saw off, line up the mark with the blade, making sure that the entire kerf will be in the waste. Turn on the saw and pull it through the board. *Always keep your arms and hands out of the blade path and return the saw to the rear of the track after each cut.*

You can make multiple cuts of the same length by placing a stop on the fence at the proper position and then by positioning each board against the stop. Try not to hit the stop too hard with the board to keep from moving the stop. You can use a commercial stop or simply clamp a small scrap to the fence.

You can also make rip cuts with the radial-arm saw up to the length of its arm. Lock the saw head in position on the arm and rotate it 90°. Place the board against the fence and feed it into the saw.

Table Saw   The blade on a table saw should be set so that only about ⅛ of an inch protrudes above the board being cut; this is not only safer, it also helps to minimize chipping. Don't make any adjustments to the saw while it is running. When cutting on the table saw, the good side of the board should be up. *Stand off to the side of the blade line to avoid being hit if the board kicks back.* When the saw is running, keep your hands at least 6″ away from the blade in all directions. If you need to cut something smaller than 6″, use a push stick that will keep your hands 6″ away from the blade (Illus. 59). Don't reach over the blade to catch a board; let the board fall on the floor or use a take-off table. This is a long thin table that is exactly the same height as the table-saw table. The take-off table should be placed behind the saw so that it will support the board as it leaves the saw.

To rip on the table saw, set the rip fence at the correct width. Measure from the face of the fence to the fence side of a saw tooth that is set in the direction of the fence. This will put the entire saw kerf in the waste. Turn on the saw and put a jointed edge against the fence. Feed the board into the saw, making sure that you keep the edge of the board against the fence.

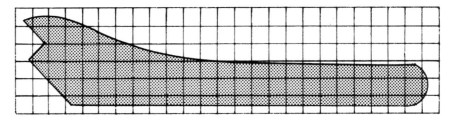

1 square = ½ inch

Illus. 59. A push stick is a necessity when using a table saw. This shape is comfortable to use, but you can make a simple push stick by cutting a notch in a scrap of wood.

Ripping long boards is usually a two-person operation. Have someone else support the boards as they leave the back of the table. That person should only support the wood; you should do all of the feeding and guiding. If you have a take-off table, you can rip long boards by yourself.

When ripping anything smaller than about 6 inches wide, you should use a push stick when the end of the board needs to be pushed past the blade. A push stick doesn't have to be fancy; a scrap of wood with a notch cut in the end will do.

To crosscut with the table saw, you need to use the mitre gauge. The mitre gauge has markings indicating degrees for angle cuts; it should be placed at 90° for square cuts. It's a good idea to check the gauge's accuracy by placing a square against the blade and the mitre gauge. Place a jointed edge against the gauge. Mark the length of the cut on the edge of the board closest to the blade, and line up the mark with the blade. Turn on the saw. Hold the board firmly against the mitre gauge, and push the mitre gauge forward to feed the board into the saw.

There are two ways of making multiple cuts of the same length using the table saw. With the first method, the fence should not be used in conjunction with the mitre gauge unless you take certain precautions; otherwise, there is a strong possibility of kickback. To use the fence as a stop and also avoid kickback, clamp a short piece of scrap to the front part of the fence. This clearance block should stop before it reaches the blade. Set the fence so that the distance between the clearance block and the blade is the length of the piece. With the mitre gauge pulled back even with the clearance block, position the board to be cut against the clearance block. Hold the board firmly against the mitre gauge and feed it into the saw. The board should not be in contact with the clearance block when the cut is complete.

The other way of making multiple cuts of the same length with the table saw is by attaching a wood extension to the face of the mitre gauge. The extension should be a little longer than the board being cut. Clamp or nail a stop block to the extension at the correct length. Then simply position the board so that it rests against the stop block and proceed as you normally would with the mitre gauge.

MAKING CURVED CUTS

So far, all of the saws described make only straight cuts. When you need to make a curved cut, you need to use a different type of saw. The handsaw most commonly used for making curved cuts is the coping saw. Three power saws often used for making curved cuts are the saber saw, the jig saw, and the band saw.

Using a Coping Saw The coping saw has a very thin blade stretched across a springy metal frame. The distance between the blade and the frame determines how deep you can cut into a board. The coping saw is one of the few western saws that cuts on the back stroke. When inserting a new blade, position it so that the teeth point towards the handle. By rotating the handle and the blade attachment at the other end of the frame, you can rotate the blade to any position relative to the frame. This feature is very useful because it lets you move the frame out of the way when you make long cuts.

Clamp the board to be cut to the bench with the cutting line overhanging the edge. Try to keep the overhang to a minimum to prevent the board from springing back and forth. For long cuts, you may need to reposition the board several times.

Hold the saw only by the handle; applying any pressure to the other end of the frame may cause the blade to come unhooked. When cutting a board that is laying flat on the bench, hold the handle of the saw under the board and follow the line on the top of the board. If the board is clamped vertically in a vise, hold the handle on the side facing you and follow the line on that side.

You can use the coping saw for making inside cuts by drilling an entrance hole inside the waste area of the cutout. Remove the blade from the saw and place it through the hole, and then reinstall it in the handle.

To make a square corner on an inside cut, cut all the way to the line from one direction and then back the saw up a little and make a smooth curve around the corner through the waste. When you have completely cut around the cutout, remove the waste and go back to each corner and cut from the other direction to square the cut.

Using a Saber Saw   The saber saw is an inexpensive piece of portable power equipment that many beginners buy soon after they start cabinetmaking. It performs basically the same function as the coping saw. The saber saw has a short, stiff blade that is moved rapidly back and forth by an electric motor.

You can make inside cuts with the saber saw by drilling an entrance hole or by plunge cutting. To make a plunge cut, hold the saw so that the front of the shoe is resting on the face of the board and the blade is almost touching the wood. Turn on the saw and then slowly lower it so that the blade begins to cut into the face of the board. Continue slowly lowering the saw until the shoe is flat against the face and the blade has cut all the way through the board. Now proceed with normal cutting.

Don't force the saber saw, or the blade may break. Since a saber saw blade is wider than a coping saw blade, it won't cut as sharp a corner. To make very intricate cuts, you may need to first remove most of the waste with a rough cut as close to the actual shape as you can make it and then go back and cut the details. To cut inside corners, use the same procedure described for the coping saw. You can make bevel cuts by adjusting the angle of the shoe.

As with all power saws, keep your fingers away from the blade while it is in motion.

Using a Jig Saw The jig saw is like a motorized coping saw. The blades are very similar, but the jig saw blade doesn't have the cross pin attachment; instead, it is clamped into a screw-tightened jaw.

The blade on the jig saw is positioned for cutting on the downwards stroke. The motor is below the table and the upper end of the blade is supported by an overarm. As with the frame of the coping saw, the distance between the blade and the overarm limits the depth of cut. The blade can be rotated 90° in the chuck to permit long cuts.

The jig saw has a hold-down attachment that keeps the board flat against the table. You need to adjust this attachment so that there will be enough force to keep the board from clattering up and down with the blade.

Cutting with a jig saw is similar to cutting with a coping saw, except that the board is moved and the saw remains stationary. You can make inside cuts in the same manner described for the coping saw. And you can make bevel cuts by tilting the table.

Using a Band Saw In production work where speed is important, you should use a band saw for making curved cuts. The band saw has a long, flexible blade joined into a continuous loop. The blade travels over two wheels, one above the table and one below the table. The blade cuts in a downwards motion towards the table. Because the blade travels in only one direction, the board doesn't need to be held down with a special attachment as with the jig saw. The band saw has a sliding bar that resembles the hold-down attachment on the jig saw, but its function is guiding the blade. You should position the blade guide near the surface of the board, but not touching it. There are two sets of blade guides, the one just described and another set below the table. These guides must be properly adjusted for the saw to cut correctly. There are guide blocks or wheels on either side of the blade and a rear guide that controls the blade's front-to-back position.

To initially adjust the guides, back off the adjustments until none of the guides are touching the blade. The blade tension should be set so that it takes a moderate amount of finger pressure to deflect the blade. Manually rotate the lower wheel and adjust the upper wheel tilt control until the blade is riding in the middle of both wheels. Stand clear of the saw and turn it on for a few seconds until the blade position stabilizes on the wheels. If the blade moves too far from the middle of the wheel, readjust the tracking adjustment.

Turn off the saw and adjust both rear guides so that they almost touch the rear of the blade. Now adjust the side guides so that the teeth of the blade are outside of the guide. Finally, move the side guides in so that they barely touch the blade on each side without deflecting it. If the guides are properly adjusted and you have a sharp blade, you can make very accurate cuts with the band saw.

Blades in a variety of styles and widths are available for the band saw. You should use blades with fine teeth for thin stock and blades with coarser teeth for thicker stock. Wide blades make straighter cuts, but they can't turn tight curves. Narrow blades are best for tight curves. Generally, most cabinet work can be done with a $\frac{1}{4}''$-wide blade. Don't force the board into the blade, and don't force a wide blade around a sharp bend.

For intricate work, it may be necessary to make relief cuts. A relief cut is a straight cut from the waste edge to the cutting line. You make the cut and then back the saw out. When backing out long distances, it's a good idea to turn off the saw so that the blade won't be drawn off the wheels. The relief cut allows you to remove a section of the waste at the point where a difficult turn must be made, permitting the blade to turn without binding. You can make bevel cuts with the band saw by tilting the table. In most cases, the band saw is not suitable for making inside cuts. To make an inside cut, you either need to make an entrance cut through a good section of the board and later glue it back together or you need to cut the blade and weld it back together inside of an entrance hole.

As always, keep all parts of your body away from the moving blade and keep the guards in place.

4
JOINERY

The separate parts of a cabinet are held together with joints. The process of cutting the joints is called joinery. Over the centuries, cabinetmakers have developed hundreds of specialized joints. Before the development of modern glues, joinery had to be quite complex; many types of self-locking joints were developed that would stay together even if the glue failed. Modern glues have simplified joinery. The main objective now is providing the greatest surface area for gluing.

It is more difficult to separate a glue joint by spreading the joint apart than it is by applying a shear force, so many joints are designed to minimize forces on the joint. Solid lumber expands and shrinks with changes in humidity, so joints used with solid lumber need to allow for dimensional changes. Man-made materials, such as plywood and particle board, are dimensionally stable, but they require specialized joints that account for their unique properties. The type of joint used with particle board is particularly important because, while very strong in compression, particle board has a low shear strength.

Sometimes joints are used for purely decorative reasons. They may or may not actually contribute to the strength of the cabinet. Decorative joints can range from simple, exposed dowels to hand-cut dovetail joints.

Joinery Tools

Various tools are used in the process of making joints, but three are used so extensively that they can be called joinery tools; they are the chisel, the backsaw, and the router.

CHISEL

A chisel is simply a heavy blade set into a handle, but it can perform a number of different operations (Illus. 60). The blade is similar to a plane iron, only it's stouter. It can therefore withstand pressure without the support the plane iron receives from the other parts of the plane. The chisel is used mainly for chopping and paring.

Chopping is the process of cutting at approximately a 90° angle to the face of the board. It is usually done with the aid of a hammer or mallet. Chopping is usually used for defining the edges of a section to be cut out with the chisel. Chopping around the edges of a cutout cuts the wood fibres so that they won't tear past the line (Illus. 61).

Chopping is also used for removing large amounts of wood and bringing a cut to its approximate depth. Hold the chisel so that the bevel is facing the wood and the blade is at about a 60° angle. Use a hammer or mallet to drive the chisel, and chop into the wood, as shown in Illus. 62. Notice that the cut is made across the grain. Use a

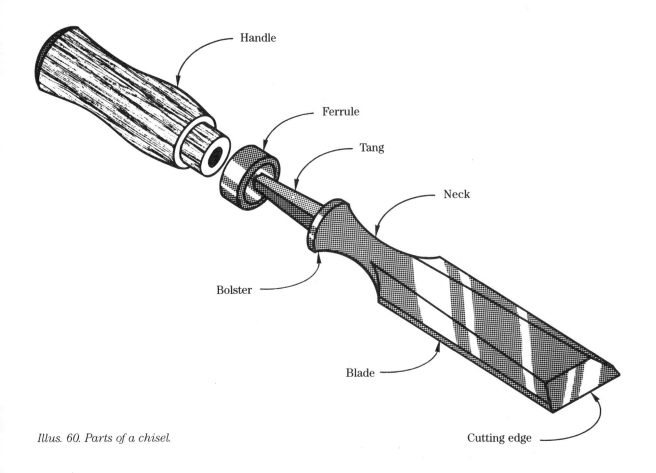

Illus. 60. Parts of a chisel.

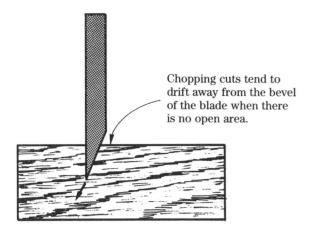

Chopping cuts tend to
drift away from the bevel
of the blade when there
is no open area.

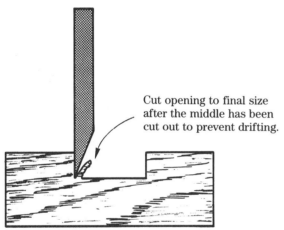

Cut opening to final size
after the middle has been
cut out to prevent drifting.

Illus. 61. Chopping cuts with a chisel.

Make stop cuts.

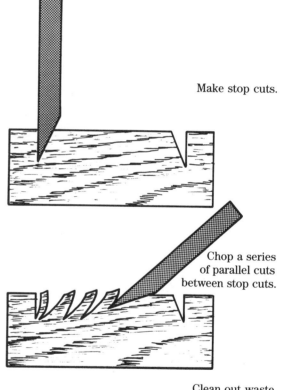

Chop a series
of parallel cuts
between stop cuts.

Clean out waste
and square up.

*Illus. 62. Using a chisel for removing wood between
stop cuts.*

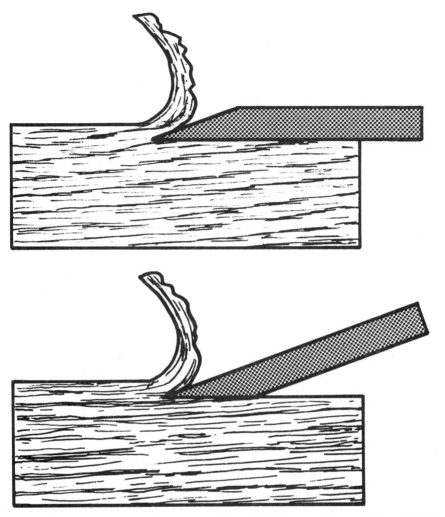

Illus. 63. You can make paring cuts with the chisel in one of two positions. With the bevel up and the back of the blade flat against the surface, you can make fine cuts although you are limited by the length of the chisel blade (top). With the bevel down and flat against the surface, you can make cuts of any length (bottom).

chisel that is approximately the same width as the cut you are making. Stop the cut a little short of the correct depth. Make a series of parallel cuts in this manner—from one end of the cutout to the other. Break out the loose chips, and then begin using the chisel for paring.

When paring, the chisel blade resembles a plane iron in the way it shaves off a slice of wood. Paring is used for removing wood inside of a cutout and for smoothing the surface of the wood at the bottom of the cutout area. You can pare with the grain or across the grain. You can tap the handle with a hammer or mallet, or you can use body force to move the chisel. *Whatever method you use, remember to keep both hands behind the cutting edge of the chisel to prevent accidents if the blade should slip.* When paring, the board should be firmly clamped down. There are two ways you can hold the chisel for paring. For roughing out a cutout, hold the chisel so that the bevel of the blade is facing the wood. This places the handle on an angle away from the wood, making the chisel easy to hold and control. To make a very smooth finishing cut, you can pare with the flat back of the blade resting against the wood. This places the handle down low against the wood, making the chisel awkward to use in some situations (Illus. 63).

Paring all the way across a board can lead to tear-outs at the edge. To prevent this, pare from both sides towards the middle (Illus. 64). Giving a slight twisting motion to the chisel will help to cleanly shear off the fibres when paring end grain or across the grain.

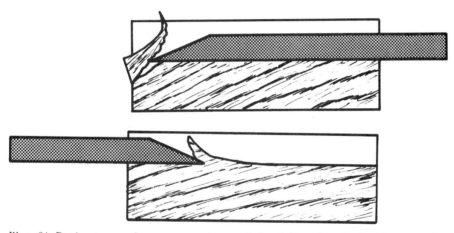

Illus. 64. Paring to an edge can cause tear-outs (top). Pare from both sides towards the middle to prevent this (bottom).

BACKSAW

The backsaw and its cousins, the tenon saw and dovetail saw, are very useful for making joints. The backsaw has a stiffener along its back that keeps it straight and eliminates whipping. You hold a backsaw with its teeth flat against the wood, instead of at an angle, as you would hold a panel saw. You make the cut across the entire surface at once; this means that the cut will be very straight and that you can stop the cut part way through the board and get a flat-bottomed cut. This is very important for making certain joints, such as the rabbet and dado. The teeth on a backsaw are finer than those on most panel saws, so there is less tearing and chipping. A backsaw is often used with guide blocks or a mitre box to hold the saw in exact alignment.

ROUTER

The router is basically an electric motor that turns at a high speed of 11,000 to 23,000 rpm. The motor is mounted in an adjustable base that controls the depth of cut. A chuck or collet is connected to the motor shaft and different bits or cutters can be mounted in the chuck.

Many types of bits are available for the router. Specially shaped bits are used for making decorative edges; but for joinery, the most useful bit is simply the straight bit. Straight bits come in several sizes. You can get a bit that will cut the exact size of the groove you need, or you can use a smaller bit and make more than one cut. Another useful joinery bit is the rabbeting bit. This bit has a guide post called a pilot that rubs against the edge of the board. The pilot keeps the cut parallel to the edge. If the edge is straight, the cut will be straight. The pilot bit will also follow a curved edge, so it is very useful for making joints in curved parts. More expensive pilot bits have small ball bearings mounted on the pilot; this makes the bit less likely to burn the edge.

You can guide a router freehand to make rough cutouts or to do decorative carving; but for most joinery tasks, you need to use some type of guide to keep the router straight. Using an auxiliary fence is one way to guide the router. The fence attaches to the router base and will guide the router parallel to an edge of the board.

Another way of guiding the router is by clamping a board that has a straight edge to the work and letting the base rub against the board. If it is important for the router not to stray from the line in either direction, as when making a dado, then you can use two boards, one on either side of the cut. By using clamped boards as a guide, you can make cuts that are not parallel with an edge of the board. This can be useful if you need to make joints at odd angles.

A third way of guiding the router uses a special template-following collar that is mounted around the bit on the base of the router. The collar is used with a template usually made of ¼″ hardboard. The collar will follow the shape of the template exactly. The template size is slightly larger than the actual cutout to allow for the thickness of the collar. This type of guide is useful for making mortises or for cutting gains for hinges.

You can mount the router in an accessory table, which makes it operate in the same way as a small shaper. The router table incorporates an adjustable fence that can be used for guiding the work. A router table is a useful accessory for working with small parts because the wood is moved instead of the router.

The router can throw wood chips at high velocity, so always wear eye protection. Keep a firm grip on the router so that it won't get out of control if the bit grabs.

The Five Basic Joints

Out of the hundreds of joints developed, five have become so popular that they can be called the basic joints of cabinetmaking. They are butt, rabbet, dado, mitre, and half-lap. You can cut all of these joints with simple hand tools or with power equipment. Using these five basic joints, you can build almost any type of cabinet.

As you advance, you will want to use some of the more advanced joints, but you will probably still find that the five basic joints will fulfill most of your needs.

The five basic joints are recommended for all materials—solid lumber, plywood, and particle board. Some of the more advanced joints, on the other hand, are designed specifically for solid wood and won't perform well when used with man-made materials.

BUTT

The butt joint is the simplest joint to cut. However, the butt joint requires some type of reinforcement to give it strength and it's not self-aligning during assembly, so the butt joint is not always the simplest one to use.

You can use the butt joint to make a corner or to edge-join two boards into a larger panel. When a butt joint is put together so that the end grain of one part attaches to the long grain of another part, the joint must always be reinforced. Otherwise, the difference in expansion and shrinkage between end grain and long grain will eventually cause the joint to fall apart. When boards are joined long grain to long grain and a fairly large gluing surface is present, as is the case when two boards are joined to form a larger panel, no reinforcement is necessary when using modern glues.

You can use the butt joint to make two types of corners. One type of corner is used when you are making face frames. The end of one

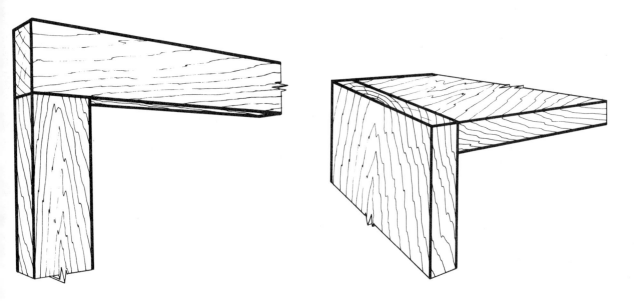

Illus. 65 (left). You should use this type of butt joint for making face frames. Illus. 66 (right). You can use this type of butt joint for joining the sides to the top or bottom of a cabinet.

board is joined to the edge of another (Illus. 65). The other type of corner is used for a situation such as joining the side to the top of a cabinet. In this case, the square end of one board is attached to the flat face of the other board (Illus. 66). You can also use butt joints to join parts, such as shelves, to the sides of a cabinet (Illus. 67).

The ends must be cut perfectly square and the face must be truly flat or the contact point will be too small for a good glue bond. Small projects that won't be subjected to very much stress can use butt joints that are simply glued and firmly clamped; but in most cases, the butt joint must be reinforced in some manner. The simplest type of reinforcement is nailing through the joint. Screws are another form of simple reinforcement. However, both of these methods leave visible holes in the exterior of the joint that must be filled when appearance is important.

A reinforcing block strengthens a butt joint and allows screws to be put in from the back (Illus. 68). A smaller reinforcing block without screws is called a glue block. You need to spread glue on the sides of the glue block and press it in place, and then rapidly rub it back and forth in place until the glue grabs. The reinforcing block is clearly visible from the inside of the joint; if this is not desirable, then dowels are a good alternative.

Dowel joints are fairly easy to make, and they adapt well to production-line work. They have therefore become very popular in inexpensive, mass-produced cabinetry. However, dowel joints that join end grain to long grain tend to loosen over time.

The simplest type of dowel joint uses the dowel in much the same way as you would use a nail or screw. When used in this manner, the joint is frequently called a pegged joint (Illus. 69). The hole for the dowel is drilled after the joint has been assembled, and the dowel is driven into the hole and cut off flush. This type of dowel joint will be much stronger if the dowels are angled slightly, as shown in Illus. 70. Dowels can shrink and become loose in their holes; angling them makes it more difficult for the parts to separate than if you used straight dowels.

When you do not want the end of the dowel to show, you should use a blind dowel joint (Illus. 71), although this joint is not as strong as the pegged joint. With the blind dowel joint, neither end of the hole comes to the surface of the board and the holes must be drilled before the joint is assembled. You can lay out the position of the holes manually or use one of several types of jigs to align the holes.

To manually align the holes, clamp the two boards together, as shown in Illus. 72. Use a square to mark the position of the holes across both boards at once. Use a marking gauge or set the blade of a combination square to act as a marking gauge, and mark the middle line of the holes. Make sure that you hold the marking gauge against the same face on both parts to compensate for any error.

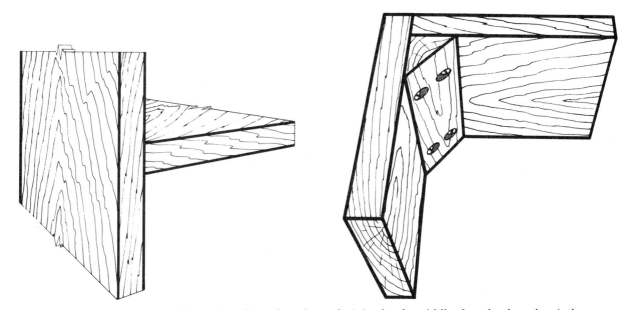

Illus. 67 (left). You can also use butt joints when a board must be joined to the middle of another board, as is the case when attaching shelves. Illus. 68 (right). A reinforcing block provides long grain-to-long grain gluing surfaces and also conceals screws.

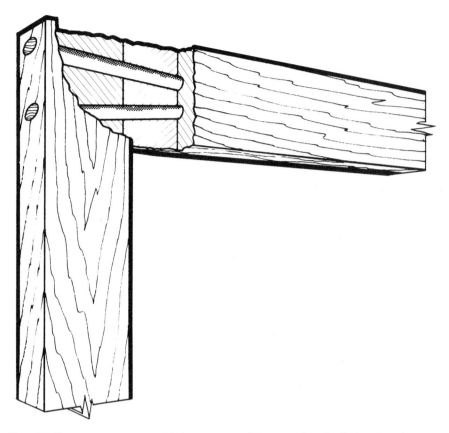

Illus. 69. You can use a pegged joint, such as this one, when building face frames. Angling the dowels increases their holding power.

Dowel centers are an easy way of locating blind dowel holes. Drill the holes in one of the parts and then insert the dowel centers into the holes. The dowel centers come in several popular sizes that fit most standard-dowel sizes. In the middle of the dowel center there is a small point. This point makes a mark indicating the middle of the hole on the corresponding part. Simply clamp the two parts together temporarily in their correct alignment to make the marks. Dowel centers have the advantage of automatically compensating for errors in layout (Illus. 73).

A dowelling jig is a tool that automatically centers the drill bit and guides it to make a straight hole. You must lay out the positions of the holes with a square as described for manual layout, but it is not necessary to mark the middle line. Even though the jig automatically compensates for boards of varying thickness and approximately centers the drill bit for each thickness, it is a good idea to place the jig so that it faces the same way on both parts to compensate for errors in centering.

The brad-point drill bit is the best type to use for doweling because it doesn't wander from the mark as twist drills do.

The holes should always be a little deeper than the length of the dowel to allow for expansion and shrinkage and to allow a space for excess glue. You can use a piece of masking tape wrapped around the drill bit to indicate the depth, or you can use a commercial drill stop to keep all of the holes the same depth.

Dowels used in joints should be chamfered at the ends to allow easy insertion into the holes, and they should have a small groove in their side to allow glue to escape from the holes. You can buy ready-made dowels that are cut to length and chamfered and have spiral or straight grooves. You can also buy dowelling in 3' lengths and cut your own dowels. Scratch a groove in the side of the dowel with an awl. The groove doesn't have to spiral as it does in the commercial variety; a straight groove will do.

Apply glue to the mating surfaces of the boards. Drip a little glue

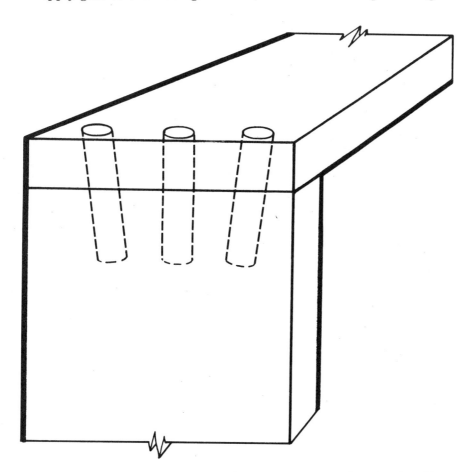

Illus. 70. You can also use pegged joints when joining the top to the sides of a cabinet. Note that the middle dowel is straight and the two outside ones are angled.

into the dowel holes, and then use a splinter to spread the glue around inside the holes. Don't use too much glue or the joint won't pull together.

Another way of reinforcing a butt joint is by screwing on steel reinforcing angles. The flat kind frequently used works well. However, the type called a chair brace is more rigid; its shape helps to hold the joint square and it has less tendency to bend.

Another reinforcement similar to the angle brace is the knock-down fitting. This is a brace that comes in two parts; one part fits on each board. The two parts can be locked together or taken apart at any time. This type of fitting is sometimes used in commercial cabinets so that they can be shipped flat to save shipping costs. The cabinets can easily be assembled on the job. There are more details on knock-down fittings in Chapter 5.

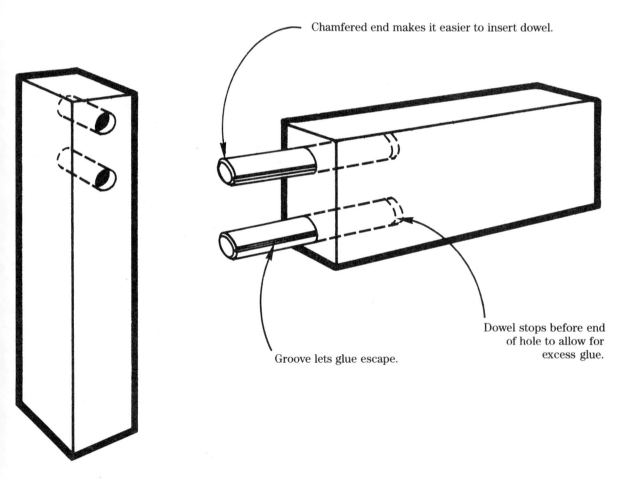

Chamfered end makes it easier to insert dowel.

Groove lets glue escape.

Dowel stops before end of hole to allow for excess glue.

Illus. 71. Blind dowels are completely concealed. Care must be taken to allow clearance for excess glue, or else hydraulic pressure may split the wood or hold the joint open when clamped.

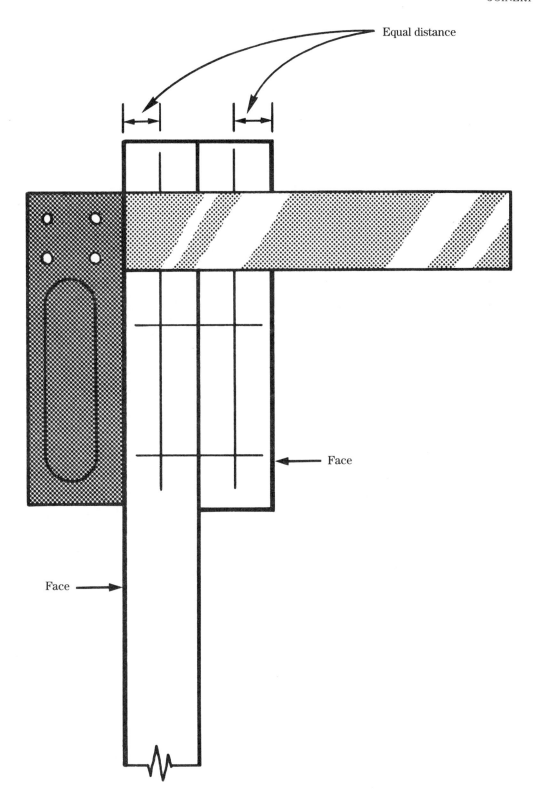

Equal distance

Face

Face

Illus. 72. To mark dowel positions, place the parts together with the faces to the outside. Measure from the face of each board.

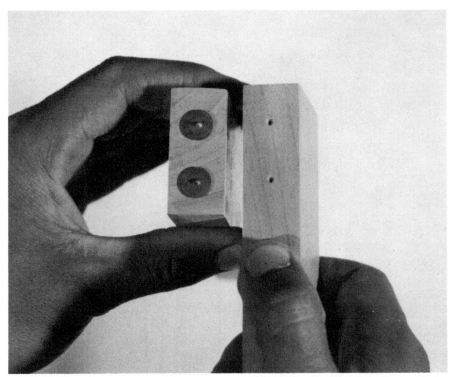

Illus. 73. Dowel centers provide an easy and accurate way of transferring hole positions from one board to the other.

Splines are thin strips of wood that are sometimes used to rein-force a butt joint (Illus. 74). The splines are usually about ⅛ or ¼ inch thick for use with ¾"-thick lumber. Thicker lumber requires a thicker spline. Splines may be made of solid wood, plywood, or hardboard. Hardboard is easy to work with, and it makes a very strong spline. This is especially true of the tempered hardboard. You can also use plywood, especially when you need a thicker spline. If you use solid wood for a spline, the grain should run across the width. This is 90° from the direction you normally orient the grain of a board. If the grain of a spline runs lengthwise, there is a tendency for the spline to split along the grain at the joint line.

You can cut the slots for the splines with a handsaw. Mark the middle of the joint and draw a line on either side of the middle, indicating the width of the spline. Make a saw kerf on each of those lines, keeping the saw inside the line. You can usually break out the thin strip of wood left in the middle by giving the saw blade a little twist. For larger splines, you may need to make several kerfs be-tween the two outer ones.

You can easily make the kerfs with a table saw. If you use a wide blade, you may only need to make one kerf for a ⅛″ spline. Set the rip fence to center the blade in the joint and raise the blade so that the depth of cut is a littler greater than one-half the width of the spline. Most of the time, you can use a spline that is about ¾ of an inch wide.

You can use a router to cut the groove for a spline. Use a bit that will make a groove the correct size for the thickness of the spline you are using. When you are making the groove in the face of a board, use an auxiliary fence or a board clamped to the workpiece to guide the router. Or you can mount the router in a router table and use the fence to guide the work. To make a groove in end grain, clamp a piece of scrap to both sides of the workpiece to make a wider base for the router to sit on and then set the router fence to ride against one of the scrap boards. The router is very good for making blind grooves that don't extend to the edge of the board. You use blind grooves where you don't want the spline to show.

Spread glue on the spline and on the mating surfaces of the joint and then assemble.

A variation on the spline is the commercially made spline shown in Illus. 75. This type of spline is known as a compressed-wood spline, or it is sometimes called a biscuit because of its shape and embossed pattern. You need to make a special blind cut for this type of spline. There are several types of machines that make this cut, ranging from high-speed production units to an accessory for a standard router.

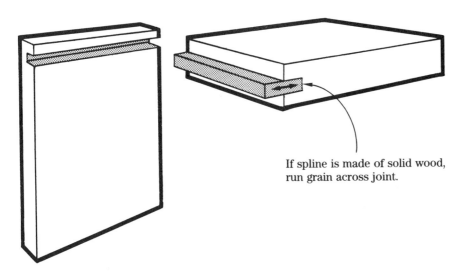

If spline is made of solid wood, run grain across joint.

Illus. 74. A spline-reinforced butt joint has greater shear strength.

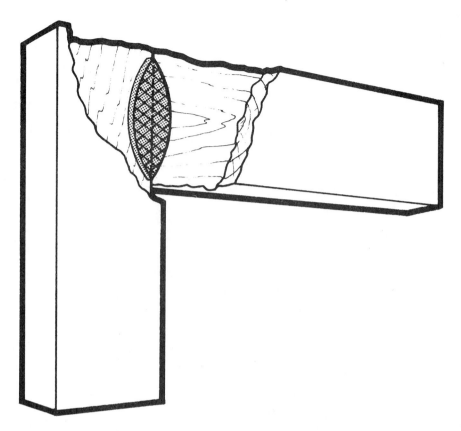

Illus. 75. A compressed-wood spline expands as it absorbs moisture from the glue, making an extremely tight-fitting joint.

Since the slots are a little longer than the splines, parts can be shifted into alignment during assembly. Long joints require several splines. Thicker boards may require that two parallel sets of slots be made for added strength. This type of spline is very well suited for particle board joints because it doesn't weaken the board very much; since the slots are not continuous, it doesn't form a break line in the middle of the particle board.

The splines are made from beech, and they are compressed during manufacturing. As they absorb the wet glue, they expand in the slots, making a very tight joint that is less apt to loosen than a normal spline or a dowel joint.

Edge-to-Edge Butts   One of the most useful types of butt joints is the edge butt, which is used for joining two or more narrow boards into a large panel. In this instance, you are gluing long grain to long grain, which is the strongest combination. A tight-fitting glue joint of this type is so strong that further reinforcement is usually not necessary. Dowels or splines can be used with this type of joint, but more to assist in aligning the board.

For this type of joint to have maximum strength, the two edges must come together tightly. One way to make sure that the edges will meet perfectly is by clamping the two boards together so that the edges are up and the face sides are out (Illus. 76). Now plane both edges at the same time. When the boards are joined together, any deviation from an exact 90° angle will be matched by a complementary angle on the other edge. This way there will be no gaps and the boards will lay perfectly flat. Be sure to align the faces, as shown in Illus. 76.

When gluing up panels from plain-sawn lumber, reverse the direction of the annual rings, as shown in Illus. 77. If the end grain doesn't show a pronounced ring pattern and you can't decide how to place the board, don't worry about it. Boards with the greatest tendency to cup will have a pronounced ring pattern.

Quarter-sawn lumber doesn't have as great a tendency to cup, so you don't need to worry about it when you are gluing up panels. However, there is a difference in the rate of dimensional change between old wood—where the rings are near the middle of the tree—and young wood—where the rings are near the outside of the

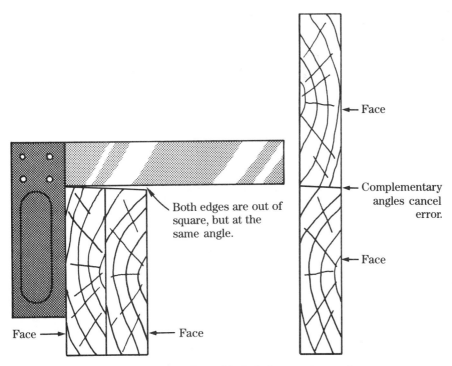

Both edges are out of square, but at the same angle.

Complementary angles cancel error.

Face

Face

Face — Face

Illus. 76. Two boards planed together with their faces out cancels any error.

Alternating direction of rings cancels out tendency to cup.

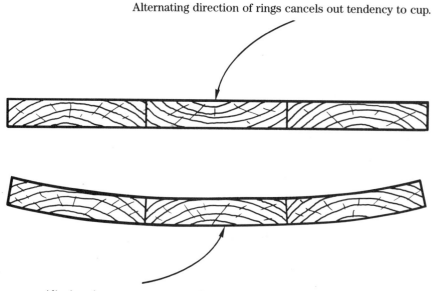

Illus. 77. Plain-sawn lumber should have alternated growth rings when you are gluing up large panels.

Aligning rings exaggerates tendency to cup.

tree. To compensate for this, some cabinetmakers glue quarter-sawn panels with old wood to old wood and young wood to young wood (Illus. 78). If the curvature of the rings is difficult to determine, don't worry about the alignment.

As boards shrink and swell, the portion that is about 6 inches from each end changes more drastically than the rest of the board. The end grain both absorbs and loses more moisture because of the exposed fluid channels present. To compensate for this, some

Old wood to old wood or young wood to young wood equalizes shrinkage.

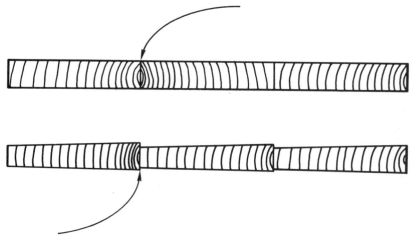

Illus. 78. You should glue quarter-sawn lumber into panels with old wood against old wood and young wood against young wood.

Young wood to old wood causes unequal shrinkage at joint.

cabinetmakers add a little spring to an edge joint, as shown in Illus. 79. After the edges have been fit to each other, take a very thin shaving from the middle of each edge. When the boards are clamped together, this puts additional pressure on the ends of the joint so that they are less likely to open up if shrinkage occurs.

Take a thin shaving from the middle. Gap is exaggerated here for clarity.

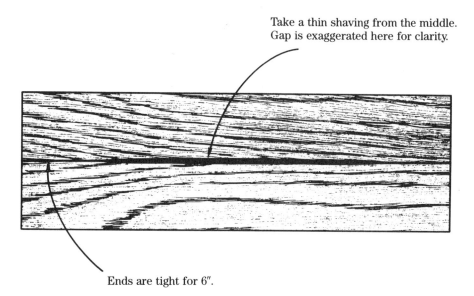

Ends are tight for 6″.

Illus. 79. Putting a little spring into a joint compensates for the greater shrinkage that occurs at the ends of the boards.

RABBET

The rabbet joint, shown in Illus. 80, is much stronger than the butt joint. Not only does it have a greater glue surface, but it also reduces shear forces because the lip supports the weight instead of just relying on the glue. There is no standard depth for a rabbet, but it is frequently ⅜″ for a ¾″ board. A rabbet cut this depth provides 50 percent more gluing surface than a butt joint (Illus. 81).

It is easy to make a short rabbet with hand tools; but for rabbets that are more than about 12 inches, it's easier if you use power tools.

Although you can cut a rabbet freehand, you will obtain more accurate results if you use guide boards clamped to the work to keep the saw square and in proper position (Illus. 82). Cut a strip of wood to the thickness of the wood to be left after the rabbet is finished and then nail it to a backing board, as shown in the photograph. Place the work on the backing board with the end resting against the strip. Clamp a scrap of wood along the cutting line, as shown in Illus. 82; this will guide the saw straight and square. Make the cut to the desired depth, using either a panel saw or a backsaw.

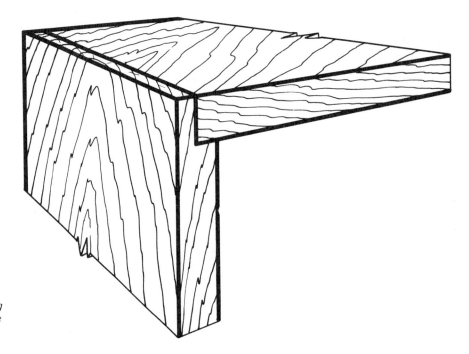

Illus. 80. A rabbet joint is frequently used for joining the sides of a cabinet to the top and bottom.

The backsaw is a little easier to handle because the stiff back keeps the saw from whipping. Hold the saw against the thickness strip and then make the second cut to complete the rabbet.

You can use a similar method for cutting a rabbet on a table saw. Set the fence to make the vertical cut first, as shown in Illus. 83. You should set the blade height to the width of the rabbet.

There are two schools of thought on how to make the second cut. With both of these methods, the blade height is set to the depth of

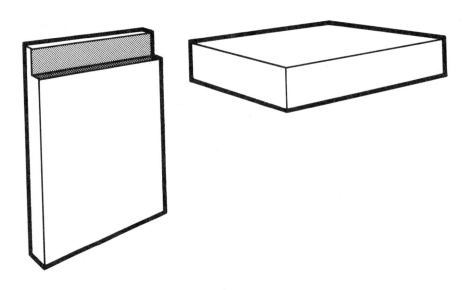

Illus. 81. In this exploded view of a rabbet joint, the shading indicates the cut-out area.

Illus. 82. You can use scrap wood to make a simple backsaw guide for making rabbets. Rest the backsaw against the guide blocks while cutting to keep the cuts square.

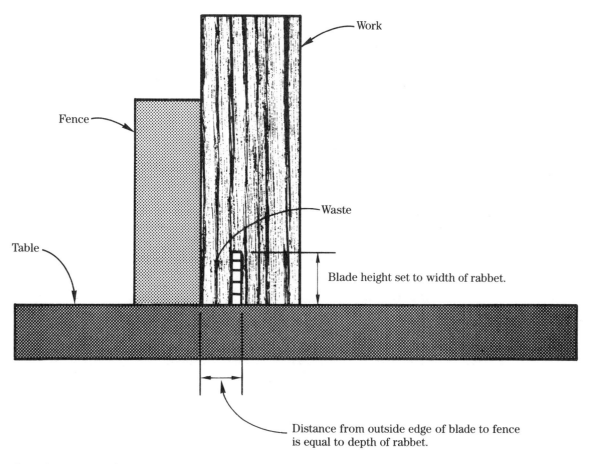

Illus. 83. Making the first cut of a rabbet on the table saw.

the rabbet. The way most professionals make the second cut is by setting the fence for the width of the rabbet, as shown in Illus. 84. This method is very accurate, and you can use the same setup for boards of various sizes without any adjustment. The only problem with this method is that there is a tendency for the waste piece to kick back out of the saw as the cut is completed. You can minimize this problem by using a push stick with a deep notch so that the push stick will push the waste through as well. The other method of making the second cut eliminates the problem of waste kickback; but it is not as accurate because, if the board wanders from the fence, the rabbet will be too large. This method requires a different setup for pieces of differing dimensions, and it won't work with very large boards. Illus. 85 shows the setup for this method. The part is placed between the fence and the blade so that the waste isn't trapped there.

A board that is bowed may lift slightly from the table during the cut. This will leave a small piece of wood in the corner of the rabbet that must be removed. You can easily remove it with a sharp chisel, or you can run a knife blade against both edges of the rabbet so that the tip cuts into the wood to be removed.

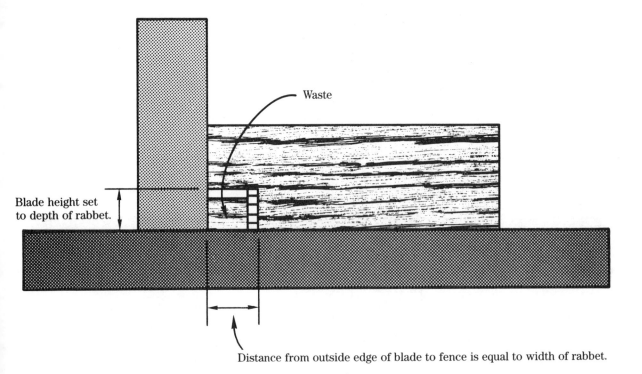

Waste

Blade height set to depth of rabbet.

Distance from outside edge of blade to fence is equal to width of rabbet.

Illus. 84. This method of making the second cut may kick back the waste, so use caution.

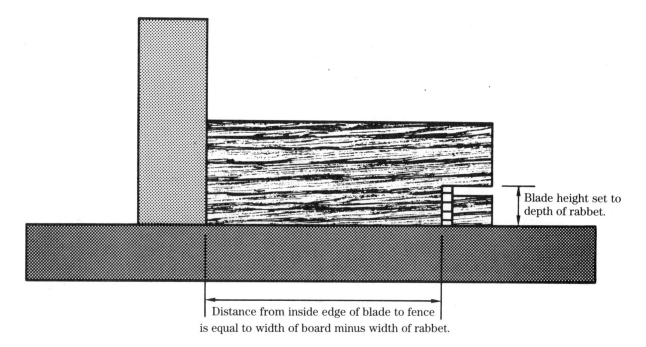

Blade height set to depth of rabbet.

Distance from inside edge of blade to fence
is equal to width of board minus width of rabbet.

Illus. 85. This alternate method of making the second cut prevents kicked-back waste, but you can't use it for large boards.

You can also make rabbets using a table saw or a radial-arm saw with an attachment called a dado blade. Set the blade to make a cut slightly wider than needed. You can use the mitre gauge or the rip fence to guide the board. If you use the rip fence, clamp or screw a piece of wood to the fence to protect it from the blade. Lower the blade below the table and position the fence so that the auxiliary wood fence is over the blade. Now turn on the saw and raise the blade to create a cutout in the wood fence. Turn off the saw and position the fence to make the proper-width rabbet (Illus. 86). There is more information about the dado blade in the next section.

You can also use a router to make rabbets. You need an auxiliary fence or you can clamp a board to the work to guide the router. Set the router fence to the width of the rabbet, and set the cutter depth to the depth of the rabbet. A ¾″ cutter will make a rabbet in one pass; if you don't have a bit this large, you can make more than one pass to cut the rabbet.

If you don't have a fence for your router, simply clamp a board to the work so that when the base of the router rubs against the board, the cutter will be in the proper position to make the joint. A special bit, called a rabbeting bit, makes using the router even easier. This bit has a small pin, called a pilot, that rubs against the uncut edge of

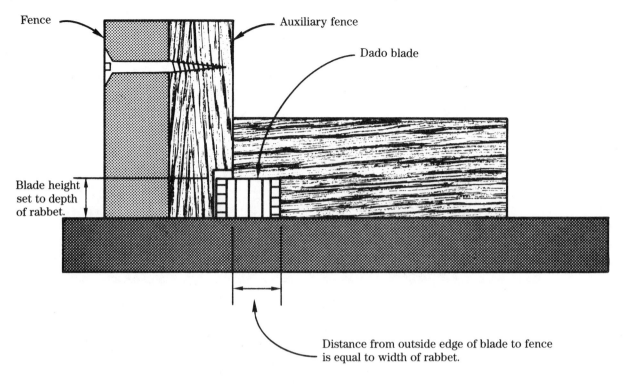

Illus. 86. A dado blade makes a rabbet in a single operation. The auxiliary wood fence prevents the metal fence and the dado blade from coming in contact with each other.

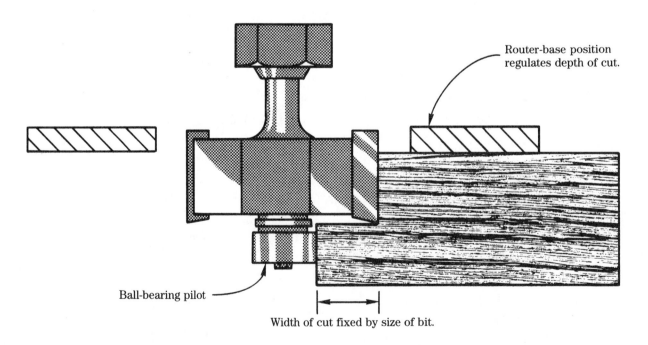

Illus. 87. A special rabbeting bit for the router makes a rabbet in a single operation.

the board to guide the bit. In more expensive models, a ball bearing is attached to the pilot (Illus. 87). The size of the bit determines the width of the cut, but the depth can be adjusted. This type of rabbeting is especially useful when the rabbet is very long, as is the case when a rabbet is used to attach the back of a cabinet or when a rabbet must be cut on a curved edge.

The jointer can also cut rabbets. Most jointers have a ledge that is designed to support the uncut part of the board when making a rabbet. The guard usually must be removed for this operation, so exercise caution. Set the jointer fence to the width of the rabbet and set the depth-of-cut adjustment to take a moderate cut. Run the board over the jointer and then adjust the depth of cut about ⅛ of an inch deeper. Continue in this manner until you reach the desired depth.

When you assemble a rabbet joint, be sure to apply glue to both surfaces of the joint. A well-made rabbet that is glued and clamped will hold without reinforcement. However, rabbets are frequently reinforced with nails, as shown in Illus. 88.

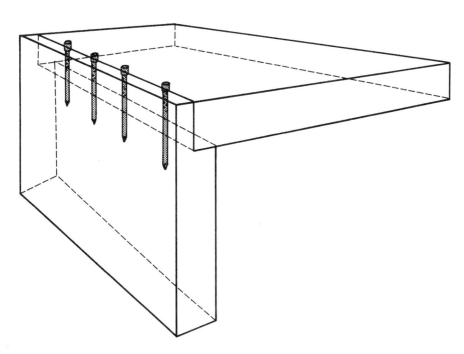

Illus. 88. Nails placed this way will lock a rabbet joint together.

DADO

The dado shown in Illus. 89 and 90 is a very strong joint. A dado that is cut to a depth one-half the thickness of the board provides twice

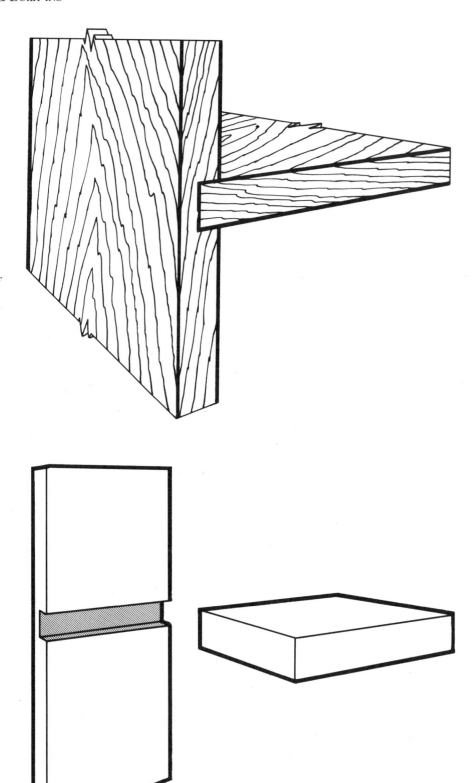

Illus. 89. A common way of attaching shelves to the side of a cabinet is by using a dado joint.

Illus. 90. In this exploded view of a dado joint, the shading indicates the cut-out area.

as much gluing surface as a butt joint, and shear forces are totally eliminated because the board is supported on both sides by a lip. The dado is used for attaching shelves—or dividers, in drawer construction—and, in some cases, for attaching the top and bottom of a cabinet. A major advantage of the dado is that it is self-aligning; once the parts are assembled, the joint will hold the parts in alignment as the clamps are applied. The dado will also hold a slightly cupped or warped board flat, and it will help prevent boards from cupping after assembly.

In the traditional terminology of cabinetmakers, "dado" only refers to this type of joint if the joint is cut across the grain; if it is cut with the grain, it is called a groove (Illus. 91). Modern materials, such as particle board and plywood, have no definite grain direction, so this distinction has become somewhat obsolete. Therefore, many modern cabinetmakers use the term dado to describe any joint of this type.

To cut a dado by hand, use a saw to make cuts at each side of the joint, stopping at the proper depth. Clamping a guide block to the board will help keep the cuts straight (Illus. 92). If the board is narrow enough to fit in the mitre box, use it to guide the saw. Next,

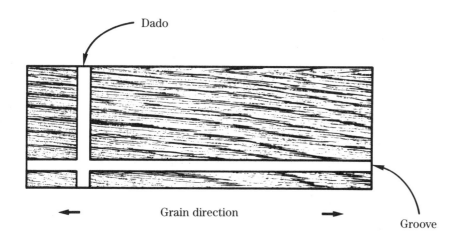

Dado

Grain direction

Groove

Illus. 91. Adhering to the strictest definition, you can only call this type of joint a dado if it is cut across the grain; otherwise, it's called a groove.

some people prefer to make several saw kerfs between the two sides, whereas others go straight to chiseling.

You use a chisel to remove the wood between the saw cuts. Hold the chisel with the bevel facing the wood, and pare off the wood in fairly heavy cuts until you reach the approximate depth. Smooth the bottom and bring the dado to the exact depth by taking lighter paring cuts.

Illus. 92. To cut a dado by hand, make stop cuts with a backsaw. A guide block clamped to the work helps keep the backsaw square. Remove the wood between the stop cuts with a chisel.

You can also use two specialized planes, the router plane and the plow plane, to remove the wood between the saw kerfs.

You may prefer cutting the dado with a portable circular saw. Set the blade depth to the depth of the dado. Use a fence or a guide board to guide the saw, and make a series of cuts inside the area to be dadoed. Use a chisel to clean out the cut in the manner just described.

If you use an attachment called a dado blade, you can use a table saw or a radial-arm saw for cutting dadoes. There are two types of dado blades available.

One type actually consists of two blades that make the side cuts and a set of chippers that removes the wood between the cuts. The chippers come in several thicknesses, and can be arranged to make cuts in varying widths. You can make small adjustments in thickness by cutting out paper or cardboard washers and placing them between the chippers. When you use several chippers at once, space them equally around the circle, instead of grouping them all together.

The other type of dado blade is the wobbler. It has a single blade mounted in the middle of a set of tapered washers. Rotating the washers causes the blade to wobble on the saw arbor; the greater the wobble, the wider the cut will be. This type of dado blade is easy to adjust because it doesn't need to be removed from the saw arbor for adjustment. Since it is so adjustable, it's easy to make minor variations in thickness. The cut made by a wobbler is slightly rounded at the bottom because the blade travels in an arc from side to side. In most cases, this isn't a problem; but if you need a flat bottom, use the other type of dado blade or flatten out the cut with a chisel.

Set the blade height to control the depth of the dado, and use a rip fence or mitre gauge to guide the board.

When dadoing plywood, it may be necessary to apply masking tape to the surface of the work to prevent chipping. In severe cases, score the face of the plywood with a sharp knife before cutting the dado.

A router is very useful for making dadoes. Because you move the router instead of the board, it's easier to handle large boards with a router than with a table saw. For boards up to ¾″ thick, you can get a cutter that will make the dado in one pass; but to make wide dadoes, you will need to make more than one cut. Since it is important for the dado to be straight on both edges, use a guide board on both sides of the router to prevent the router from straying from the line. You can make a simple dado guide for your router that will speed up the process (Illus. 93). Clamp guide boards to a scrap and make a test cut with the router. Adjust the guide boards until the cut is exactly the right width. Now screw boards across the ends of the guide boards to hold them at the correct width. Use a square to position the end blocks (Illus. 94). With the end blocks in place, you can remove the clamps and use the guide over and over. You can

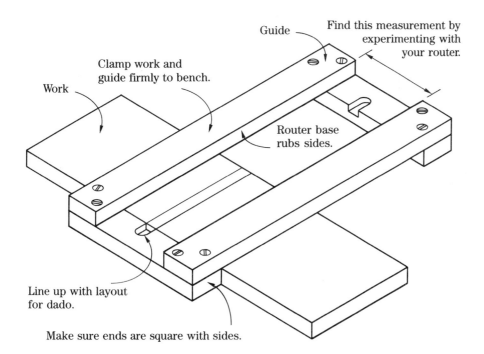

Guide

Find this measurement by experimenting with your router.

Clamp work and guide firmly to bench.

Work

Router base rubs sides.

Line up with layout for dado.

Make sure ends are square with sides.

Illus. 93. With a router guide, it's easy to make multiple dadoes.

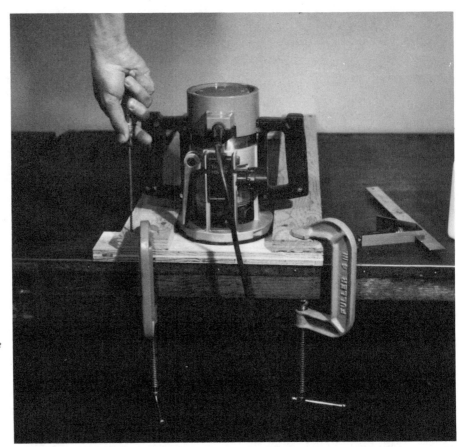

Illus. 94. When building the guide, leave the cross pieces long. Put the router in position and clamp the guides in place. Screw the guides to the cross pieces. Finally, trim the cross pieces to length.

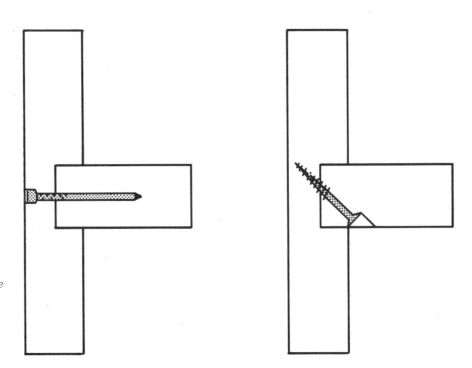

Illus. 95. You can reinforce dadoes with nails or screws. If you want concealed reinforcement, angle the fasteners in from the bottom.

place the end block against an edge to square the guide since you used a square to position the ends. The first time you use the guide, continue the cut part way into the end blocks; you can use this cut to position the guide in the future. Simply line up the cut in the end block with the layout lines on the board.

A tight-fitting dado that can be clamped while the glue dries usually doesn't require any reinforcement. If you can't clamp the joint or if the project requires additional strength, you can reinforce a dado with screws or nails. When appearance isn't important, you can drive nails or screws into the end of the board through the side; but when this isn't desirable from an aesthetic point of view, toenail or drive screws at an angle, as shown in Illus. 95,   so that they can't be seen from the outside of the cabinet.

MITRE

The mitre is an attractive-looking joint that you should use when appearance is important. Since it hides the end grain of both parts, it is frequently used with plywood or particle board. Usually you use a mitre to join two boards at a right angle—in which case, you make the cut at 45°. However, you can use a mitre to join two boards at any angle. When you desire an angle other than 90°, the mitre cut is exactly one half of the desired angle.

Even though a mitre joint offers about 40 percent more glue area than a butt joint, it is still a fairly weak joint. In most cases, it is best to reinforce it, especially if the joint will carry a structural load.

There are actually two types of mitres. One type is the face mitre, which is used for joining parts such as the stile and rails of a cabinet or picture frames (Illus. 96). With the face mitre, you make the cut on the face of the board. The other type of mitre is the edge mitre, which is used for joining parts such as the sides and top of a cabinet (Illus. 97). With the edge mitre, you cut along the end or edge of the board.

To cut a face mitre (Illus. 98) by hand, you can simply use a combination square to mark a 45° angle and then you can cut the joint freehand; but for more accurate work, you usually need a mitre box. A mitre box is a guide that holds the saw straight and at the correct angle. Although several types are commercially available that use various means of guiding the saw, you can make a simple mitre box out of three pieces of wood, as shown in Illus. 99.

It is best to use a backsaw with a mitre box, but you can also use a panel saw with the type of mitre box in Illus. 99. Place the mitre box

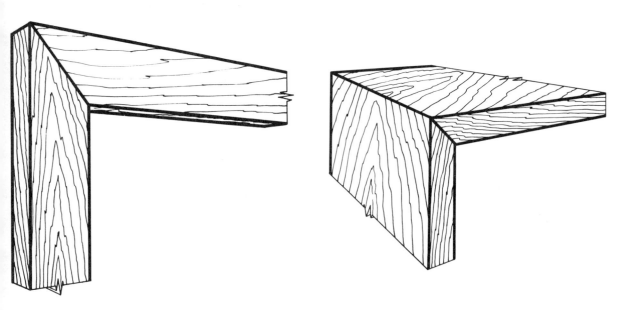

Illus. 96 (left). You can use a face mitre to join face-frame members. Illus. 97 (right). You can use an edge mitre to join the sides to the top of a cabinet.

on the bench so that the lip hangs over the edge to stabilize it. Put the part to be cut into the box with its edge against the back of the box. Put the saw into one of the 45° slots and make the cut, holding

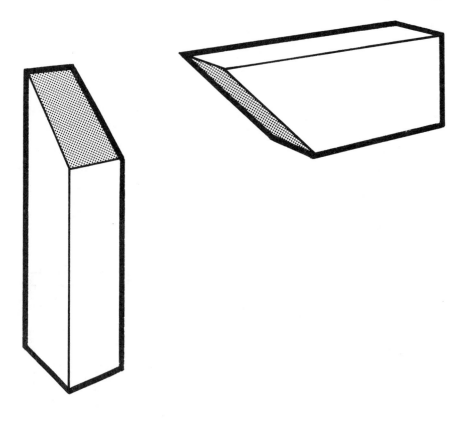

Illus. 98. In this exploded view of a face mitre, the shading indicates the mating surfaces.

the saw flat against the board so that it cuts uniformly across the entire surface at once (Illus. 100).

For a mitre to fit correctly, either both cuts must be exactly 45° or the angles must be complementary; that is, they may not be exactly 45°, but the total of the two angles must be 90°. For example, if one cut is 44½°, then the complementary angle would be 45½°. You can take advantage of this information when cutting mitres to compensate for small inaccuracies in your mitre box or in any of the other cutting devices described later. Make the first cut with the board face up; make the second cut with the board face down and on the opposite side of the saw. This procedure automatically ensures that the angles will be complementary even if they are not exactly 45°.

When you are cutting both mating parts from a single board, it is

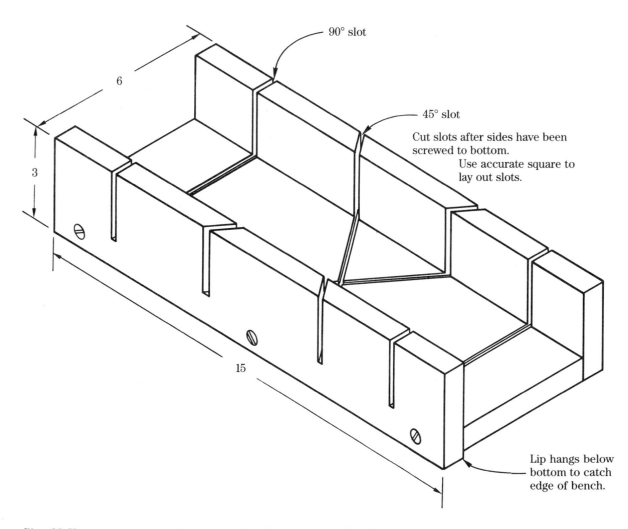

Illus. 99. You can construct a simple mitre box from three boards. A hardwood, such as birch or maple, will provide longer service.

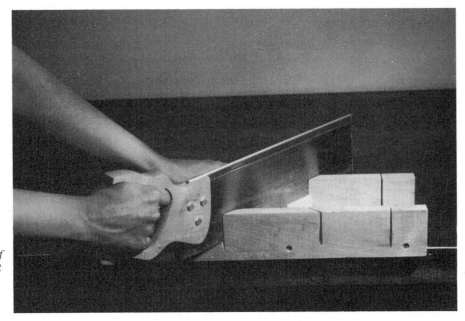

Illus. 100. To use a mitre box, place it on the bench so that the front lip catches on the edge. Place the part to be cut against the rear of the box and line up the cut with one of the slots. Put a backsaw in the slot and make the cut.

sometimes possible to make both cuts at once; to do this, the board must have two good faces. Simply make one cut and turn one of the parts over. It is not always possible to use this method because cutting a board face down can leave chips along the face of the joint. Also, irregularly shaped parts, such as mouldings, can't be cut this way. In these cases, you should try to get the angle as accurate as possible and you should cut both parts face up. If the joint is slightly off, refer to the section on fitting that follows.

You can use the radial-arm saw to cut face mitres by rotating the arm to the proper angle. Whenever possible, use the method of cutting one part face up and the other face down and on the opposite side of the blade to ensure a good fit.

A special saw, called a power mitre box, can be used for cutting face mitres. Similar to a portable circular saw mounted in a mitre box, it can be adjusted to any angle.

You can use a table saw to make this type of mitre by setting the mitre gauge to 45°. You can use the same method described earlier to get complementary angles, or you can make the simple accessory in Illus. 101 that will enable you to cut complementary angles with both parts face up.

When you use the table saw, make sure that the two sides that are used to guide the cut are exactly 90° apart because all future cuts will rely on this initial setup. Check the angle with a square for accuracy. The size of the guide depends on your saw; the base of the triangle should be equal to twice the distance from the blade to the outside edge of the mitre gauge when the gauge is set to 90°. Attach the guide to the mitre gauge with screws through the holes provided for attaching an auxiliary fence. Set the mitre gauge for 90°, and make the first cut with the edge of the part against one side of the guide. Make the second cut with the edge of the part against the second side of the guide. You need to make both cuts with the boards face up. As long as the guide was accurately made, you will get perfect-fitting mitres even if the mitre gauge is slightly off.

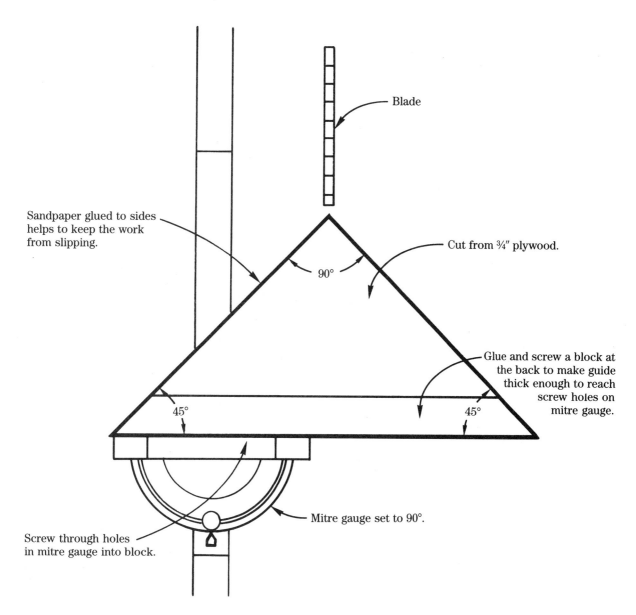

Illus. 101. This simple attachment for a table-saw mitre gauge produces better-fitting mitre joints than the mitre gauge alone. Make sure that you cut mating parts on opposite sides of the guide.

To make edge-mitre joints, you need to cut along the edge or across the end of the board. You can cut a narrow board in a mitre box by placing it on its edge; but for anything wider than 2 or 3 inches, you need to use a different technique (Illus. 102).

One method of cutting edge mitres by hand involves the use of a plane. This method works best with solid lumber on edge grain; it isn't very effective on end grain or with man-made materials. In these cases or for very long joints, power equipment can be very helpful. To lay out the mitre, draw a line along the back of the board that is exactly the same distance from the edge as the thickness of the board. An easy way to do this is by using a scrap of the same thickness to mark the line. Place the board against a bench stop with the back up; use a block plane to cut away the corner of the board between the edge and the line. Hold the plane approximately 45° to the surface of the board (Illus. 103). Continue planing until the plane iron touches both the face corner and the line. This should produce a perfect 45° mitre. Check the angle with a combination square to make sure. Fix any deviations from the correct angle with light planing strokes.

Since the jointer has an adjustable angle fence, you can use this same technique with the jointer. Set the fence to 45° and keep cutting until you reach the corner.

The portable circular saw has an adjustable angle shoe, so you can cut this type of mitre by setting the angle to 45° and cutting along the edge of the board. A guide board clamped to the work will make the cut more accurate.

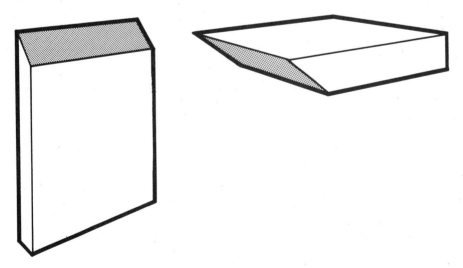

Illus. 102. Because of the length involved, it is difficult to cut edge-mitre joints with a handsaw.

Illus. 103. You can use a block plane to make edge-mitre joints by hand if they run with the grain.

Using a table saw is one of the best ways of cutting edge mitres. Set the tilt arbor so that the blade will cut a 45° angle. When it is possible, set the fence so that the board will be between the fence and the blade and the waste piece will be on the outside. When the board is too large for you to be able to do this, add an auxiliary wood fence to the rip fence to protect it from the blade and position the fence close to the blade. Lower the blade as you position the fence, and then turn on the saw and raise the blade until it slightly cuts into the auxiliary wood fence. Place the edge to be mitred against the fence and make the cut. The waste piece will be trapped between the fence and the blade when you are using this method, so there is a possibility that the waste may kick back at the end of the cut. *To avoid being hit in case of a kickback, don't stand directly in line with the blade.*

Fitting When you can't use the complementary angle method of cutting mitres, you may have to do some fitting to get a perfect mitre joint. The best way of testing a face mitre is in a mitre clamp. This is a special type of clamp that holds both parts exactly square. With the parts clamped, you can see how well the mitre fits. The parts should make equal contact along the entire joint line. If they touch at one end of the joint and there is a gap at the other end, there are several ways you can correct the problem.

The mitre clamp has a slot for a saw; place a backsaw on the joint line so that the points of the teeth on one side are lined up with one of the joint faces. Cut straight down the joint line. This will make a complementary angle cut on the adjoining part. It will also make the part about ⅟₁₆ of an inch shorter, so allow extra length for fitting if you anticipate that you will need to fit the joints. Reposition the parts in the clamp and they should fit well.

You can also use a block plane to fit the joint. With the parts clamped together, hold the thin edge of a square so that it lines up with the face of one of the mitre cuts. Use the opposite side of the blade as a guide for drawing a line on the other side of the joint. This will give you a complementary angle. Remove the part from the clamp and place it in a vise so that the mitre cut is level. Use the block plane for cutting to the line. Plane from the inside corner to the outside corner to avoid tearing out the grain.

A disc sander or a stationary belt sander are excellent tools for fitting mitre joints. Mark the joint in the same manner described for the block plane. Hold the part flat on the sander table and make sure that the table is square with the sanding disc or belt; then sand to the line.

To fit an edge mitre, dry-assemble the joint and use a square to hold the parts at a 90° angle. Examine the joint to determine where wood needs to be removed and then use a block plane to trim the joint.

Reinforcing Mitre Joints When a mitre joint carries a structural load in a cabinet, you should reinforce it. You can use nails or screws if they won't mar the appearance of the joint. For maximum strength, alternate sides so that the nails or screws tie the joint together from both sides.

Dowels are frequently used for reinforcing mitre joints. Drill the holes so that they are square with the mitre cut, as shown in Illus. 104.

Splines are very useful for reinforcing mitre joints. You can use any of the previously described methods for cutting the grooves. For edge mitres, you should cut the grooves square with the mitre cut, as shown in Illus. 105. You can reinforce face mitres with two different types of splines. The spline in Illus. 106 is similar to the spline used for edge mitres. You should cut the spline oversize and then trim it to final size and shape after the joint has been assembled and

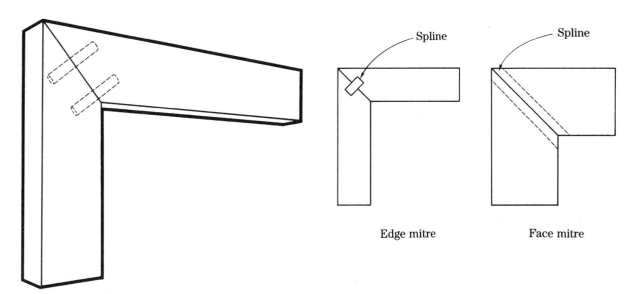

Illus. 104 (left). When you use blind dowels to reinforce a mitre joint, you should place them at a 90° angle to the face of the joint (45° to the edge of the board). Illus. 105 (right). You can use splines to reinforce both edge mitre and face mitre joints.

the glue has set. To install the type of spline in Illus. 107, cut the parts as if a spline isn't being used and assemble the joint. After the glue has set, cut the slot for the spline through the corner of the

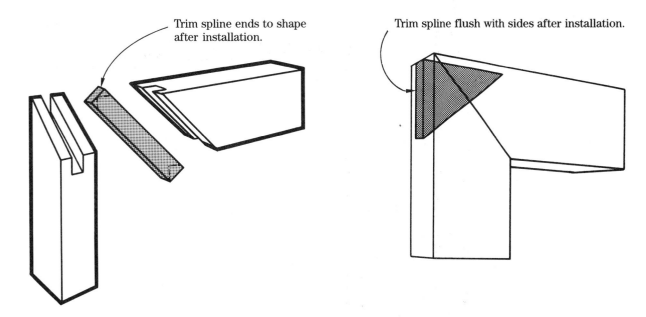

Illus. 106 (left). In this exploded view of a splined face mitre joint, the shaded area represents the shape of the spline when it is first placed in the joint. The dashed lines indicate the shape of the spline after it has been trimmed. Illus. 107 (right). You need to cut the groove for this type of spline after the joint has been assembled. You should make the spline oversize and then trim it to shape after inserting it.

joint. Install the spline oversize and then trim it after the glue has set.

When the inside of the joint won't show, glue blocks or reinforcing blocks are often used.

HALF-LAP

You should use the half-lap joint to join two narrow boards where they cross or meet at a corner. This type of joint is especially useful in building the framework of a cabinet carcass (Illus. 108). Because of its large long-grain contact area, the half-lap joint is very strong.

You cut the end lap in much the same way as a rabbet. Make the shoulder cut first, and then cut in the other direction to remove the waste (Illus. 109). You make the cross lap the same way as a dado. Cut saw kerfs on both sides of the joint and then remove the waste with a chisel (Illus. 110).

You can cut half-lap joints with a router. Place scraps of the same

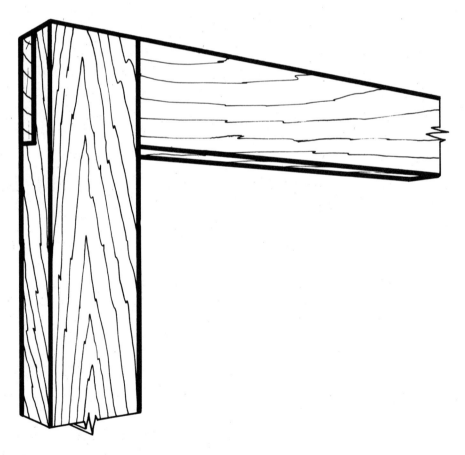

Illus. 108. You can use the half-lap joint to join face frames or for structural framing inside a cabinet.

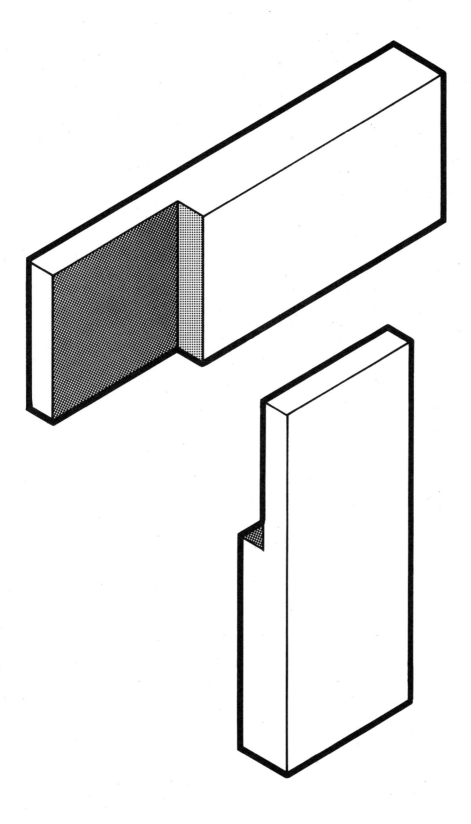

Illus. 109. In this exploded view of a half-lap joint, the shading indicates the cutout area.

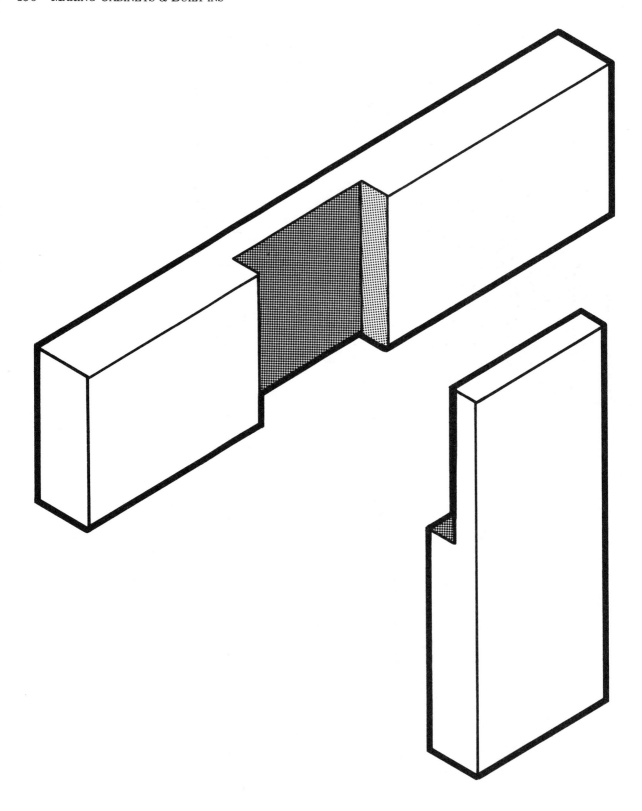

Illus. 110. You can also use half-lap joints for joining boards that don't meet at the corner.

thickness on both sides of the board to support the router base. Clamp on guide boards that will help you cut the shoulders straight.

You can also use the radial-arm saw or the table saw to cut half-lap joints. Use a dado blade and make several cuts to get the correct width.

You can reinforce this type of joint with short nails driven in through the back.

Advanced Joints

If you master the five basic joints, you can build almost anything you want; but as you progress, you will probably want to try some of the more advanced joints that offer additional strength or beauty.

MORTISE-AND-TENON

You use the mortise-and-tenon joint in the same places that you use a dowel-reinforced butt joint, but the mortise-and-tenon provides much more strength because of its large long-grain contact area (Illus. 111). A mortise is a rectangular hole cut into the wood, and a tenon is a projection on the mating part that fits into the mortise.

You should use this type of joint only with solid lumber; it is not suited for plywood or particle board.

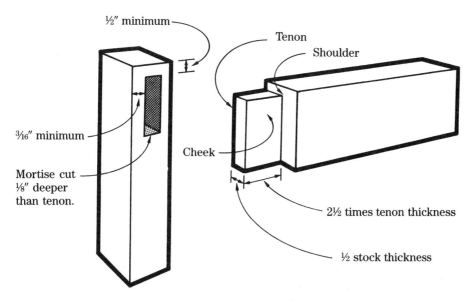

Illus. 111. You should use mortise-and-tenon joints when great strength is required.

The mortise should be about one third of the total width of the board. So, for ¾″ lumber, you should use a ¼″ mortise. Try to leave about ¾ of an inch between the end of the mortise and the end of the board. Usually it's a good idea to leave the parts to be mortised slightly long and then trim them to length after the joint has been assembled (Illus. 112). This provides some extra backing to prevent the wood from splitting while you are cutting the mortise. Lay out the mortise and then drill a series of holes inside the lines to the desired depth. Use a chisel to clean out the wood between the holes and square up the corners (Illus. 113).

Cut the tenons with a backsaw. Make the long cuts first, stopping

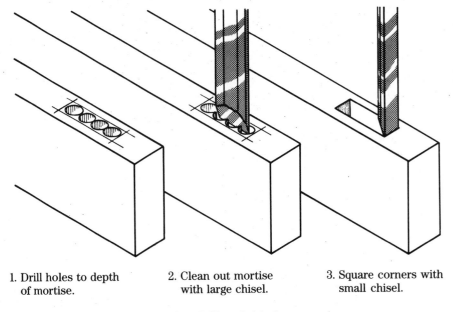

1. Drill holes to depth of mortise.

2. Clean out mortise with large chisel.

3. Square corners with small chisel.

Illus. 112. Cutting a mortise with a drill and chisels.

at the line for the shoulder cut. Make the shoulder cut to remove the waste (Illus. 114). If the tenon is too large, you can trim it with a rasp.

You can also cut tenons with a table saw. You can use a standard blade and make a series of cuts the same way as you would by hand, or you can use a dado blade and do all of the cutting from the side of the board. You will have to make several passes over the blade to get the proper-length tenon.

A router accessory is available that will allow you to make both the mortise and the tenon with a router.

Trim flush after assembly.

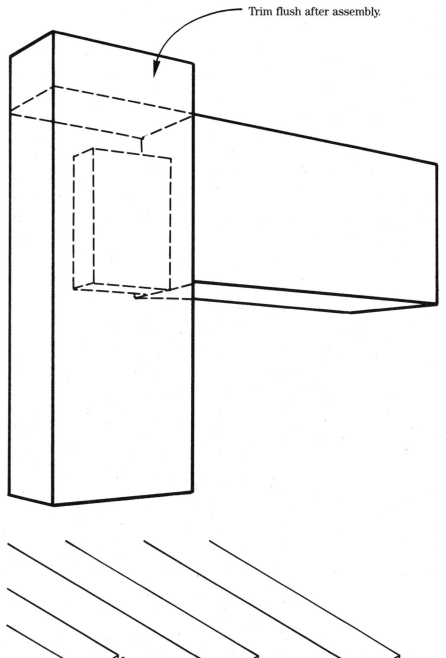

Illus. 113. When the mortise is cut near the end of the board, leave the board long during the cutting and assembly to reinforce the end of the mortise. After assembly, trim the board to length.

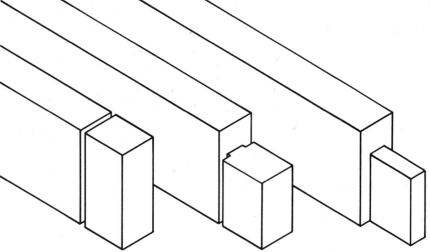

1. Make shoulder cuts.   2. Cut tenon to width.   3. Cut tenon to thickness.

Illus. 114. Steps in cutting a tenon.

BOX JOINTS

The box joint is a strong joint for joining corners. It is useful for anything that resembles a box—drawers, for example (Illus. 115). The box joint is a machine joint, which is designed to be cut with power equipment.

To make a box joint on the table saw, add an auxiliary wood fence that is about 4 inches high and 20 inches long to the mitre gauge. Set a dado blade to make a cut equal to the desired width of the pin (finger) of the box joint. Set the blade height to equal the thickness of the board plus $\frac{1}{32}$ of an inch. Cut through the wood fence with the dado blade, and then make a wood key block that will fit into the slot and project about $\frac{3}{4}$ of an inch from the face of the fence. Glue the

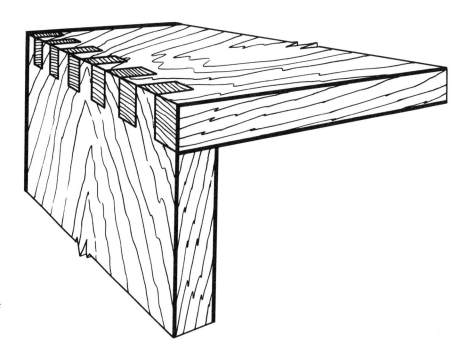

Illus. 115. A box joint offers both strength and decoration.

key in place. Reposition the fence on the mitre gauge so that the key block is separated from the side of the blade by the width of one pin.

You can cut both pieces at once by clamping them together and offsetting them by the width of one pin. Make the first cut by butting the edge of the board against the side of the key block. Reposition the work so that the cut just made is over the key block and then make the next cut. Continue in this manner until all of the pins have been cut.

You can also make box joints using a router with a commercial template.

DOVETAILS

Dovetails are considered by many to be the mark of true craftsmanship. They form a strong, interlocking joint that is very useful in drawer construction (Illus. 116). The best dovetails are hand cut because the size of the pin can be tailored to the size of the part and the type of wood used. Softer woods require larger pins (Illus. 117).

You can also use a router to make dovetails. Although the standard type of dovetail jig for a router doesn't offer any choice in pin size and the pins are often too small for softer woods, an improved type of dovetail jig allows you almost as much freedom in designing dovetail joints as hand cutting does.

Dovetails can be used with solid wood only. Pins made of particle

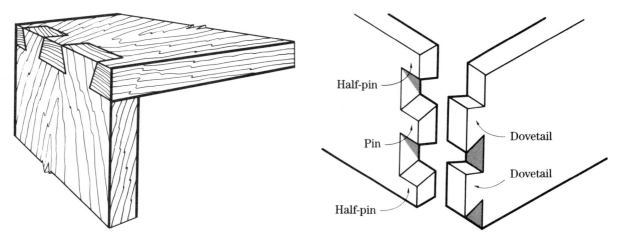

Illus. 116 (left). The dovetail joint is often used in drawer construction. It can also be used for joining the side to the top of a cabinet. Illus. 117 (right). Parts of a dovetail joint.

board will crumble and break off. The plies in plywood form a break line that will cause the pins to break. Because of consumer demand for dovetailed-drawer construction, many commercial cabinets employ machine-cut dovetails with plywood and particle board; but the resulting joint is weaker than a rabbet or dado when it's used with these materials.

You need to use a sliding T-bevel to lay out the angles of a dovetail (Illus. 118). The angle used depends on the type of wood. For softwood, use a 1:6 ratio. Hardwoods require a 1:8 ratio. To set the T-bevel to the correct ratio, place it against a square. For a 1:6 ratio, the blade of the T-bevel should be 1″ out of square at a point that is 6″ from the pivot. For a 1:8 ratio, use the same procedure, but the blade should be 1″ out of square at a point that's 8″ from the pivot.

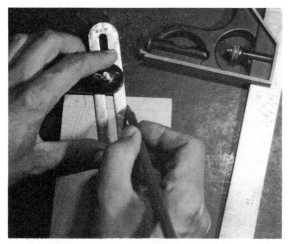

Illus. 118 (left). Use a sliding T-bevel to mark the angles of the dovetails. Mark the straight cuts with a square. Illus. 119 (right). Use a coping saw to make the cut across the bottom between the pins and dovetails.

Commercial dovetail gauges are available that are preset to the proper angles. Lay out the dovetails so that you get a half-pin at the top and the bottom. Mark the waste with an *X* so that there won't be any confusion as you cut.

Cut the dovetails first; then use them to mark the position of the pins. Use a backsaw or a dovetail saw to make the side cuts, and then complete the cut by cutting across the bottom with a coping saw (Illus. 119). Use a sharp chisel to smooth the cuts and trim right to the line.

There are many variations on the dovetail. You can vary the spacing of pins and dovetails to create decorative patterns. And you can cut half-blind dovetails so that the ends of the dovetails won't show on the face of the other board. You can cut these dovetails in the same manner as previously described, but you must cut the pins with a chisel. You can use a router with a dovetail jig to cut half-blind dovetails.

There are hundreds of other joint variations. If you are interested in trying some of them, consult a book on advanced joinery.

5
ASSEMBLY TECHNIQUES

After you have cut the joints, the parts will be ready to be assembled. Glue is the cabinetmaker's primary fastener; all other types of fasteners are simply ways of reinforcing a glued joint. Clamping plays a vital role in producing a strong glue joint.

Glue

Although glue has been used for centuries, scientists are still probing the secrets of how glue actually sticks. We do know that glue bonds in two ways—physically and molecularly. A physical bond results when the glue seeps into the pores of the wood and hardens. A molecular bond occurs when molecules in the glue attach to molecules in the wood. Most wood glues exhibit both kinds of bonding to varying degrees.

The strength of a glue line between two wood surfaces depends on the type of glue, how well the joint fits, and whether end grain or long grain is being glued. A tight-fitting joint is much stronger than a loose one. Some types of glue will fill gaps in a joint, but most glues perform best when the glue line is thin. End grain doesn't glue as well as long grain; that is why many joints have been developed to maximize the long-grain contact. When you are gluing wood long grain to long grain, the bond is so strong that no other reinforcement is needed if the joint is tight fitting and has been properly clamped. Joints involving end grain are much weaker, and usually require some type of reinforcement.

TYPES OF GLUE

Many types of glue are available and modern technology is producing new types continuously. Out of all these glues, two have emerged as the foremost glues of the modern cabinetmaker; they are polyvinyl acetate (PVA) and aliphatic resin.

Polyvinyl Acetate Glue   The glue most often used by beginning cabinetmakers is PVA. Because of its milky-white appearance, it is usually referred to as white glue. PVA's long-setting time is an advantage for beginning cabinetmakers. It allows them time to reposition parts and change alignment as they assemble the cabinet.

Since PVA is not waterproof and heat will soften the bond, this type of glue should not be used when moisture or heat will be present.

Aliphatic Resin Glue   The professional's choice for an all-around cabinetmaking glue is aliphatic resin. This type of glue is usually referred to as carpenter's glue or woodworking glue. It resembles white glue, except it is slightly yellow, and it is stronger and more water resistant than white glue. Aliphatic resin's faster setting time and initial tack can be advantageous for the experienced cabinetmaker, but they can also be drawbacks if parts need to be repositioned after the initial assembly.

This type of glue is very good for glue blocks because it has a strong initial grab that will hold the glue block in place without clamps.

Since aliphatic resin sets up hard, sanding it off the surface of the wood is relatively easy. PVA glue, on the other hand, will soften from the heat generated by sanding, so it smears when you try to sand it off.

While cabinetmakers tend to use PVA and aliphatic resin most of the time, they use many other types of glue for specialized applications.

Contact Cement   To apply plastic laminates, veneers, and edging strips, it's best to use contact cement. Its main advantage is that it doesn't require clamping. You apply it to both surfaces and allow it to dry. As soon as the surfaces touch, they begin to bond. This means that it's necessary to pay careful attention to the initial alignment of the parts. Once the parts are in contact, you need to apply additional pressure to make a firm bond.

Contact cement can form an extremely strong bond when it's used for applying surface materials, such as plastic laminates or veneers, but it doesn't have the type of strength required for use in joints.

Contact cement is water and heat resistant.

There are two types of contact cement available, solvent-based and water-based. The solvent-based cement is extremely flammable and produces toxic fumes. It is for professional use only. Advances in water-based contact cement technology have made the safer water-based contact cement an attractive substitute for the solvent-based glue. Many professionals have now switched to the water-based glue.

Panel Adhesive Panel adhesive was developed for use in the building trades to attach wall panelling and plywood. It can be useful to the cabinetmaker for operations such as applying a panelling skin to a skeleton-frame cabinet. The adhesive comes in a caulking tube and it is applied with a caulking gun. Unlike most glues, it is meant to be applied in beads. It has a very high initial tack, so it will hold parts in place without clamping.

Hide Glue This is the traditional cabinetmaker's glue, and it still offers some advantages for fine cabinetry work. It comes in dry flakes, which are first softened in water and then heated to the proper working temperature. Special electric glue pots keep the glue at the working temperature. You must apply and clamp the glue while it is still hot. Hide glue is especially good for glue blocks because it grabs so fast.

This type of glue forms a very strong bond and has exceptional shear strength. It won't stain surrounding wood, and produces an almost invisible joint. On the other hand, hide glue is very susceptible to water and heat, and certain microorganisms can destroy it.

A modern variation of hide glue is liquid hide glue. This liquid form requires no heating. It has many of the same advantages and disadvantages of the original hide glue, but it has a longer setting time.

Urea Resin Glue Commonly called plastic resin glue, this type of glue is frequently used in production cabinet work. It comes as a powder and must be mixed with water before use. Once mixed, it has a limited life, so it must be mixed just before use. It is highly resistant to water, and produces a bond that is stronger than the wood if the joints fit well. But if the joints don't fit well, this type of glue won't fill any gaps. The glue line must be uniform and thin. A thick glue line tends to crystalize and become very weak.

Hot Melt Glue Hot melt glue is a polyethylene-based plastic that softens when heated. It comes in small sticks that are placed in a special heat gun. This type of glue is especially suited for small detail work because it sets as soon as it cools, so no clamping is needed. When you use hot melt glue, you must assemble parts quickly before the glue begins to cool.

Resorcinol Resin Glue When you need the greatest water resistance, you should use resorcinol glue. This type of glue is not frequently used in cabinetmaking because it has a deep red color that makes the glue line visible. It comes in two parts, a powder and a liquid. *Dust from the powder is toxic, so avoid inhaling it as you mix the two parts together.* This glue has a very limited working time of 3 hours maximum after mixing, so only mix as much as you can use in that time.

Epoxy Glue Epoxy glue is also an extremely waterproof glue. It comes in two parts that must be mixed immediately before use. Its main advantage for the beginning cabinetmaker is its ability to fill gaps. You can salvage a poorly fitting joint by using epoxy glue. It is rather expensive; so unless you need its gap-filling properties, you might as well use other glues.

Acrylic Resin Glue For even greater strength and gap-filling properties, you should use acrylic resin glue. As with epoxy, it comes in two parts that need to be mixed just before use. This glue is even more expensive than epoxy, but it has unlimited gap-filling abilities. This makes it ideal for repairing broken parts because it will even fill in for missing fragments of a part.

Casein Glue Casein glue is made from milk. It is an old product that still has some advantages. It comes as a powder that must be mixed with water before use. Although this glue is very water resistant, it's not considered waterproof. It will adhere to oily woods, such as teak, that don't work well with other types of glue.

APPLYING GLUE

You have two conflicting objectives when applying glue. You want to provide enough glue so that the joint will be strong, not "glue starved"; but you don't want to apply more glue than is necessary because the glue will drip out of the joint and mar the surface of the wood.

The best way to make sure that you have just the right amount of glue is by spreading a thin, even coat on both mating surfaces. Use your finger, a scrap of wood, a putty knife, or a disposable plastic knife to spread the glue. The common practice of running heavy beads of glue and hoping that they will spread out as the parts are assembled leads to gaps where there is no glue and areas with too much glue that oozes out of the joint. On parts where you are especially concerned with the glue oozing out, stop just short of spreading the glue to the edge.

The ideal amount of glue will form a small bead along the glue line as the joint is clamped, but the glue won't spread from the bead.

The best way of removing glue from the surface is by allowing the glue to dry until it is no longer tacky but not quite set hard and then shaving it from the wood with a sharp chisel. The practice of removing glue with a damp rag while the glue is still wet actually tends to force the glue into the wood, sealing it. This will produce noticeable glue marks when you apply a finish.

Clamping

There are many types of clamps, but three types are the favorites of cabinetmakers; they are C-clamps, hand screws, and bar clamps (Illus. 120). C-clamps and hand screws are used for similar kinds of clamping. The hand screw is more versatile, but also more expensive; therefore, many beginners start out with C-clamps. Because bar clamps are used for joining small boards into larger panels and are used in all stages of cabinet assembly, they are almost indispensable to the serious cabinetmaker.

HAND SCREWS AND C-CLAMPS

You need to use either hand screws or C-clamps to clamp parts where the distance is less than about 8 inches. For example, you would use them to clamp a half-lap joint together. They are also very useful for clamping boards to the workbench while you are performing operations such as planing or routing.

C-clamps have a C-shaped iron body and a threaded screw for exerting pressure. A small, round shoe on the end of the screw is

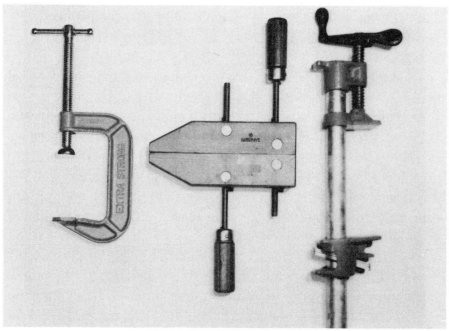

Illus. 120. Left to right: C-clamp, hand screw, and bar clamp.

attached by a ball joint, allowing the shoe to sit squarely. Because the anvil and shoe are so small, the C-clamp will dent most wood, even with moderate pressure; so you should always place a piece of scrap wood between the clamp and the piece being clamped.

C-clamps tend to cause parts to creep out of alignment as you tighten them. This is because the anvil and shoe are not always in perfect alignment. Watch for this as you tighten the clamps, and correct any creeping before the glue sets.

Hand screws have two threaded screws instead of one, as with the C-clamp. Because of their large maple clamping surface, hand screws are less likely to dent the wood; on important work, however, you should still put a block of wood or a piece of cork between the work and the clamp.

The two screws permit the jaws to be placed on surfaces that aren't parallel; but for most work, you will want the jaws to be parallel. To get the jaws parallel, hold one handle in each hand and crank the clamp around. When one end of the jaws is closed, let that handle slip in your hand and continue spinning the clamp until the other end has closed as well. The jaws will now be fully closed and parallel. To open the jaws and keep them parallel, hold both handles tightly again and spin the clamp in the opposite direction. The jaws will open up evenly. Stop when the jaws are far enough apart to slip easily over the parts to be clamped. To tighten the clamp, turn both handles at the same time in the same direction.

BAR CLAMPS

Bar clamps are very important in cabinetmaking because they are available in lengths that are long enough to use in the assembly of large cabinets. For example, you can use bar clamps to clamp both sides of a cabinet in place at the same time. Most bar clamps are very similar; their main difference has to do with the type of bar they use. Heavy industrial types have an I-beam type of bar that resists twisting and bending, but they are expensive and you are limited to certain lengths. Most beginning cabinetmakers prefer the type that employs iron-plumbing pipe as the bar. You can get the pipe in any length you want, and you can even use pipe couplings to lengthen it. This is very useful when you are building long units such as kitchen cabinets.

Edge-Joining Lumber   One of the main functions of bar clamps is edge-joining narrow boards into larger panels. Chapter 4 discussed how to prepare the edges for this procedure. The minimum number of clamps that you can use for joining boards into panels is three. You must have at least one clamp on the opposite side of the panel, or the clamping pressure will cause the panel to cup. Larger panels require more clamps.

Always alternate clamps on either side of the panel to even out the stresses. Place a board along each edge to protect the edges of the panel from the jaws of the clamps. If you have difficulty lining up the boards, clamp boards crosswise at the ends of the panel with C-clamps or hand screws to help hold the boards in alignment. Placing wax paper between the cross boards and the panel will prevent the cross boards from being glued to the panel by squeezed-out glue. Tighten the clamps evenly, working from the middle to the ends, until the joints are tight and a small bead of glue is squeezed out (Illus. 121). Don't overtighten the clamps, or too much glue may squeeze out of the joint and weaken it, or the clamp may break.

Assembly   The use of bar clamps makes cabinet assembly easier to do and stronger. Even if you are using screws or nails, hold the parts in place with bar clamps while you install the fasteners. This will ensure that all the joints are pulled in tight. Dado joints only require clamping from one direction because they have a lip on both

Illus. 121. Here narrow boards are being joined into a wide panel. The C-clamps and plywood strips at the end help to keep the boards in alignment. The plywood strips on the edges prevent the bar-clamp jaws from denting the edge of the panel.

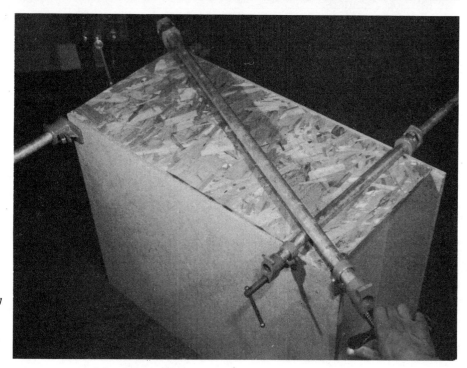

Illus. 122. Bar clamps are very useful for assembling cabinets. The clamp running diagonally between the corners pulls the cabinet into square.

sides. It's best to clamp rabbets from both directions to make sure they are seated firmly against the shoulder.

You can also use bar clamps to help square assemblies. To check the bookcase just described for square, use a tape measure to diagonally measure the distance from corner to corner. Both diagonals should be the same distance. If they are not, place a bar clamp diagonally across the corners that are the farthest apart and tighten the clamp until both measurements are equal. Leave the clamp in place until the glue has dried or until fasteners have been installed that will hold the cabinet square (Illus. 122).

Fasteners

You need to use fasteners when joints need reinforcement or when it is impractical to clamp a joint. Out of the many types of available fasteners, screws and nails are the most useful for cabinetmaking. However, special features are necessary with particle board because of its unique properties.

NAILS

There are five types of nails that are usually used in cabinetmaking: common, box, finishing, casing, and brads.

Of the five types, common nails are the largest in diameter. They have large flat heads. Common nails are only used in the roughest parts of cabinet work, such as making a sub-base for a built-in cabinet. Because of their large diameters, they tend to split the wood.

Box nails resemble common nails; but they are thinner, so you can use them in thinner wood with less chance of splitting the wood. They are used in areas where their heads won't show—attaching the back of a cabinet, for example. The large heads are especially useful when attaching thin materials because they won't pull through as easily as the smaller heads.

Finishing nails are even thinner than box nails, and they have small heads that you can set below the surface of the wood. Finishing nails are the most common type of nail used in cabinetmaking.

Casing nails are similar to finishing nails, but they are the same diameter as box nails and their heads are tapered, giving them more holding power. Use casing nails when you need more strength, but set the heads below the surface.

Brads are the thinnest nails available. Their heads resemble the heads on finishing nails. They come in lengths from ⅜″ to 1½″. The length of brads is designated in inches, whereas all other nails are designated by a penny size.

The Penny System The length of most nails is designated by an old English system, called the penny system. The abbreviation for penny is *d*. Although no one knows exactly how the penny system originated, it may have had something to do with the cost per hundred; now it has simply become an arbitrary measure of length.

Standard nail sizes start at 2d, which is 1″ long, and end at 60d, which is 6″ long. There is no uniform formula for converting penny size into inches, but there are a couple of rough estimates you can make. Between 2d and 16d, each standard size is ¼ of an inch longer than the last, beginning at 1″ for a 2d nail. The standard sizes run consecutively up to 10d, but then they skip to 12d and then to 16d. Another way of estimating the length in inches of a penny size up to 10d is by dividing the penny size by 4 and adding ½ of an inch. Using this method to find the length of a 6d nail, you would divide 6 by 4, which comes to 1½, and then add ½, which gives you a total of 2″ for the length of a 6-penny nail.

Nails are usually sold by the pound. Obviously, you will get a lot more small nails than large ones in a pound, so you need to estimate how many nails you will need. A pound of 3d finishing nails will contain approximately 900 nails, so a pound of these nails will last a long time. On the other hand, a pound of 16d common nails will only contain about 50 nails. Here are the approximate number of nails per pound for some finishing nails frequently used in cabinet-making: 4d = 600, 6d = 300, 8d = 200, and 10d = 125.

Choosing a Nail The type and length of nail you choose depends on the thickness of the lumber, the strength required, and the type of head that's needed.

The length of the nail shouldn't be too long, or the point will break through to the face of an adjoining board; but it should be long enough to give adequate holding power. As a general rule, a nail should be four times the thickness of the board it is driven through. For a ¾″-thick board, this would be 10d. Of course, if the other board isn't thick enough for a nail this size, you must use a shorter nail. Generally, for cabinet work, a finishing nail is the best choice; but for added strength, you can use a casing nail. In situations where the head won't show, a box nail is a good choice because of its greater holding power.

Driving Nails You can usually drive a nail directly into any wood that has a specific gravity of less than 0.5 (see Chapter 1). With harder woods, you need to drill a pilot hole before you drive the nail, or the wood will probably split. The pilot hole should be slightly smaller than the nail so that the wood will grip the nail tightly.

Nails will hold better when you drive them into edge grain rather than end grain; so when you have a choice, choose edge grain. Usually you don't have a choice, and you have to take what you get. If you angle nails so that they point in towards each other, they will have greater holding power. Drive one nail in straight first to keep the parts from slipping out of alignment. Use a hammer that is heavy enough to drive the nail easily; a hammer that is too light may actually bend the nail. A 16 oz. hammer is usually used for cabinet work. Hit the nail squarely with the middle of the face of the hammer. Avoid the urge to drive the nail in with one blow. Using several lighter blows will give you more control and it actually makes the nail grip better. If you have trouble with nails bending, it could be that the work isn't supported well enough. Try to place the work so that you are hammering against something solid. If it isn't possible to brace the work in some other way, hold a hammer in back of the area you are nailing (the heavier the hammer, the better). The weight of the hammer will steady the board, and the hammer will slap back after each blow, counteracting any spring in the board.

You need to use a nail set to drive the nails below the surface so that the heads can be hidden with putty. The set has a cup-shaped depression in its end that cuts into the head of the nail to keep it from slipping. You will need several sizes of nail sets for setting large and small nails. Don't set the nail too deep or it will lose most of its hold on the wood; about $\frac{1}{16}$ of an inch below the surface will provide enough room for the putty.

Power Nailers   There are special guns for driving nails and staples. Most nail guns operate on compressed air, but there are also power nailers that run on electricity. For small fasteners there are hand-operated guns that are similar to staple guns. Power drivers are useful when you will be doing a lot of repetitive nailing. Power-driven staples are especially good for applying $\frac{1}{8}''$ or $\frac{1}{4}''$ backs to cabinets. The bridge of a staple resists pulling through these thin materials better than a nail head. Epoxy-coated staples are very useful for fastening particle board. The friction from driving the staple melts the epoxy, gluing the staple to the board. For $\frac{3}{4}''$-thick particle board, a $2''$ epoxy-coated staple with a $\frac{3}{8}''$ bridge will fasten boards face to edge with no splitting.

When you are using a power driver, don't overdo it. Because this tool is easy to use, people have a tendency to put in too many nails or staples. Too many fasteners in a confined area will split the wood and make the joint weaker than if fewer fasteners were used. *Power drivers can shoot a fastener with great force, so never pull the trigger unless the gun is pressed against a board.*

SCREWS

Screws hold better than nails, and they will help to pull joints together. Screw sizes are designated by a number indicating the diameter of the screw and by the length of the screw in inches. The smallest screw diameter is 0, and the largest commonly found is 24. For cabinetmaking, sizes 4 through 12 are the most frequently used; and of those sizes, 6 and 8 are probably used more than any others.

Wood screws come with three basic types of heads: flat, round, and panhead (Illus. 123). Flatheads are meant to be countersunk flush or below the surface. Oval-head screws are a variation on the

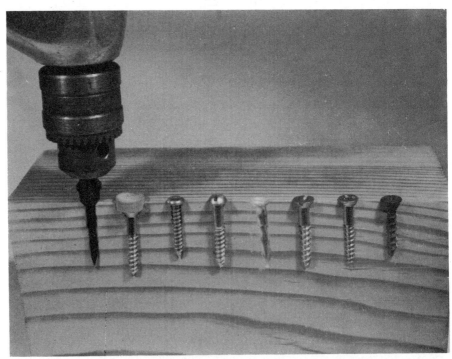

Illus. 123. Left to right: 1. Drilling a pilot hole with a special drill that makes the thread-clearance hole and the shank-clearance hole, and countersinks in a single operation; 2. a standard flathead wood screw countersunk below the surface with a dowel plug inserted to hide the screw; 3. a panhead sheet-metal screw; 4. a round-head wood screw; 5. a properly drilled pilot hole showing thread clearance, shank clearance, and countersinking; 6. a standard-slotted flathead wood screw; 7. a standard wood screw with a Phillips flathead; and 8. a dry-wall screw.

flathead; they require countersinking, but their tops extend above the surface for decorative purposes. Round heads need no countersinking; their heads extend above the surface. Panhead screws extend above the surface as round heads do, but their heads are flattened on top. Most cabinet work is done with flathead screws. Two types of screwdrivers are commonly used with wood screws, the straight blade and the Phillips. When given the choice, most cabinetmakers prefer Phillips head screws because the screwdriver is less likely to slip out of the heads and mar the wood. Phillips heads are also easier to drive with an electric drill or power screwdriver. Some large production shops have begun using a type of screw that has a square hole in its head. This type is especially well suited for power drivers.

The threads on a traditional wood screw are fairly shallow, and the shank is the same diameter as the outside of the threads. This type of screw requires a two-step pilot hole. First, a hole slightly smaller than the root diameter of the threads should be drilled the entire length of the hole; then the hole should be enlarged for the length of the shank to the same diameter as the shank. There are special drills that will do this job in one operation and also countersink if needed (see Illus. 123). The shank allows the screw to turn freely in the outside board, while the threads bite into the inside board. This enables the screw to pull the two boards tight.

When appearance is important, you can countersink screws beneath the wood surface and put putty over them or you can place dowel plugs in the hole to cover the screw heads.

The traditional wood screw is an old design with several disadvantages. As a result, the case-hardened, extruded-thread wood screw has been developed. This type of screw is commonly called a drywall screw because it was originally developed for attaching dry wall in building construction.

The dry-wall screw has very deep, sharp threads and a much smaller root diameter than the traditional wood screw. The shank is smaller than the threads, so it doesn't require a separate clearance hole. This type of screw is designed to be driven into woods with a specific gravity of less than 0.5, without a pilot hole. The point is very sharp to aid in starting the screw, and the head is a modified type of flathead that will pull flush in these softer woods. Harder woods require a pilot hole and countersinking, but a shank-clearance hole is not necessary.

The face-frame screw is a variation on the dry-wall screw. With the face-frame screw, you don't have to drill a separate pilot hole in hardwoods because it has a drill-like point that makes its own pilot hole. Although you can drive these screws by hand, they were specifically designed for power drivers. Most production shops have switched entirely to this type of screw. They are usually sold by the pound, the way nails are.

PARTICLE BOARD FASTENERS

Particle board is made up of many short wood fibres; because these fibres are shorter than those in solid wood, screws and nails don't hold very well. Particle board also has different holding characteristics on its face and edge. A fastener installed in the face of a piece of particle board will hold approximately twice as well as the same fastener installed in the edge of the board. Although the fasteners described in this section can be used with many materials, they are most advantageous with particle board.

Since a fastener attached to the face of a piece of particle board will hold better than one attached to the edge, particle board fasteners are designed to be attached to the face of both boards. One such fastener is the knock-down fitting (Illus. 124). This type of fitting has two separate parts that attach to the inside faces of boards that meet at a corner. They both have a large surface-contact

Illus. 124. A knock-down fitting allows screws to be attached to the face of both parts and provides greater holding power than screwing into the end of a particle board part.

Illus. 125. The bolt-and-cross dowel fastener overcomes the poor screw-holding characteristic of particle board by employing the threaded-metal cross dowel.

area, and are attached with several screws that enter the face of the board. The plates are attached before assembly; during assembly, the two parts are locked together with a screw or cam. You can assemble and disassemble knock-down fittings many times, so they are especially useful for cabinets that are frequently moved. Many commercial cabinets employ knock-down fittings to save shipping space. The cabinets are shipped flat and assembled on the job.

Another way of increasing the holding power of particle board is by installing an insert that is stronger than the board. Two commercial fasteners that employ this principle are the bolt-and-cross dowel and the cam fitting. The bolt-and-cross dowel uses a metal dowel with a threaded hole. A hole is made in one board for the cross dowel, and a smaller hole is made through the face of the other board and into the edge of the board with the cross dowel. A metal bolt installed from the face of the outside board connects with the cross dowel, pulling the joint together (Illus. 125). A shop-made substitute for this type of fastener employs a wood dowel instead of the metal one. You need to glue the dowel into the hole and then drive a wood screw through the other board and into the dowel. Although it's not as strong as the metal version, this method provides more strength than if you simply screwed into the edge of the particle board.

The cam fitting operates in a similar manner, but the cross dowel has a cam slot in it. Instead of twisting the bolt to tighten the connector, you twist the dowel.

Large, coarse threads hold better in particle board than small, fine threads, but very large fasteners weaken other parts because they require such large holes. The threaded insert solves this problem. It is a metal plug that has large, coarse threads on the outside and a small threaded hole in the middle (Illus. 126). To install a threaded insert, drill a pilot hole that is slightly smaller than the insert. Use a countersink to chamfer the edge of the hole to prevent bulging around the insert. Some inserts have a hexagonal hole for an Allen wrench; others have a slot for a standard screwdriver. Screw the insert into the pilot hole as you would a wood screw. The top of the insert should be slightly below the wood surface. You can attach the hardware or mating part with a small machine screw that fits the hole in the insert.

Illus. 126. A threaded insert has coarse wood screw threads around its outside diameter, providing greater holding capacity in particle board. In the middle of the insert, there is a smaller hole threaded for a machine screw. This insert has a hexagonal hole part of the way that accepts an Allen wrench; other types have a slot that accepts a standard screwdriver.

6
CARCASSES

The main assembly of any cabinet is called the carcass. Additional parts, such as doors and drawers, attach to the carcass. There are three ways you can make a carcass: by skeleton-frame construction, case construction, and panel construction. Backs, bases, and cornices are also considered part of the carcass.

Skeleton-Frame Construction

Skeleton-frame construction is similar to the framing of a house. The framework is made of small parts put together in the shape of the cabinet; then the framework is covered with a thin "skin" that hides all of its details. (Illus. 127). The framework is made of solid wood, usually an inexpensive species. The skin is usually plywood, but you can also use particle board or hardboard.

To assemble the framework, you can use dowel joints, mortise-and-tenon joints, or half-lap joints. Mortise-and-tenon joints and half-lap joints are stronger than dowel joints. Since the framework isn't visible in the finished cabinet, half-lap joints are often used because they are easier to make than mortise-and-tenon joints. Frame members are usually 1½" wide; avoid widths greater than 4" to prevent problems associated with dimensional change in the frame members.

You can build frames individually, and then treat them as solid boards for subsequent operations. For example, you can make the side frames of a cabinet with rails placed wherever a joint with

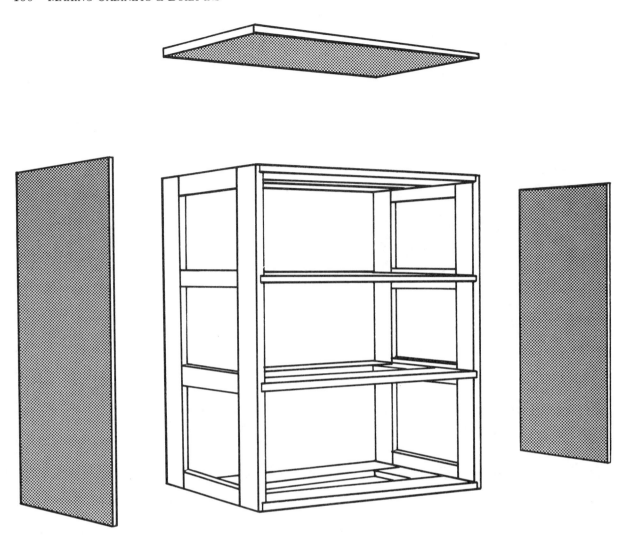

Illus. 127. Skeleton-frame construction uses a thin skin that covers an inner framework.

another part of the cabinet will be made. Once you have built the
side frames, you can cut rabbets and dadoes in them for the top,
bottom, and shelves or drawer guides, as if the frames were solid
pieces. The frames that fit into these joints can also be constructed
beforehand, and the frames can be assembled into a carcass as if
each frame were a solid board.

Once you have assembled the frames, skin them over with a thin
(usually ¼″ or ⅛″) sheet of plywood, particle board, or hardboard.
Built-in cabinets made in this manner can be skinned with wall
panelling to match the room. You can glue on the skin without using
any fasteners if sufficient clamps are available, or you can glue the

skin and then nail it with small brads. You can also use contact cement or panel adhesive to apply the skin.

The skin adds rigidity to the frame. Complex corner joints are not necessary when skinning the frames. Simple butt joints are usually used; but if both faces will show, you can use a mitre joint. When an edge of the frame will show around a drawer or door opening, you can cover the frame with decorative stiles and rails. Stiles are the vertical members of the frame and rails are the horizontal members. You can also use one of the edge treatments described in Chapter 1, such as veneer tape.

Case Construction

Case construction is probably the most widely used method of making carcasses among modern cabinetmakers. The parts of the carcass are each made from a single board. Plywood and particle board are very well suited for this type of construction (Illus. 128). You can also use solid lumber with this method; but in larger cabinets, dimensional stability can be a problem. When you use solid

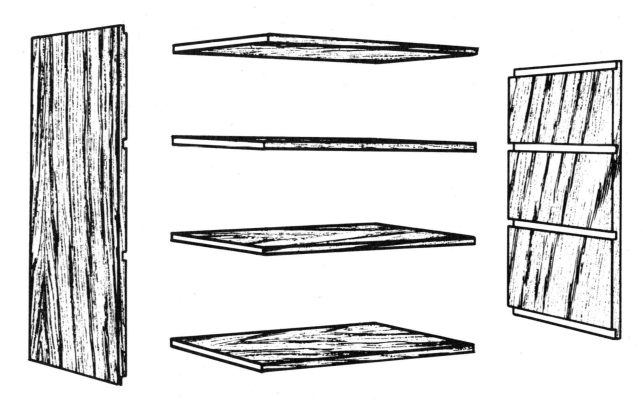

Illus. 128. In case construction, each part of the carcass is made from a single board.

lumber, the grain should be in the same direction on all of the parts in the carcass.

You should not mix solid wood with plywood or particle board when using this type of construction. For example, if you used solid wood for the sides of a cabinet and plywood for the top and bottom, the sides would change in width with changes in humidity, whereas the top and bottom would remain stable. This would eventually cause the joints to pull apart. You can use solid wood for small parts, such as stiles and rails or reinforcing blocks, in a plywood or particle board cabinet because the narrow width of these small parts isn't affected by dimensional change very much.

Dadoes and rabbets are the most common types of joints used in case construction. However, you can use mitre joints when both faces will show. Decorative stiles and rails are often used on the front edges of this type of carcass to cover the exposed edges and to provide a solid attaching point for hinges.

Panel Construction

The best method of carcass construction using solid wood is panel construction (Illus. 129). This form of carcass construction has evolved over many years to accommodate the dimensional changes that are constantly occurring in solid wood. As with skeleton-frame construction, the carcass is made of many small parts joined into a framework, but in this case the framework is visible.

As previously mentioned, the vertical members of the frame are called stiles, and the horizontal members are called rails. A frame member between two panels is called a mullion (Illus. 130). Frame members are usually 1½" to 2" wide, but you can use any dimension up to 4". Stiles and rails wider than 4" are subject to dimensional change, so they should be avoided in most cases.

A groove cut into the inside edge of the frame holds a panel. The panel is slightly smaller than the space allowed, and it is not glued in place. This leaves the panel free to expand and contract without distorting the carcass. The frame members are always long and narrow, with the grain running with their length, so there is little dimensional change in the frame. The result is a very stable carcass. Because of this stability, you can mix plywood and solid wood in the same carcass. You can make the top and bottom of plywood and the sides of solid wood in panel construction without any problems.

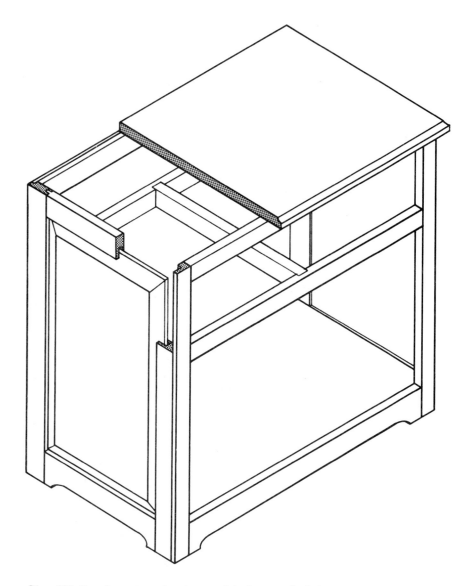

Illus. 129. Panel construction is one of the best methods in terms of accommodating for dimensional change in solid wood.

The simplest type of panel construction is shown in Illus. 131. The frame has no decorative edge and a thin, flat panel is used. Besides solid wood, you can use plywood, particle board, or hardboard for the panel. The man-made materials can be glued in the groove. In this case, dimensional stability is not the main concern; the frame is simply used to strengthen a panel that would not be strong enough on its own.

You can cut the groove on a table saw using a dado blade or with a router or shaper. You can cut short grooves by hand using the

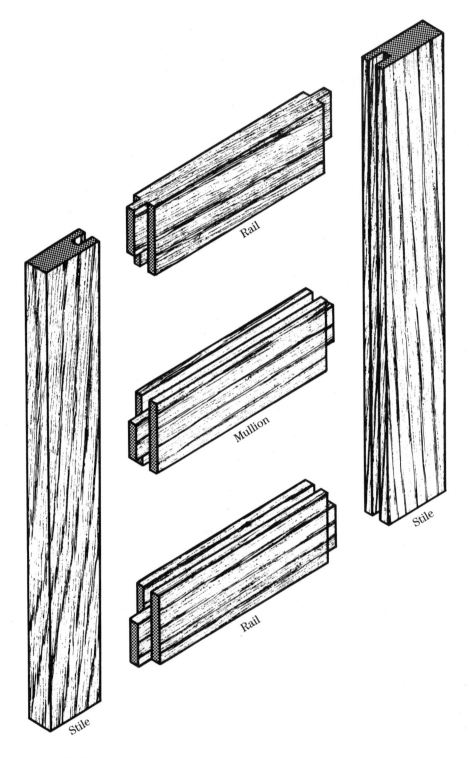

Illus. 130. Parts of a panel frame.

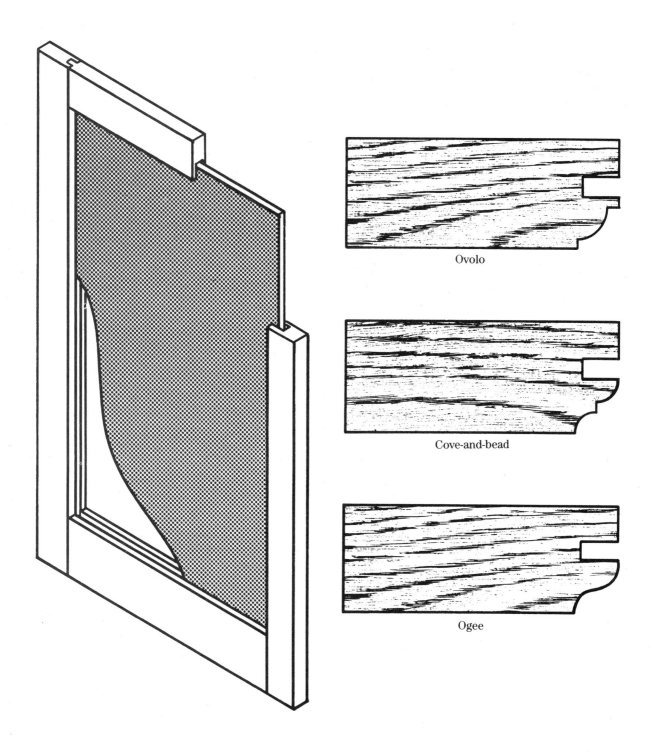

Ovolo

Cove-and-bead

Ogee

Illus. 131 (left). The simplest type of panel construction uses a thin, flat panel. Illus. 132 (right). Decorative sticking.

methods described in Chapter 4 for dadoes. To cut a long groove by hand, you need to use a plow plane.

Frequently, a decorative edge, called sticking, is added on one or both sides of the groove. Ovolo, cove-and-bead, and ogee are three popular designs (Illus. 132). A shaper or router is usually used to cut the sticking. In the past, special planes were used for making sticking. Some moulding planes are still available, though not as many as

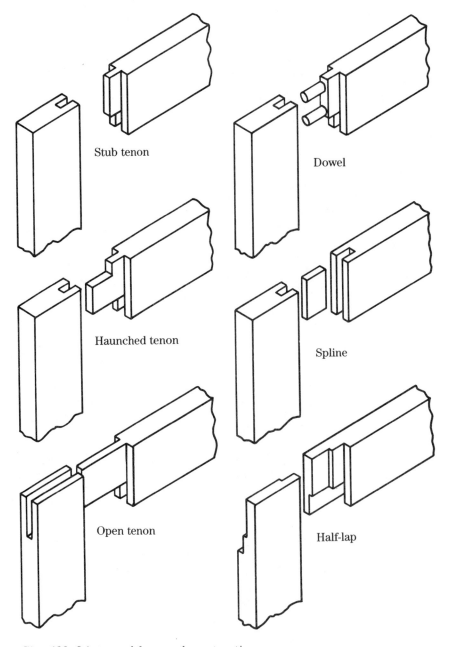

Illus. 133. Joints used for panel construction.

in the past. Cabinetmakers who prefer to use only hand tools still use moulding planes for this purpose.

The frame members are usually joined with mortise-and-tenon joints (Illus. 133). A short tenon that fits into the groove made for the panel is called a stub tenon. The stub tenon is acceptable when a great deal of strength is not required, but a full-length tenon provides greater strength. You need to use a haunched tenon so that the exposed end of the groove will be filled. If the groove won't show, then it is not necessary to use this tenon. It's easier to cut an open tenon than a mortise, so an open tenon is sometimes used when the edges of the frame are concealed. You can also use dowel joints; in which case, you will still cut a stub tenon on the end of the rail to fit into the groove on the stile. A spline joint offers about as much strength as a stub tenon and is simpler to make. To cut a groove in the ends of the rails, use the same saw setup that you used to cut the grooves for the panels. *Exercise care when making this cut on a table saw. Be sure to keep your fingers well away from the blade.* Using a tenoning jig that clamps the board in place is the safest way to handle cuts on the end of narrow parts. You can use half-lap joints, but they are not as simple as those normally used because an added step is necessary to make the projection that fills the groove.

When you use decorative sticking, the end of the rail must have an opposite matching cut to fit over the edge of the stile. This is called a coped joint (Illus. 134). To accomplish this, you should use special matched pairs of shaper cutters.

You may use a raised panel both for appearance and to give the added strength available from a thicker board. The panel can be bevelled on both sides or only on the front. When both sides are bevelled, you can use a full ¾"-thick panel and it will still be flush with the frame. If only one side is bevelled, then you need to use a panel that is ½" or ⁷⁄₁₆" thick to keep the front surface flush with the frame. You can use a ¾"-thick panel if you don't mind having the panel extend past the frame.

You can cut the bevel on a table saw. Set the blade to a 10° tilt and raise it 1¼" above the table. Position the fence ³⁄₁₆" away from the blade. Hold the panel upright with its back against the fence. *This operation must be done without the guard, so use caution and keep your hands well clear of the blade.* It will be easier to keep the panel from rocking if you attach a board to the fence that extends higher than the fence to help support the panel. Another

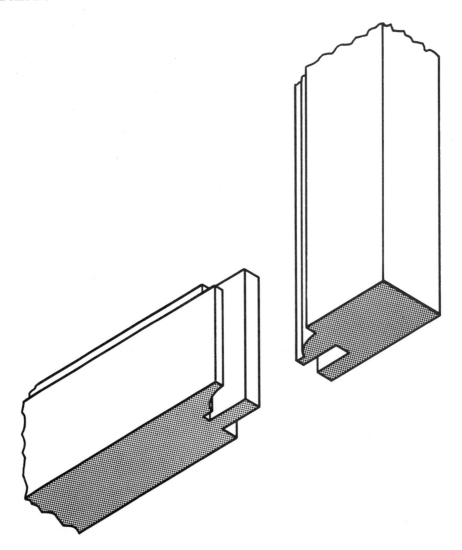

Illus. 134. A coped joint.

method of guiding the panel is by cutting a spacer that is the same width as the rip fence; sandwich this spacer between the back of the panel and a scrap board about the same size as the panel. If you place the spacer in the middle of the panel, you can make two cuts on opposite sides of the panel before you have to reposition the spacer. Clamp this assembly together and place it on the saw so that it straddles the fence. This method will practically eliminate any rocking or wandering from the fence.

A bevel cut on a table saw will usually require a lot of hand sanding to remove the saw marks. Using a planer blade will help to minimize the marks. A special type of blade that has an abrasive coating on the side will further reduce the marks left by the saw.

A shaper is often used to produce the bevel on a panel. Shaper cutters can produce a curved bevel or a bevel with a dual angle.

You can use a plane to cut the bevel by hand. Planes are the original tool used for this operation, and have been used for centuries. Although you can use special panel-raising planes, you can produce a simple raised panel with a block plane. Lay out lines on the panel to indicate the thickness of the edge and the end of the bevel on the face. Cut the cross-grain bevels first so that any tear-outs will be removed when you cut the other bevels. Hold the plane at the approximate angle of the bevel and chamfer the corner. Keep cutting down the corner until you are near the layout lines. Hold the plane at the angle necessary to meet both lines, and clean up the bevel with a few fine cuts.

Whenever possible, stain the panels before assembly; that way, if they shrink, there won't be a noticeable light line at the joint between the panel and the frame. Since the panel is loose in the frame, it can sometimes shift too far out of alignment. This is not noticeable with flat panels; but with a raised panel, there may be a noticeable difference in the width of the exposed bevel from one side to the other or the panel may tilt slightly. To prevent this, put a 1"-long bead of silicone caulking in the middle of the top and bottom grooves. The caulking will glue the panel in place, but it is also flexible enough to allow panel movement. By gluing only the middle of the end-grain part of the panel, the panel will expand and contract evenly on either side of the glued section, maintaining an equal exposure on both side bevels.

Face Frames

Face frames are stiles and rails applied to the front edges of the carcass. You use them for hiding the exposed edges of the carcass and for providing a solid attaching point for hinges (Illus. 135).

Face-frame members are generally ¾" thick and 1½" wide. You can also use frame members that are 2" wide. You can use other dimensions for face frames, but avoid frame members wider than 4" to prevent problems with dimensional change. The face frame is frequently attached to the edges with a butt joint; since this is long-grain-to-long-grain contact, the butt joint is fairly strong. If you want to minimize the size of the face frame's exposed edge, you can cut a rabbet around the edge of the frame.

Face frames are frequently attached with finishing nails. You can usually straighten long frame members that are slightly warped or bowed as you apply the nails. Nail the face frame in place at one end;

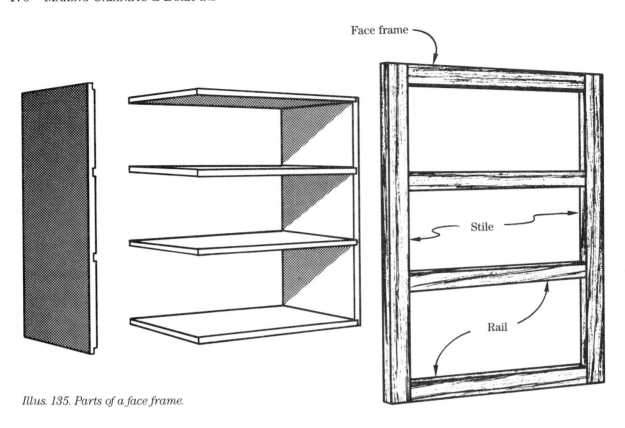

Face frame

Stile

Rail

Illus. 135. Parts of a face frame.

then use the leverage provided by the length of the board to pull it into place, and then nail it progressively to the other end.

Tops

With a high cabinet, where the top is above eye level, you can usually treat the top the same way as a shelf or the bottom of the cabinet; but you must give special attention to the top of a low cabinet because it affects the appearance of the cabinet (Illus. 136).

When you use solid wood for a cabinet top, there is a tendency for the top to cup. Changes in humidity can cause large dimensional changes in the wide panels used for tops. A 12″-wide top can change as much as ¼″ in width as a result of changes in moisture content. Therefore, you must pay special attention to keeping the top flat and allowing for dimensional change.

You can use cleats to help keep the top flat (Illus. 137). Don't glue the cleats to the top. Attach the cleats with screws placed in slotted holes to allow for expansion and shrinkage. Use round-head screws with a washer to keep the screw head from pulling through the slot.

Underside of top is flush with lower edge of front rail.

Top fits into dado.

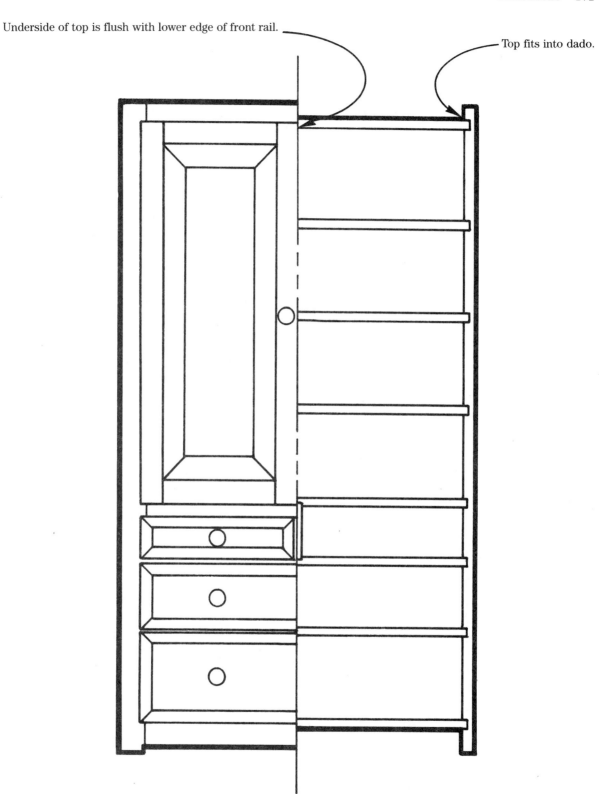

Illus. 136. When the top is above eye level, it can be attached the same way as a shelf.

If you don't allow for dimensional change in this way, the top is apt to crack as the wood shrinks.

You can also use end caps to keep the top flat (Illus. 138). A tongue cut on the end of the top fits into a groove cut into the end cap. End caps can cause the top to split if you attach them incorrectly. You should only glue the cap to a section about 4 inches wide in the middle of the top. You need to leave the rest of the tongue and groove free to move as the top shrinks and expands.

Traditionally styled cabinets usually have a top that is not an integral part of the cabinet. A subframe is integral to the carcass, and the top is screwed from underneath to the subframe. If the top is solid wood, it should not be glued and the screw holes should be enlarged in the subframe or slot-shaped to allow for dimensional changes in the top (Illus. 139). You can glue and screw a plywood or particle board top to the subframe with no provision for expansion. Counter tops of built-in cabinets are attached this way (for more details, see Chapter 10).

Instead of attaching the top to a subframe, you can use small brackets to attach the top. The brackets can be made from wood or metal. You make the wood type (Illus. 140) by cutting a ¼″ × ½″ rabbet on the edge of a 2″-wide strip of wood. This strip should have the grain running across its width, instead of along its length as is usual. After you've made the rabbet, cut the strip into 1½″ lengths. Drill a hole in the middle of each bracket for a screw. Cut a ¼″ × ¼″

Don't glue cleat to top.

Only apply glue to middle area.

Illus. 137 (left). Screw holes in the cleat should be slotted. Use a washer on the screw to keep the head from pulling through the slot. Illus. 138 (right). When you use end caps, apply glue only to the middle area of the tongue so that the top can freely expand or contract.

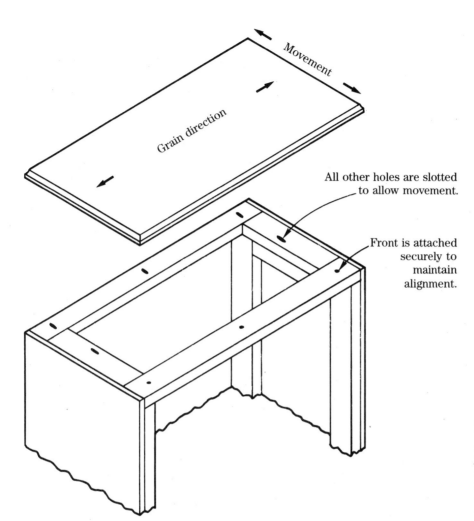

All other holes are slotted
to allow movement.

Front is attached
securely to
maintain
alignment.

Movement

Grain direction

*Illus. 139. When a solid
wood top is attached to a
subframe, use slotted holes
for the screws everywhere
except along the front. Attach the front securely to
maintain proper align-
ment.*

dado ½″ down from the top-inside edge of the sides of the cabinet.
Position the top on the sides, and place the brackets so that the
projecting tongue fits into the dado in the side. Attach the bracket
to the top with a screw. You can glue the brackets to the top, but
don't let any glue get on the parts that touch the sides. Space the
brackets 4″ to 6″ apart, all along the dado. You can use the same type
of brackets to attach the top to the front and back rails, but you
need to make the tongue longer and the dado deeper. Position the
bracket so that the tongue is only halfway into the dado. This will
allow the tongue to move in and out of the dado as the top shrinks
and swells.

The metal type of bracket (Illus. 141) works in exactly the same
way, but the dado is narrower and usually a saw kerf is all that is
necessary. You can purchase the metal brackets ready-made, or you
can make your own by bending strap iron in a vise.

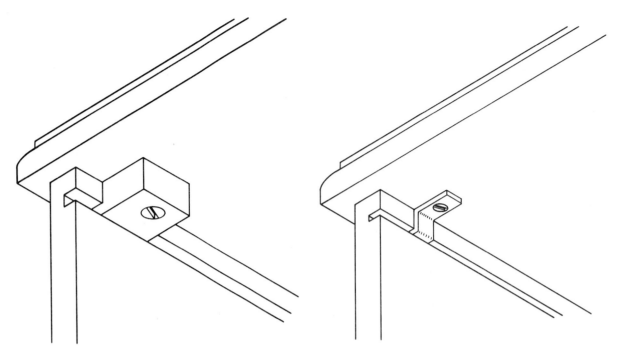

Illus. 140 (left). You can use wooden brackets that fit into a dado in the side to attach the top, and they allow for dimensional change. Illus. 141 (right). Metal brackets for attaching the top are commercially available, or you can make them by bending strap iron.

Some modern designs call for a top that is integral with the carcass. Case construction is usually used for the rest of the carcass when an integral top is needed. An integral top usually doesn't overhang the edges, so mitre joints are usually used to hide the end grain. Sometimes the joinery is used for decorative effect; should this be the case, you can use exposed dovetails or box joints to attach the top.

Backs

The back of a cabinet is an important structural member of the carcass. It holds the entire cabinet square. If you build an open-backed cabinet, you need to include extra bracing to keep the cabinet square. Backs are usually made of ¼" plywood or ¼" or ⅛" hardboard. You can simply butt the back in place, but this leaves an exposed edge along the side of the cabinet. A better method is providing a rabbet along the back edges of the sides where the back can fit (Illus. 142). Usually the back can overhang at the top and bottom, unless the top shows; then you also need to make a rabbet at the top.

You should attach the back after you have assembled the rest of the carcass. Check the carcass for square by measuring diagonals from corner to corner. Both measurements should be equal. Use a square placed at several joints as an additional check. If the cabinet is out of square, try to rack it into square before applying the back. If you can't do this, then put the back in place and put several nails in one side but leave the other edges free. It is usually possible to apply hand pressure to the back and one side to rack the cabinet into square. If you still can't square the cabinet, then place a bar clamp diagonally across the corners that were the farthest apart and tighten the clamp until the cabinet is square. Now nail the back in place.

Backs are not usually glued. However, when you use man-made materials, you can glue the back in place without any problem and the cabinet will be strengthened. Short box nails will hold better than brads because their large heads won't pull through the back. When a power stapler is available, staples offer the greatest holding power because the bridge prevents the staple from pulling through

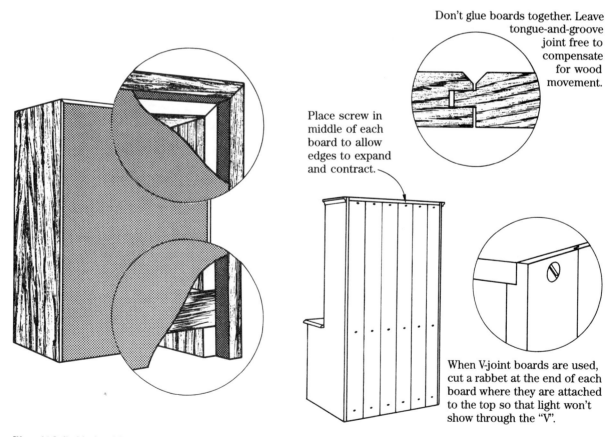

Don't glue boards together. Leave tongue-and-groove joint free to compensate for wood movement.

Place screw in middle of each board to allow edges to expand and contract.

When V-joint boards are used, cut a rabbet at the end of each board where they are attached to the top so that light won't show through the "V".

Illus. 142 (left). A rabbet is one of the best joints for attaching the back to a cabinet. Illus. 143 (right). On an authentic antique reproduction, you can use tongue-and-groove boards for the back.

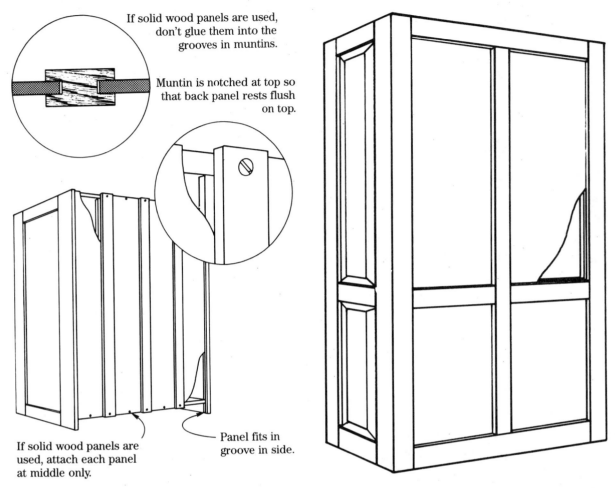

If solid wood panels are used, don't glue them into the grooves in muntins.

Muntin is notched at top so that back panel rests flush on top.

If solid wood panels are used, attach each panel at middle only.

Panel fits in groove in side.

Illus. 144 (left). The muntin back is another type of back you can use in antique reproductions. It is also useful when you need to make a back larger than the standard 4 × 8 sheet size. Illus. 145 (right). The panelled back offers more rigidity than the muntin back.

the back. Space the nails 4″ to 6″ apart around all four edges. For added strength, you can use screws instead of nails.

If you are building an antique reproduction and you want it to be authentic, you can't use man-made materials for the back. Several types of backs were used before the advent of plywood. You can assemble tongue-and-groove strips, which are similar to the type used as flooring, into a large panel for a back (Illus. 143). Screw or nail the boards only in the middle of their widths and don't use glue on the tongues or grooves.

Another type of back, called a muntin back, uses thin pieces of solid wood joined together by muntins, which are narrow uprights made of thicker wood and grooved on both edges (Illus. 144). You can also use muntins for joining man-made materials when the back is too large to be cut from a single 4′ × 8′ sheet.

A tongue-and-groove back or a muntin back won't hold the carcass in square as rigidly as a back made from a single sheet of
plywood or hardboard. A type of antique back that does add rigidity
to the carcass is the panel back (Illus. 145). It is made the same way
as the panelled sides discussed earlier. Usually flat panels are used,
but bevelled panels will also work.

Cornices

A cornice is a decorative moulding that is applied to the top of high
cabinets. Modern designs usually eliminate the cornice, but for traditional cabinets a cornice is still employed (Illus. 146). Cornice

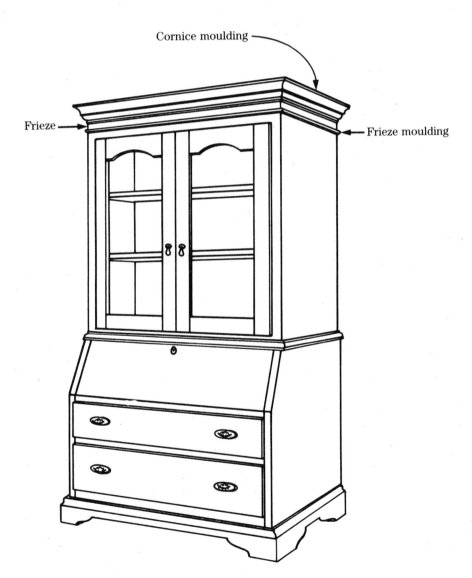

Cornice moulding

Frieze

Frieze moulding

*Illus. 146. The cornice is a
decorative detail frequently
used at the top of antique
cabinets.*

moulding is commercially available, or you can make your own. If you make the rest of the carcass from a dimensionally stable material, such as plywood, you can attach the cornice directly to the carcass. When you use panel construction, you can attach the cor-

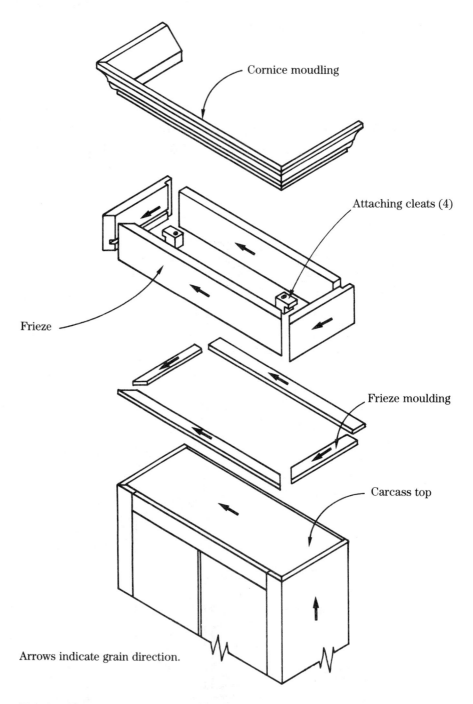

Cornice moudling

Attaching cleats (4)

Frieze

Frieze moulding

Carcass top

Arrows indicate grain direction.

Illus. 147. This type of cornice construction allows for dimensional change when you use a solid wood case type of construction for the carcass.

nice directly to the top rail. This method will also usually work with solid lumber if the sides aren't wider than about 8 inches. Since the grain direction of the moulding is 90° to the grain direction of the side, differences in expansion will create problems when the sides are wider than 8″.

To solve this problem, attach the cornice to a separate part, called a frieze. The frieze is a box-shaped unit, shown in Illus. 147. The grain direction is indicated by arrows. Apply the cornice moulding to the frieze. Since the grain of the frieze runs in the same direction as the cornice moulding, no problems will result from dimensional change. Apply a thin strip with a rounded edge to the bottom of the frieze assembly so that the rounded edge projects slightly past the rest of the carcass. This strip is called a frieze moulding, and it hides the joint between the carcass and the frieze. Attach the frieze as-.sembly to the carcass with screws, but do not use glue. The screw holes should be slotted, or wood brackets similar to the ones described for attaching tops should be used to allow for shrinkage and swelling.

Bases and Legs

A cabinet that rests on the floor needs some type of base or legs. Bases, also called plinths, can be an integral part of the carcass or a separate part. You can create a simple base by installing the bottom of the cabinet in a dado that is spaced about 3 to 4 inches above the bottom of the side; by using a filler board (also called a toe kick) across the front, you can complete the base.

In some designs, the toe kick may have a decorative shape along its bottom edge (Illus. 148). Frequently, the toe kick is recessed into the cabinet about 2 to 3 inches. This creates a toe space that allows people to stand closer to the cabinet without bumping their toes against the toe kick (Illus. 149). You can notch back the sides to meet the toe kick or you can leave them full-width. To attach the toe kick, you can use butt joints, rabbets, or mitres (Illus. 150). In some designs, the toe space extends around the sides as well. This gives the impression that the cabinet is floating above the floor. The effect is heightened if you paint the toe kick black. To achieve this effect, you must use a separate assembly for the base (Illus. 151).

A separate base also makes it easier to add additional bracing in the middle and at the back of the base. Bases for large cabinets, especially built-ins, can be made from 2 × 4 lumber; smaller cabinets use 1 × 4 lumber. Some traditional designs employ a separate base that extends past the carcass, instead of being recessed. If it is not visually objectionable, you can attach the base with nails or screws driven down through the bottom of the cabinet. Otherwise, add screw blocks to the base and attach it from underneath.

A base with a flat bottom will tend to rock if the floor has any minor irregularities. The base should only contact the floor at the corners. To achieve this, you can attach small feet called floor glides.

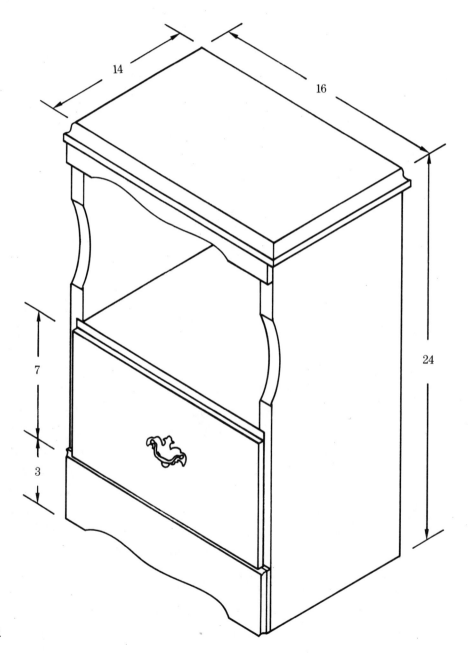

Illus. 148. This nightstand uses the simplest type of base. The bottom is dadoed into the sides and the toe kick is attached to the front.

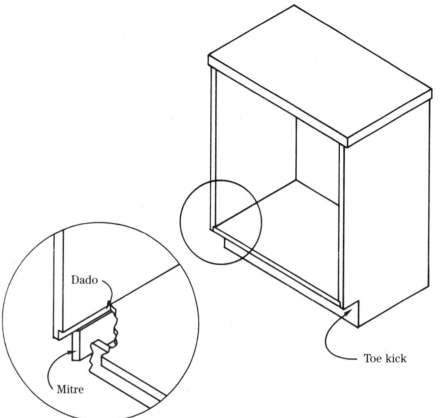

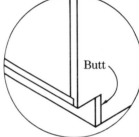

Illus. 149. To provide a toe space, you need to set the toe kick back from the front of the cabinet. In this instance, the sides are notched back and a mitre joint joins the toe kick to the side.

If you don't use floor glides, remove a small amount of wood from the middle of the bottom of each part of the base. An easy way to do this is by using a jointer. If the jointer has an adjustable outfeed table, set the infeed table for about a ⅛ of an inch cut and adjust the outfeed table so that it is level with the infeed table. Hold the board slightly off the table for the first 4″ so that no cut is made, and then lower the board to the table and push it through until the cut is 4″ from the other end. Lift the board from the jointer. If you can't adjust the outfeed table, then two passes over the jointer will be necessary. Follow the procedure just described for the first cut. This will produce a tapered cut because you haven't lowered the outfeed table. Next, turn the board end for end and follow the same procedure again. This may still leave a high spot in the middle of the board; if this is objectionable, you can remove it with a hand plane.

Bases for built-in cabinets are usually left flat on the bottom, and shims are used to compensate for irregularities in the floor.

Illus. 150. Alternate joints used to attach the toe kick to the side.

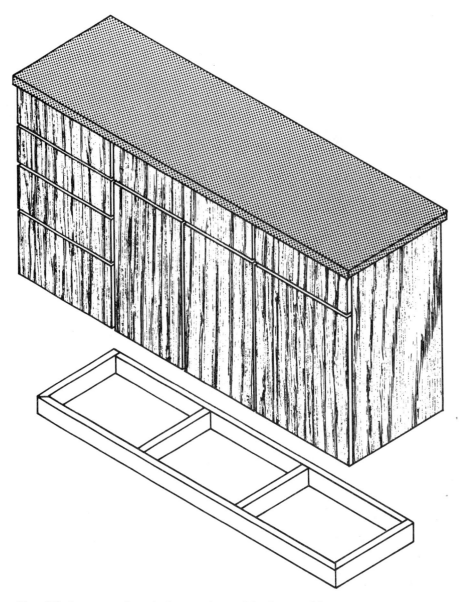

Illus. 151. A separate base is frequently used for large cabinets.

Bracket feet are sometimes used in place of a base (Illus. 152). They resemble the corners of a base with the middle part cut away, and are usually cut in a decorative pattern.

A glue block inside the corner of the bracket foot actually carries the weight of the cabinet. The glue block should extend slightly past the bottom of the foot; if you use a floor glide, it should be attached to the glue block. This block must be constructed in a special way to prevent cross-grain shrinkage and swelling from splitting the foot. The block is glued up in segments. The first segment is positioned with its grain running in the same direction as the grain in one side of the foot, and every other segment is turned 90° to the grain of the last segment. The resulting block is similar to plywood with very thick plies. This procedure provides long-grain gluing surfaces for both sides of the foot, while keeping the grain in the block running in the same direction as that in the foot.

When a cabinet is designed to sit more than a few inches above the floor, legs are usually used. Simple, tapered, lathe-turned legs are frequently used in modern designs, whereas ornamentally turned legs are often used with period cabinets. Many modern designs use a square leg or a square, tapered leg. The square leg is simple enough to make; the square, tapered leg is more difficult.

One method for tapering the legs involves using a jointer. Determine the amount of taper per foot required and set the jointer depth of cut to that figure. Make a mark on the leg that is 1′ from the end. With the jointer turned off, move the guard back and place the leg over the cutters so that the mark is in the middle of the cutter head. The part of the leg to be tapered should be on the infeed table. Lift the end of the leg on the outfeed table so that the leg is not touching the knives, but it is still holding the guard open. Use a push block on the infeed side. Turn on the jointer and lower the leg until it touches the knives and then push the leg through. Repeat this process on all sides of all of the legs, and then change the depth of

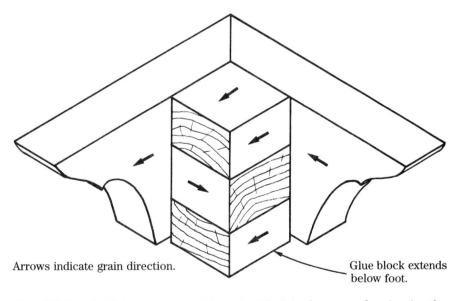

Arrows indicate grain direction.   Glue block extends
                                                    below foot.

Illus. 152. Bracket feet are supported by a glue block in the corner. Laminating the block, as shown here, prevents problems caused by cross-grain expansion and provides long-grain gluing surfaces on both parts.

cut to about ⅟₁₆ of an inch. Place the leg with the small end facing the cutter and the tapered section flat on the infeed table. Push the leg through the jointer, keeping the taper flat against the table. Continue taking cuts in this manner on all sides of the leg until the entire leg is tapered.

Factory-made legs are available in many sizes and styles—from simple, tapered legs to cabriole legs. Commercial legs can be very useful for the beginning cabinetmaker. They are usually attached with a metal plate that is threaded to accept a threaded bolt in the leg. The plate attaches to the bottom of the cabinet with screws (Illus. 153).

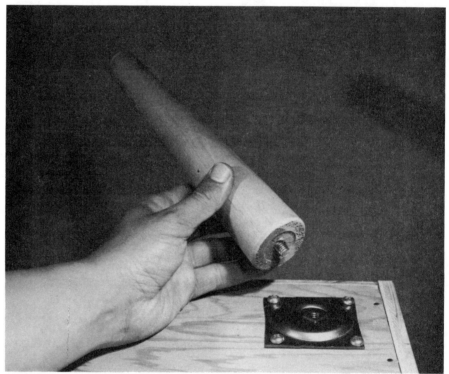

Illus. 153. Commercial legs are usually attached with a threaded plate screwed to the bottom of the cabinet.

ATTACHING LEGS

You can purchase mounting plates similar to the type used on commercial legs for attaching shop-built legs to a cabinet. If the load the legs must carry won't be too great and if the bottom of the cabinet lends itself to this type of attachment, the use of mounting plates can be an effective method.

You can also attach turned legs by turning a round tenon at the top of the leg. The tenon fits into a corresponding hole bored into the base. You can bore the hole at an angle if you plan on angling the legs. You can simply glue the tenons into the hole; but for a stronger joint, cut a slot in the tenon and drive a wooden wedge into the slot from above when the leg is in place. If you don't want the top of the tenon to show through the bottom of the cabinet, you can make a blind hole if you stop boring before the bit emerges from the base. A Forestner bit is best for this operation because it doesn't have a long middle spur that will break through the wood before the hole is at an adequate depth. You can wedge this blind joint with a foxed wedge. You need to place the point of the wedge into the slot before inserting the leg in the hole. As you insert the leg, the end of the wedge will hit the top of the hole, and it will be forced into the slot as you drive the leg home. You may need to experiment with scrap to get the proper size for the wedge. If it is too long, you won't be able to drive the leg all the way in; if it is too short, the wedging won't be effective.

If you use a skeleton frame, you can incorporate the legs into the frame. For square legs, simply extend the corner frame members past the bottom of the cabinet. When turning round legs, leave a square section at the top that can be attached to the frame before you apply the skin.

You can also make a separate base where you can attach the legs. The legs can be attached to the rails with dowels or mortise-and-tenon joints.

7
SHELVES

Shelves are an important part of most cabinets. Shelves may be permanently attached to a cabinet or they may be adjustable. Fixed shelves form a part of a cabinet's structure and add more strength to the cabinet. Adjustable shelves, on the other hand, add little strength to a cabinet, but you can move them to accommodate different-sized objects.

Design Considerations

Shelf size should be determined by the type of objects that will be stored on the shelf. You can place small paperback books on 6″-wide shelves with 8″ spacing between the shelves. A common size for a bookshelf that will accommodate a variety of books is 8″ wide with a 10″ spacing. Very large books and loose-leaf binders require shelves that are 12″ wide and 14″ apart. Record albums will fit comfortably on 14″-wide shelves spaced 14″ apart. Overhead food-storage shelves are usually 12″ to 14″ wide, whereas below-counter shelves are about 24 inches wide. When you use fixed shelves, be sure to measure the things you intend to store on the shelves before you lay out the shelf spacing. It's frustrating to find that the item you had intended to place on a shelf is ¼″ too tall to fit between the shelves. That's why adjustable shelves are so popular; you can adapt the shelves to fit new items at any time.

Materials differ in terms of their stiffness and load-carrying capacity, so the material you use will affect the way you design the shelves. In cabinetmaking, most shelves are made of ¾"-thick material. The thicker the material, the greater the load-carrying capacity.

The distance between supports is a critical factor in shelf design. When a middle support is not desirable, the length of the shelf is limited by the maximum distance the material you are using can span without support. Solid lumber is the stiffest material that is used for building shelves. The actual load-carrying capacity varies among wood species. For light loads, ¾" solid wood shelves can be up to 48" between supports. Generally, 36" between supports is best. Plywood is not as stiff as solid wood. Although ¾" plywood can span 48" if the load is very light, 36" is usually considered maximum. For a heavy load, 30" between supports is best. Particle board is the least stiff of the products that are used for making shelves. The maximum distance particle board can span without deflecting under load is about 30 inches. In most cases, supports should be spaced 24" apart. Illus. 154 shows the results of a test using 12"-wide shelving. A load was placed on each shelf and the deflection was measured. The actual measurements will vary depending on wood species and other factors, but this chart will give you an idea of the amount of sag to expect.

You can increase the load-carrying capacity of a ¾"-thick shelf by applying a 1½"-wide facing strip to the front edge of the shelf, as shown in Illus. 155. You can achieve even greater strength by applying a similar strip to the rear of the shelf. You can increase the load-carrying capacity of fixed shelves if you attach the shelf to the back of the cabinet. Nail through the back into the shelf, spacing the nails about 4 inches apart.

Fixed Shelves

Fixed shelves are usually attached with dado joints. The dado provides a lip to support the shelf and plenty of glue-surface area. When you use plywood or particle board, you should usually conceal the joints with edging strips (for more details, refer back to the section on edge treatments in Chapter 1). The end of a dado joint in solid lumber can be quite attractive and, in most cases, there is no need to conceal it; but if you prefer having the joint not show on the front of the cabinet, then you can use a stopped dado instead (Illus. 156).

The easiest way to cut a stopped dado is with a router or a radial-arm saw because you have greater control. You can also cut a

Recommended Maximum Shelf Length
(Without Middle Support)

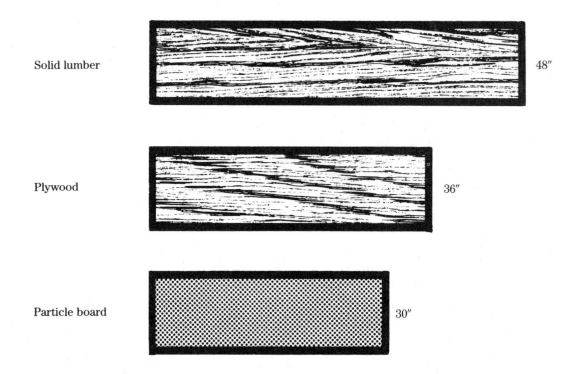

Solid lumber   48"

Plywood   36"

Particle board   30"

Load	25 lbs.				50 lbs.			
Shelf length (inches)	24	30	36	48	24	30	36	48
Solid lumber	*	*	*	*	*	*	$\frac{1}{16}$	$\frac{1}{8}$
Plywood	*	*	$\frac{1}{16}$	$\frac{1}{8}$	*	$\frac{1}{16}$	$\frac{1}{8}$	$\frac{1}{2}$
Particle board	*	$\frac{1}{16}$	$\frac{1}{4}$	$\frac{3}{8}$	*	$\frac{1}{8}$	$\frac{1}{4}$	$\frac{5}{8}$

Shelf Sag (Deflection in Inches)

*No significant sag.

Illus. 154. Recommended maximum length for ¾"-thick shelves with no middle support. The table gives the deflection obtained when sample shelves were loaded with 25-pound and 50-pound weights.

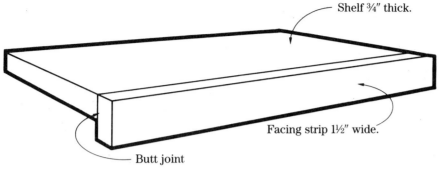

Shelf ¾″ thick.

Facing strip 1½″ wide.

Butt joint

Reinforce with glue and nails, dowels, or splines.

Alternate rabbet joint

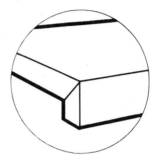

Alternate mitre joint

Illus. 155. A 1½″-wide facing strip applied to the front of a shelf increases the shelf's load-carrying capacity and also hides plywood or particle board edges.

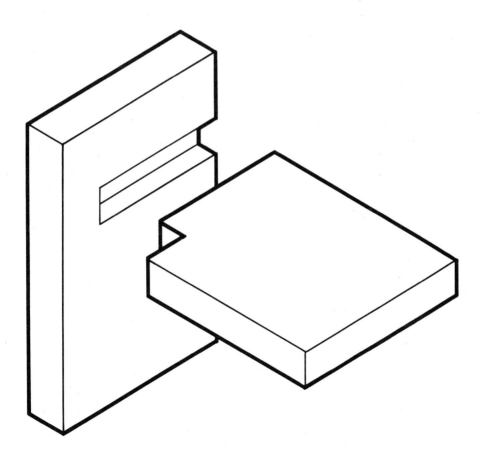

Illus. 156. A stopped-dado joint can be used to conceal the shelf-to-side joint in solid lumber construction.

stopped dado with a table saw, but you have to make a mark on the fence that indicates the front of the blade and a mark on the side of the board opposite the dado that indicates where to stop the dado. Stopping before the end of the cut can be difficult when the parts are large. Turn off the saw and wait for the blade to stop before you remove the board from the saw. If you remove the board with the saw running, there is a chance that the board will move out of line with the saw and, at the least, the dado will be enlarged and an unsightly gap will result. In extreme cases, the blade may bind and kick back the board.

The end of the dado is rounded at this point. You can use a chisel to square up the end, or you can simply make the cutout in the shelf large enough to miss the rounded section. However, if this will result in a large cutout, it's better to square up the dado because the cutout section only has the strength of a butt joint.

You can use butt joints for shelves, but they must be heavily reinforced. To reinforce a butt joint, you can use screws driven through the side into the end of the shelf. The screws should be at least 2″ long and spaced about 3 inches apart. You can also use nails, but they won't be as strong. You need to use 10d nails, spaced 3″ apart. Dowels or splines can also be used for reinforcing butt joints. Regardless of how you reinforce a butt joint, remember that the weight is being carried mostly by the reinforcement because the force on the joint is almost entirely a shear force.

Adjustable Shelves

Adjustable shelves are attached to the side of the cabinet with some type of bracket. One of the most common types has a metal standard with a series of rectangular slots spaced about ½ inch apart. A small metal clip fits into the slots and supports the shelf (Illus. 157). One of the most important things to remember when installing this type of shelf standard is that the standard should extend down to a solid support, such as a fixed shelf or the bottom of the cabinet. In an attempt to save money, some people don't start the standard at the bottom because they think that there is no need for a shelf that low; but if the standard doesn't extend to a solid support, all the weight must be carried by the fasteners that are used to attach the standard.

The fasteners are actually designed to only keep the standard in place, not to support the weight of everything placed on the shelves.

Illus. 157. Metal standards and brackets offer a wide range of shelf positions.

Three types of fasteners are usually used, and two types of fastener holes are found in the standard. One type of fastener hole is a countersunk hole that will accept a flathead screw or a special nail. You must use very short screws in order to avoid going through the other side of the board. Instead of screws, you can use special nails, which have heads that resemble the heads on flathead screws. Another type of fastener is a special type of staple, which is usually only used in production shops. A second set of holes in the standards accommodates the staples; the standards have two small holes side by side with a recessed area between them for the bridge of the staple. You need to use a special type of staple gun, which has a positioning finger that fits into one of the notches in the standard, to ensure that the staple will line up with the holes.

You can cut the standards to length with a hacksaw. Production shops use a special nipper to cut the standards. It produces a very clean square end that is similar to the factory cut. Whenever possible, leave a factory end at the bottom of the standard and cut it to length at the top. This will ensure that all of the slots will line up. If the slots are out of alignment, then the shelf will slant or rock. If you have to cut the bottom end of a standard, make sure that you keep the same distance from the first slot to the end on all of the standards. The slots are marked with a small embossed number. This helps to line up the clips when you are installing the shelves. As long as you keep a factory end at the bottom, the numbers will always line up. If you cut a long standard into smaller ones, the numbers won't always line up. It's a good practice to try to line up the numbers even if it involves some waste.

These types of standards are available for surface or recessed mounting. Most cabinetmakers prefer the recessed mount. If you use the surface mount, there will be a small gap between the end of the shelf and the side of the cabinet unless you cut a notch in the end of the shelf to fit around the standard. The recessed type fits into a groove cut in the side of the cabinet. Using a dado blade on a table saw is the easiest way to make the groove, but you can also use a router. The standards are usually placed about 1½ to 2 inches away from the front and back of the sides. Since the shelf is free to slide from front to back with this type of bracket, you shouldn't place the standard too near the back. If it is too near the back, a slight forward movement of the shelf will cause it to fall off the clips. On very narrow shelves, the spacing is decreased to about 1 inch. A decorative stile that is wider than the side can help keep the shelf in position. Usually a 1½" stile is placed on a ¾"-thick side so that the extra width extends into the area for shelves. The shelves are made to fit behind the stile. This eliminates any front-to-back movement.

Another popular type of adjustable shelf bracket consists of a small, L-shaped metal bracket that has a short metal dowel attached to it. This type of bracket doesn't need a standard. The dowel fits into a hole drilled into the side of the cabinet. You must cut the shelf slightly smaller than the distance between the sides to accommodate the thickness of the metal bracket. The bracket hangs with the lower part of the "L" facing down so that it supports the shelf, while the shelf presses against the side of the "L," holding the dowel firmly in its hole. This type of bracket is almost completely concealed when installed; only the bottom of the "L" is visible from the bottom of the shelf. There is also a plastic version of this type of shelf bracket. It will fit in the same-size holes as the metal bracket. The plastic version has a larger exposed area under the shelf, so it is more visible (Illus. 158).

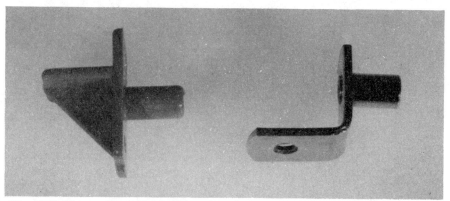

Illus. 158. These adjustable shelf brackets fit into holes drilled into the side of the cabinet. The metal one, on the right, is almost concealed with the shelf in place, whereas the plastic one, on the left, is more visible.

Since you drill the holes for the brackets in the sides, you can determine how much adjustability you want. You may decide to make a continuous row of holes spaced 1″ apart, or you could drill three or four holes on either side of a shelf position to allow for some adjustment. You could simply drill holes in one position for each shelf, and then drill more holes later if you need to move a shelf. Regardless of the way you choose to drill the holes, it is important for the holes to line up or the shelves will rock or slant. Use a story stick to lay out the holes, or make a template from a strip of hardboard and drill holes in it to act as a drilling guide. A piece of pegboard makes an excellent drill guide (Illus. 159). Cut a piece that is the same size as the side of the cabinet, and draw lines that indicate which row of holes to use. Keep front-and-back spacing the same so that the template can be reversed for use on both sides. Always position the template with the same end at the bottom.

Another variation on this type of shelf bracket uses holes drilled in the side; but instead of the usual bracket, a piece of ⅛″ welding

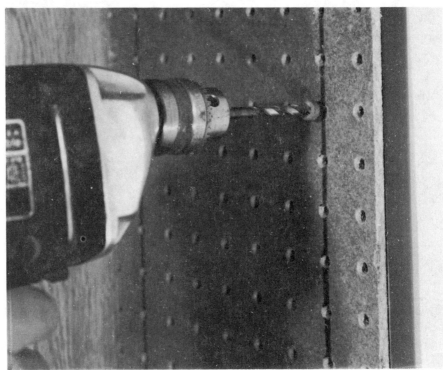

Illus. 159. Pegboard makes a good drill guide when you are making multiple holes in the cabinet side for adjustable shelf brackets. A drill stop on the drill keeps the holes a uniform depth.

rod is bent so that its ends fit into the holes and the rest of the rod extends about ⅜ of an inch past the side. A saw kerf cut into the end of the shelf slides over the rod (Illus. 160). For a totally concealed installation, stop the saw kerf about ¼ of an inch from the front of the shelf. Drill ⁵⁄₃₂″ holes at the desired locations on the side of the cabinet.

Adjustable shelves may seem to be a fairly modern development, but actually they have been used for a long time. If you are building an antique reproduction and you want to use adjustable shelves, you can make wooden brackets that will be appropriate for the time period. One of the simplest types of wooden brackets is very similar to the metal L-bracket just described. It uses a series of holes drilled into the sides, but the shelves rest on wooden pegs instead of metal brackets. You can use a short length of dowel to support the shelf. The dowel can be exposed on the underside of the shelf, or you can conceal it by cutting a stopped groove where it can fit on the underside of the shelf (Illus. 161). Following the same concept, you can whittle brackets from wood that will fit into the holes. The design of these brackets is similar to the design of the plastic

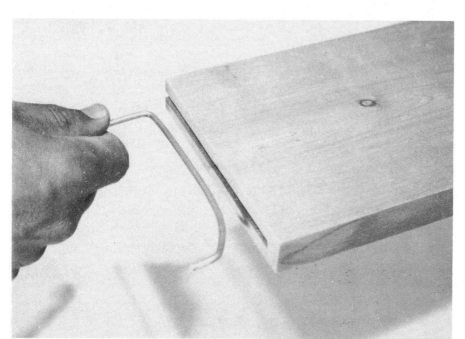

Illus. 160. You can bend a piece of welding rod into completely concealed shelf bracket. The ends fit into holes drilled into the side of the cabinet. The rest of the bracket fits into a slot cut in the end of the shelf. If you use a table saw to cut the slot, bend the rod as shown to conform to the curved end of the slot. When you use a router to make the slot, you can make 90° bends at both ends of the bracket. To install the shelf, insert the brackets in both sides of the cabinet and slide the shelf in from the front.

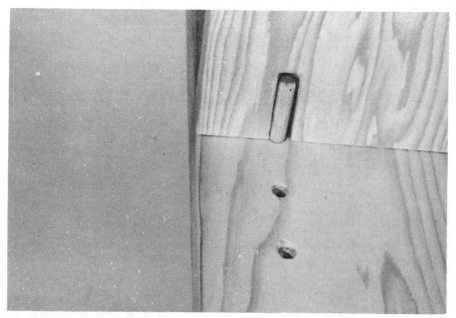

Illus. 161. A length of dowel inserted in a hole drilled in the side of the cabinet can serve as an adjustable shelf bracket for antique-reproduction cabinetry. Cutting a small pocket in the bottom of the shelf, as shown here, conceals the dowel and prevents front-to-back shelf movement.

bracket shown in Illus. 158, but the upper projection is omitted and the shape is more graceful.

Another form of wooden bracket uses strips applied to the front and back of the sides, which have notches cut into them. A wooden cleat fits into the notches, and the shelf rests on the cleat. You need to cut the ends of the shelves to fit around the strips. You can cut the notches in several ways. Square notches are easy to cut with a dado blade. You can make rounded notches by drilling a set of holes in the middle of a board and then ripping the board down the middle. The V-notched strip (Illus. 162) is the type preferred by old-time cabinetmakers because each notch can be made with only two cuts of a handsaw. For perfect alignment of the notches, clamp both strips together back to back while making the cuts.

Illus. 162. Using notched, wooden standards is an authentic way of providing adjustable shelves for antique reproductions.

8
DOORS

When you apply doors to a cabinet, the doors often become the dominant visual feature. For this reason, the type of door you use is very important to the overall look of a cabinet.

Slab Doors

The simplest type of cabinet door you can make is the slab door. It is merely a single piece of wood cut to the correct size for the door (Illus. 163). Plywood and particle board are usually used for slab doors because of their dimensional stability, but you can glue solid lumber into slabs that are large enough for doors also. Since a slab door has no decoration other than the grain of the wood itself, the grain becomes a dominant feature. Frequently wood with a prominent grain is used for slab doors and, when more than one door is involved, the doors are usually grain-matched. A simple way to grain-match plywood doors is to lay them out on the sheet the same way they will appear on the cabinet (Illus. 164). Number the doors with an inconspicuous pencil mark so that you can install them in the correct order.

The slab door is usually used with modern-styled cabinets; to adapt the slab door to other styles, some type of decoration is usually applied to it. A type of decoration that is frequently used simulates a panel door. You can make a simulated panel door by applying mouldings to the door or by cutting a bevelled edge on the door, as shown in Illus. 165. Another method involves cutting a decorative groove in the face of the door with a router. Special bits are available for this purpose. An adjustable metal guide is available that guides the router around the door. It has several attachments that will make an arched top cut or various corner designs.

You can make your own template that does the same thing, but it won't be quite as versatile. Cut a piece of ¼″ hardboard the same size as the door, and then cut the desired shape out of the middle. Use a template-following collar on the router. Clamp the template to the door at the top and one side. Make the cuts across the bottom and the other side; then reposition the clamps to the areas that you have already cut and make the remaining cuts. With this type of template, you need a different one for each size door.

Illus. 163. The slab door is easy to make and install.

Illus. 164. Woods with bold grain patterns, such as oak, are frequently used for slab doors. Cutting the adjacent doors from a single piece of wood assures grain matching. Part of the grain is lost in the saw kerf, so use the thinnest blade possible when you want very accurate grain matching.

Illus. 165. A bevelled edge on this glued up solid wood slab door gives it more of an antique look.

Panel Doors

The panel door is frequently used for traditional-style cabinets (Illus. 166 and 167). It is constructed in the manner described in

Illus. 166. The flat panel doors of this antique washstand are the major visual focus.

Chapter 6. Since the construction details of the door are the main visual focus, wood with a more subdued grain is usually best for this type of door.

Since doors receive a lot of stress, you should join the stiles and rails with strong joints. Mortise-and-tenon joints are recommended, but you can also use dowel joints.

Glazed Doors

A glazed door is very similar to a panel door, except you use a piece of glass or plastic instead of a panel (Illus. 168). From a safety standpoint, acrylic plastic is better than glass because it won't shatter into sharp pieces. The only problem with acrylic plastic is that it isn't as hard as glass, so it tends to get scratched easier. Tempered glass combines the safety of plastic with the hardness of glass, but it must be special-ordered to size and it can't be cut into smaller pieces once it is tempered.

A glazed door can have a single pane or several small panes. When you use the smaller panes, you can assemble them with lead chan-

nels—in which case, the wood frame is the same as a single pane—
or you can place the panes in a wood frame consisting of small
muntins.

Constructing the frame is similar to constructing a frame for a
panel door, but rather than using a groove for the panel, you need to
make a rabbet for the glass. The rabbet is open to the back of the
door and, once the door is assembled, the glass is held in place by a
small strip of wood, called a stop. You need to attach the stop with

*Illus. 167 (left). These raised panel doors give a traditional look to built-in cabinets. Illus. 168 (right). The glazed
doors on this bookcase protect the contents while also allowing them to be seen.*

very small brads driven parallel with the glass. Use a small tack hammer or a special brad driver, and drill pilot holes to avoid breaking the glass as you drive the brads (Illus. 169). A type of plastic stop is available that makes glass installation easier. It is a barbed spline that fits into a kerf cut around the edge of the rabbet. You don't need any nails; the stop simply snaps into the kerf.

Illus. 169. The glass fits into a rabbet cut in the door. Using small brads, nail a small strip of wood, called a stop, in place to hold the glass in the rabbet. Don't glue the stop in place so that you will be able to replace the glass in case of breakage. Normally, the stop is stained before installation; it is left unfinished in this photo for contrast.

Cleated Doors

For a rustic look, a cleated door is frequently used. This type of door is made of several pieces of solid lumber held together with cleats. You can place the cleat on the back of the door, or you can use it as a decorative detail on the front.

Tongue-and-groove lumber is often used in this application. The edges of the boards may be bevelled to form a V-groove along the joint (Illus. 170). Sometimes this effect is simulated on a plywood slab door by making a series of straight cuts across the door with a router.

Door Applications

In addition to the way it is constructed, a door is also classified by the way it is applied to the cabinet. There are three ways cabinet

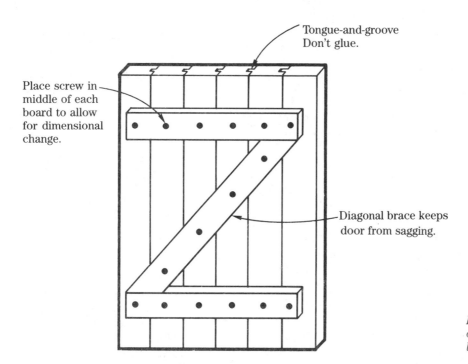

Tongue-and-groove
Don't glue.

Place screw in
middle of each
board to allow
for dimensional
change.

Diagonal brace keeps
door from sagging.

Illus. 170. Cleated doors are often used when a rustic look is desired.

doors are usually applied: flush, overlap, and lipped. You can use all of these methods with any of the types of doors previously described.

FLUSH

When you attach a flush door to a cabinet, the door front should be flush with the stiles and rails that surround the door (Illus. 171). The

Illus. 171. You need to attach flush doors with butt hinges. Careful fitting is required.

flush door is the most difficult type to fit because a gap shows all around the door. To look good, the gap must be even. To keep the gap as small as possible, you should bevel the edges of the door about 2° to the inside. This allows the door to fit tightly and still open. If the edges are square, you will need a larger gap for the rear corner to clear as the door opens.

A flush door is usually attached with butt hinges. You need to set the hinges into cutouts, called gains. Cut the gains with a chisel or a router. In some cases, a decorative type of hinge, such as a butterfly hinge, is face mounted. Hinge placement is not too critical; the hinges should be a short distance away from the top and bottom. For a shortcut, some professionals use the hinge itself as the measuring tool. Place the hinge so that it is touching the top or bottom edge, and make a mark at the other end of the hinge. Now position the hinge so that its top is on the mark. This method seems to provide a visually pleasing amount of space for a hinge of any size, and it assures that all of the hinges will be equally spaced.

A flush door requires some type of stop to prevent it from being pushed too far into the cabinet. On small doors, it may be sufficient to simply allow the door to hit the inside shelves, or a door catch may be all that is necessary. However, larger doors need a stop applied to the inside of the stile to keep the door in position.

OVERLAY

The overlay door is one of the easiest to make and fit. It fits over the front of the cabinet and, since it is larger than the opening, there is no problem in fitting it to the opening (Illus. 172). Because all of the edges of an overlay door show, you will need to use some form of edge treatment for plywood or particle board (see Chapter 1).

You need to use a special type of hinge on an overlay door. You can apply this kind of door to a stile, or you can eliminate the stile and attach the door directly to the side of the cabinet. Different types of hinges are required for each application. Overlay doors without stiles but with concealed hinges are frequently used in built-in cabinets to give a sleek, modern look (Illus. 163).

LIPPED

The lipped door has a rabbet cut around the edge so that half of the edge is inside the opening and half overlaps the outside. This type of door offers the same ease of fitting as the overlay door, but it doesn't project as far from the front. You can leave the edge square or you

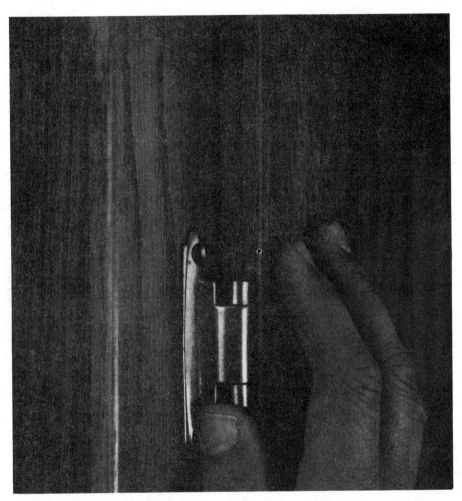

Illus. 172. Overlay doors are easy to align. Attach the hinges to the door first; then holding the door in the proper position, attach the hinges to the stile.

can round it. You can do the rounding with a shaper or router, but many cabinetmakers simply bevel the edge with a jointer or hand plane, round it with coarse sandpaper, and then smooth it with finer grades of sandpaper. Since the entire edge doesn't show, as it does with the overlay door, it isn't always necessary to cover the edge of plywood.

When two lipped doors meet without a stile between them, they are usually given a 2° bevel, as with the flush door. Another method involves making a rabbet on one door and cutting a tongue on the other door to project into the rabbet. If you use this method, the doors won't work independently; you must always open the door with the tongue last and close it first.

The hinges used with lipped doors are made to fit into the rabbet (Illus. 173). Buy the hinges before you cut the rabbet so that you can cut the rabbet to fit the hinge.

Illus. 173. Lipped doors require special hinges that are bent to fit the rabbet cut around the door.

Door Hardware

Cabinet doors need some type of hardware to enable them to function. Pulls, hinges, catches, and locks are all types of door hardware (Illus. 174).

Door pulls are available in a wide range of styles, but they can be divided into three general categories: knobs, surface-screw pulls, and rear-screw pulls. Knobs used for cabinets are usually small and attach with a machine screw through a hole in the door from the rear, or the knob has a threaded shaft that screws directly into the face of the door.

Surface-screw pulls use wood screws to attach the pull from the face side. They are often used for rustic or period cabinets. Probably the most widely used type is the rear-screw pull; it mounts with two machine screws that come from the rear of the door through holes drilled in the door. The screws are concealed with the doors closed. Carved, wooden pulls are popular for both modern and traditional cabinets. They usually are attached with screws from the rear. Many styles of carved pulls are available commercially, or you can make custom pulls of your own design. A router is very useful when you are making your own pulls.

Sliding doors require recessed pulls. The simplest type is shown in Illus. 174. Simply drill a hole in the door and press the pull into place.

There is no standard for the placement of door pulls; a lot depends on the size and style of the pull. It is common practice to place pulls near the top on low doors and near the bottom on high doors; but in some instances, the pulls are placed in the middle in both cases. A common placement would be 1½" in from the edge and 2" from the top or bottom.

The type of hinge you use largely determines the function of the cabinet doors, so carefully choosing the correct hinge is an important part of applying cabinet doors.

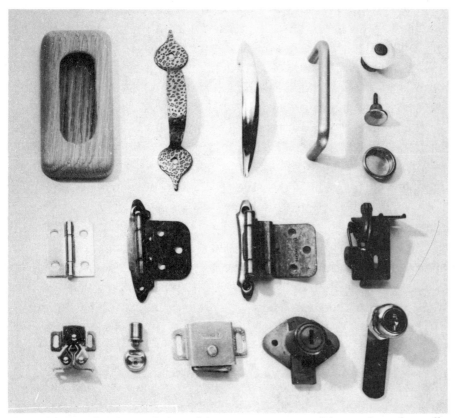

Illus. 174. Door hardware. Left to right, top row: commercial carved wooden pull; surface mount pull; two styles of rear-mount pulls; two small knobs, (top) a rear mount and (middle) one with a built-in screw for front attachment; on the bottom is a recessed sliding-door pull. Second row: butt hinge; overlay hinge; lipped-door hinge; and self-closing, fully concealed overlay hinge. Bottom row: roller catch, bullet latch, magnetic catch, door lock with screw flanges, and cam lock.

The butt hinge is the most versatile type of hinge. You can mount it on the face of flush doors or cut it into gains on the edge of the door. You can use butts to apply overlay doors by attaching the hinge to the rear of the door and the front of the stile. As versatile as it is, the butt hinge still has some limitations. It can't be used for lipped doors and, for a finished look, it should always be applied in gains. In many modern cabinets, specialized hinges are used instead of butts.

A special type of hinge designed for overlay doors has the screws that mount to the stile exposed. This make door alignment much easier since you can hold the doors in place in the closed position as you install the screws. Lipped-door hinges have a bent leaf that fits into the rabbet around the door. Some types of overlay door hinges are fully concealed. Self-closing hinges have made door catches unnecessary in many cases; they have a built-in spring mechanism that holds the door closed. When installing self-closing hinges, it is usually necessary to allow more clearance on the opposite side of the door than usual; as you tighten the screws, the spring action of the hinge forces the door slightly away from the hinge side. If you don't allow for this, the doors will bind.

You must use catches if you don't use self-closing hinges. One type is the roller catch, which is referred to as a friction catch because it holds the door shut with the friction between a spring steel clip and the plastic rollers. The bullet latch is another type of friction catch. You install the bullet latch in a hole drilled in the side of a flush door. The small spring-loaded latch fits into a strike plate mounted on the side of the stile. The magnetic catch uses magnetism instead of friction to hold the door closed. A small, powerful magnet mounts on the cabinet, and a steel plate mounts on the door.

To position a catch, mount the magnet or roller on the stile or a shelf. Attach the other part of the catch to the magnet or roller in its proper position; then shut the door. Small points on the catch will make dents in the door where you should mount the catch.

There are several types of locks that you can apply to cabinet doors. One type requires a single hole through the door, and it's attached with two wood screws. This type of lock is designed to be used with flush doors. The bolt extends from the lock flush with the back of the door, and it will lock against a stile of the same thickness as the door. You can also use this type of lock on lipped doors or flush doors with a thicker stile if you cut a mortise into the stile for the bolt to enter. Whenever two doors meet without a stile between them, this is the type of lock to use. You mount the lock on one door and you secure the other door with a barrel bolt inside. You can't use this type of lock with overlay doors unless the two doors meet and one is secured with a barrel bolt.

Another type of lock that you can use on doors is the cam lock. This type of lock requires a single hole through the door, and it is secured with a nut that threads onto the body of the lock. A washer with spurs that bite into the wood keeps the lock from rotating in the hole. This type works better on overlay and lipped doors because it is available in several lengths, so you can get one that is long enough to reach behind the stile. When traditional styling is more important than security, small mortise locks are used. The lock fits into a mortise cut in the back of the door. You cut a keyhole through the door and then place a small metal plate over the hole.

Sliding Doors

Sliding doors are also called bypass doors. You can open them without having the door project out from the cabinet, which can be an advantage when you want to leave the door open for some time; but only one side can be open at a time, which can be a disadvantage. Sliding cabinet doors are usually made from ¼" plywood or hardboard, but ½" doors are also used. The doors should be slightly wider than one half of the opening so that there will still be about a 1 inch overlap when the doors are closed.

There are several types of commercial tracks available to accommodate different-sized doors and different degrees of usage. For light usage, a plastic track works well. Heavy use requires a metal track with ball-bearing rollers. Metal ball-bearing tracks can also be used with sliding glass doors in display cabinets.

You can easily make your own wooden tracks for sliding doors that will receive moderate use. One way involves cutting two parallel grooves with a router or dado blade. The grooves should be slightly wider than the doors so that they won't bind. Make the top grooves deeper than the bottom grooves so that you can install and remove the doors after assembling the cabinet. Cut the doors so that, when the top of the door is pushed all the way into the top groove, the bottom of the door will just clear the top of the bottom track. When the door is in place, it will come part way out of the top track; but since the bottom track isn't as deep, it won't come all the way out. The grooves can't be much closer together than ¼"; otherwise, the strip of wood separating them will be too weak. This results in a gap between the two doors. You can eliminate the gap by using ½" doors and cutting a ¼" rabbet along the top and bottom of the back. The lip that is formed will fit in the ¼" groove, and the rabbeted out section will straddle the strip of wood between the two doors (Illus. 175).

Illus. 175. Two types of sliding doors using shop-made wooden tracks. The front set is made from ¼" plywood; the rear set is made from ½" solid lumber that has been rabbeted to fit the ¼" groove in the track.

Tambour Doors

The type of door used in a roll-top desk is called a tambour door (Illus. 176). It can be used vertically or horizontally. A tambour door is composed of many small strips that are hinged together with a canvas or plastic backing. The tambour door rides in a track as does a bypass door, but the track curves so that the door opens all the way and is stored inside the cabinet (Illus. 177).

Although some tambour doors are made from strips that have overlapping rabbets and tongues, most are simply made from flat strips with slightly rounded edges. If the strips have overlapping joints, the tongue must be very short and the rabbet must have plenty of clearance for the door to bend correctly. Factory-made tambours may have a plastic backing, but most shop-made tambours still use canvas for the backing.

The strips are generally ¾″ wide and ¼″ thick. This size enables

Illus. 176. Tambour doors are well suited to built-in applications as well as free-standing cabinets. Here a tambour door is being used on an appliance garage. It hides small kitchen appliances when you aren't using them, or it opens up to expose a fully usable work area. Notice how finger pulls are routed into the pull strip.

you to rip them from a ¾″-thick board. Set the rip fence to make a ¼″ cut. If you have a jointer, joint the edge of the board after each cut so that you have a good face for the strip. It is also easier to round the edges before cutting off the strip. Keep ripping strips from the edge of the board until you have enough to make the tambour. If you number the strips consecutively as they come off the saw, you can assemble the tambour so that the grain matches closely.

Illus. 177. A tambour door offers the same advantages as sliding doors, but it has an additional advantage in that the door is completely out of the way when open.

You make the pull strip from a thicker piece of wood. Cut rabbets on the ends to fit into the track. You can use a router to cut finger pulls in the strip (Illus. 176), or you can attach knobs or pulls to the pull strip.

Lay the strips in position face down on a piece of scrap plywood. Place the pull strip at the edge of the plywood so that it is level with the rest of the strips. Nail some scrap strips to the bench around all four sides of the door to hold the strips in position. Apply contact cement to the back of the strips and to a piece of canvas slightly larger than the door. When the cement is dry, apply the canvas to the back of the strips. With a sharp knife, trim the canvas to fit the door (Illus. 178).

You can make the track in two ways. The most common method involves cutting it directly into the side of the cabinets with a router. You must do this before assembling the cabinet. Make a template out of ¼" hardboard and clamp it to the side. Use a template-following collar on the router.

You can determine the proper radius for the corners by bending the completed door around different curves until you find one that works best. The width of the individual slats in the tambour determines the minimum corner radius. To make a sharp bend, the track groove needs to be wider than is necessary for straight parts of the track. You can widen the track at a sharp bend by slightly repositioning the template and taking a second pass over the curved sections of the track. This is better than cutting the entire track wide because it avoids a loose fit in the straight parts of the track. Depending on the size of the opening, the tambour may fit entirely in the side of the cabinet or the track may have to extend around the back of the cabinet to fit the open door. False sides and a false back are sometimes used to hide the tambour when it is open. Unlike the tracks for bypass doors, both tracks should be of equal depth. You must install the door during assembly.

Another way to install a tambour door involves an applied track. You can use this method to install a tambour door in a cabinet that has already been assembled. It's especially useful when you are remodeling cabinets. If you want the gentle, graceful curves found in roll-top desk design, you will have to cut the track with a router; but when the design calls for a door that is flat except for a 90° bend where it enters the cabinet, you can use an applied track.

You make the applied track by cutting a groove in a strip of

Illus. 178. Shop-built tambour doors usually have a canvas backing glued to the strips. After the canvas is in place, use a sharp knife to trim off the area that will fit in the track.

hardwood. Use a table saw with a dado blade or a router mounted in a router table.

Drill screw holes inside the track. For a ¼"-wide groove, use #6 screws. You must countersink the screws below the bottom of the track to avoid binding the door. You won't be able to fit a standard countersink into the track, so use a ¼" drill bit to countersink the holes.

Mitre the corners and then apply the track with glue and screws. If you apply the track before attaching the back to the cabinet, you can slide the tambour into the completed track from the rear. If the cabinet is already assembled, install all of the track except the front. If the track makes a bend at the rear, complete the corners (in the way that follows) before installing the door. Slide the door into the track; then install the front part of the track. When the track is in place, you need to modify the corners so that the door can make the bend smoothly. Glue corner blocks to the track as shown in Illus. 179; then use a chisel to pare away the inside corner of the track until it is about a 1"-radius curve. Smooth the curve with sandpaper.

When the track is complete, pull the door into place and install stop blocks on the rear track to prevent the door from opening too far.

Illus. 179. You can make this type of tambour door track on the table saw and then you can apply it to the cabinet with screws. Mitre the track at the corner and then glue the triangular blocks in place. Finally, use a chisel to cut the curved inner surface of the track. Sandpaper, rubbed shoeshine-fashion over the area, will smooth the curve.

9
DRAWERS

Since drawers have a reputation for being very difficult to build because of the many complex joints used in fine drawer construction, many beginning cabinetmakers are reluctant to tackle them; but strong, good-looking drawers can actually be built quite simply. Intricate drawer construction has always been a source of pride among master cabinetmakers, and the drawers are beautiful and will last for centuries; but for many applications, much simpler construction practices will suffice. Illus. 180 shows a simple yet strong drawer design, which uses only rabbet and dado joints. This design is especially well suited to plywood and particle board because these materials don't work well with the more intricate type of drawer joints.

Drawer fronts are usually made from ¾"-thick material, whereas the sides and back are usually made of ½" or ⅜" material. The sides are thinner to give the maximum amount of space inside the drawer and to save weight, but there's nothing wrong with using ¾"-thick material for the sides and back.

The front should be made of the same material as the outside of the cabinet. The sides and back are usually made of a different material. In the highest quality cabinets, solid oak is usually used for drawers. When expense is a consideration, less expensive species of solid lumber are used. Pine is often used for medium-duty drawers. Plywood and particle board are increasingly being used for drawer construction. When the drawer sides also act as runners, a hardwood is best; but when you use mechanical drawer guides, pine, plywood, and particle board are good choices.

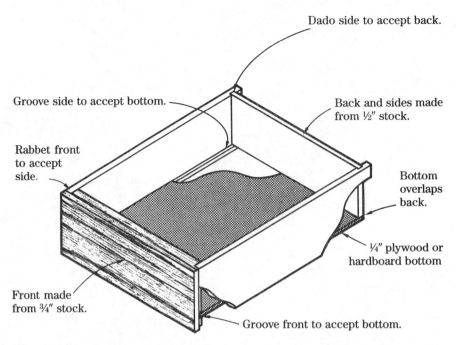

Dado side to accept back.

Groove side to accept bottom.

Back and sides made from ½″ stock.

Rabbet front to accept side.

Bottom overlaps back.

¼″ plywood or hardboard bottom

Front made from ¾″ stock.

Groove front to accept bottom.

Illus. 180. This simple type of drawer construction is strong enough for most uses.

Premanufactured drawer sides are available that cut down the time involved in making large numbers of drawers. They come in several standard widths and the groove for the bottom is precut. The tops are rounded and, in some cases, prefinished. Manufactured sides made of hardwood are available from some mail-order wood-working-supply companies. Another type of manufactured drawer side is made of a fibreboard that is similar to hardboard; the surface is covered with an imitation wood grain. Commercial shops use this material extensively, but it is not widely available to the general public. If you will be building a lot of drawers and would like to use this material, contact a cabinet shop in your area and they may sell you some of their stock.

The drawer bottom is usually made of ¼″-thick material. Plywood is the usual choice. For very high-quality work, use a hardwood-veneer plywood. Another good choice is ¼″ hardboard. A special type of particle board is used as a drawer bottom in some commercial work; it has a vinyl coating that makes the drawer easy to clean.

The first step in constructing the type of drawer shown in Illus. 180 is to measure the opening. Even if you are going to make several drawers the same way, it's a good idea to measure all of the openings and custom-fit each drawer. Cut all of the parts to rough size and then cut the groove for the bottom in the front and sides. Round off the top corners of the sides with a block plane, router, or shaper.

Notice that the back is not as wide as the sides; it stops at the top of the groove, so no groove is cut in the back. Leave ½″ between the bottom of the groove and the bottom of the sides so that there will be plenty of support for the bottom of the drawer. This groove will carry all of the weight of the drawer's contents. The depth of the groove should be about one-half the thickness of the side; so for a ½″ side, the groove would be ¼″ deep. Cut the groove wide enough for the bottom to slide in it without being too loose.

This type of drawer fits flush inside the drawer opening, so the next step is to make sure that the front fits the opening; then cut the rabbets in the ends of the front (Illus. 181). Next, cut the dadoes for the back in the sides. Leave at least ½″ between the dado and the rear of the side. Now cut the back to length and begin assembly. Since a drawer is submitted to a lot of stress as you open and close it, you need to reinforce the joints. You can use nails, screws, and

Illus. 181. A router table is a very useful tool for drawer construction. You can use it for making rabbets and dadoes, the groove for the bottom, and the dovetail dadoes described later. Notice the material being used here; it is a manufactured drawer side, made of wood-grained fibreboard. The groove for the bottom has been cut at the factory. The sides are simply cut to length and rabbeted or dadoed as necessary.

dowels for this type of drawer construction. The fasteners are driven through the side into the front and back. The joints between the front and back and the sides are all glued, but the bottom is not glued. You should cut the bottom to fit snugly in the groove. The bottom overhangs the back and should be flush with the ends of the sides.

It is very important for the drawer to be square. Place the drawer bottom up on the bench with the front facing you. Place a square in the corner formed between the front and one side. Place your hands on the back of the drawer and pull the drawer against your body. In this position, you can easily twist the drawer until it is square. When the drawer is square, make sure that the back is tight against the front and then nail it in place along the back. Use box nails because their heads will hold better than the heads on finish nails. Space the nails about 2 inches apart.

You can use the same basic construction to make a lipped drawer. A lipped drawer is easier to fit because the drawer front overhangs the drawer opening, hiding the gap around the drawer. The drawer is made in exactly the same way, except the front is larger than the opening. A ⅜" lip on all sides is usual. Cut a ⅜"-wide rabbet along the top and bottom of the front, and make the rabbet for the sides

Illus. 182. In this type of drawer construction, you use the overlay front to lock the dadoes on the sides. You use a router to cut the stopped dado in the front.

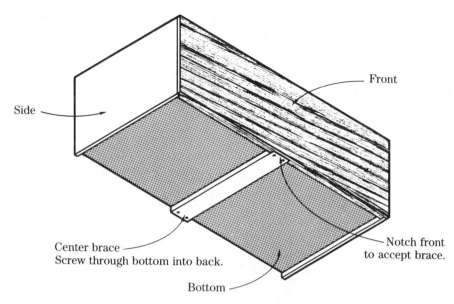

Side

Front

Center brace
Screw through bottom into back.

Notch front
to accept brace.

Bottom

Illus. 183. Wide drawers require a center brace to support the bottom.

⅜" wider than the side so that the sides will be recessed in from the sides of the front. The front edges can be rounded, as described for lipped doors in Chapter 8, or left square, depending on the style of the cabinet.

Overlay drawers are usually made with a false front. You construct the drawer as if it were a flush drawer, except you make the front from the same material as the sides and you don't need to carefully fit it to the opening. Using screws driven in from the rear, you attach a false front, which is larger than the opening, to the drawer front. This type of construction is widely used in commercial built-in cabinets. It allows the drawers to be mass produced without individual fitting, and the fronts can be adjusted to compensate for slight errors in drawer alignment.

A variation on this type of construction is shown in Illus 182. The joint between the front and the sides is a dado set in ½" from the end, the same way as the back joint. The ends of the sides fit into stopped dadoes in the false front. This is a very strong type of construction because, once the false front is screwed in place, the sides are locked. The extra strength provided by the dadoes helps to resist the stresses placed on the front joints during heavy use. This type of drawer is easy to make if you have a router and it adapts well to mass production. You can use the same dado setup for both the front and back joints and, since the sides are reversible, you don't need to worry about making the correct amount of right and left sides. Make the stopped dado in the false front with a router. If you are making a number of drawers, make a template that will guide the router and position the dado.

Very wide drawers, like those commonly found in a chest of drawers, require a center brace that helps support the bottom. To install the brace, cut a notch in the middle of the front, as shown in Illus. 183. The brace should be as thick as the distance between the drawer bottom and the bottom of the sides so that it will be flush with the sides. Screw the brace in place after installing the bottom. The screws should go through the bottom and into the front and back.

As you progress to more advanced projects, you may want to try some of the traditional drawer joints used in fine cabinetmaking. You should only use these joints when the drawer components are made of a solid hardwood such as oak. If you try to use dovetails or locked joints with plywood or particle board, the small projections will crumble off, leaving a very weak joint. You can use dovetails with

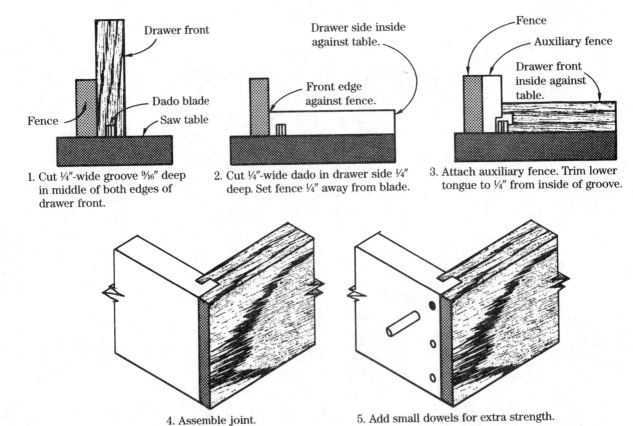

1. Cut ¼"-wide groove ⁹⁄₁₆" deep in middle of both edges of drawer front.

2. Cut ¼"-wide dado in drawer side ¼" deep. Set fence ¼" away from blade.

3. Attach auxiliary fence. Trim lower tongue to ¼" from inside of groove.

4. Assemble joint.

5. Add small dowels for extra strength.

Illus. 184. The tongue-and-lap locked joint is stronger than a simple rabbet for connecting the sides to the front of a drawer.

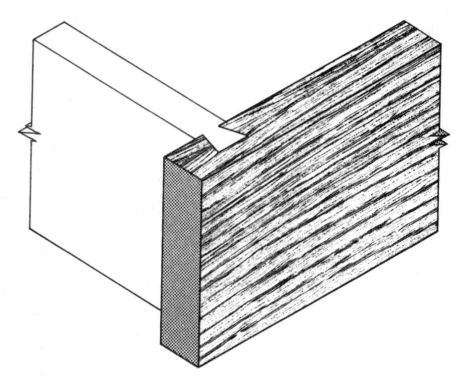

Illus. 185. The dovetailed dado is a strong joint for joining an overlay drawer front directly to the sides.

softwood, such as pine, but the dovetails should be coarser than the ones used in hardwoods (see Chapter 4).

High-quality drawers should have a groove for the bottom cut in the back. This makes the bottom stronger but also more difficult to assemble and square. The bottom must fit snugly in all four grooves or it won't be able to hold the drawer square.

The dovetail is the traditional favorite for drawer construction. Except in cases where the joinery forms a decorative part of the cabinet, half-blind dovetails are used so that they won't show from the front. An exception to this is when you use overlay false fronts. When this is the case, open dovetails can be used and hidden by the false front. Router-cut dovetails are often used in drawer construction, but hand-cut dovetails are still the mark of the highest quality construction. Making dovetails is discussed in detail in Chapter 4.

The tongue-and-lap locked joint is simpler to make than the dovetail, but it is not as strong. You can make this joint easily on a table saw. Illus. 184 explains the procedure. This joint will be stronger if it is pegged with small dowels.

You can use a dovetailed dado joint (Illus. 185) to attach the sides directly to an overlay front, with no need for a false front. Don't use this joint with pine, plywood, or particle board. You cut the dado with a router and a dovetail bit. The dado must be open at the bottom of the front and stopped at the top. You can make the dovetail on the front end of the sides on the table saw. Set the tilt arbor to the same angle as the dovetail bit and cut the angles on both sides. Set the angle back to 90° and lower the blade to make a square shoulder. You can also use this type of joint in place of the dado to join the back to the sides.

Another method of attaching the back involves using the tongue-and-dado joint (Illus. 186). First, cut a rabbet on both ends of the

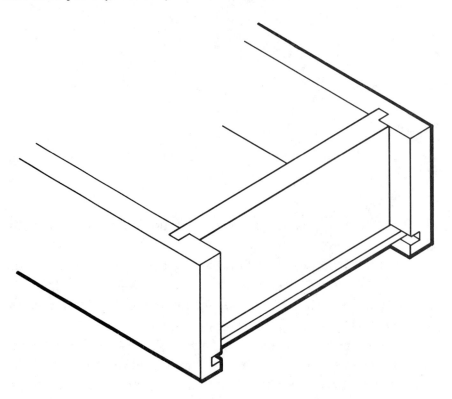

Illus. 186. The tongue-and-dado joint is sometimes used to attach the back of the drawer to the sides.

back. The tongue formed should be one half as long as the thickness of the sides. Next, cut a dado in the sides that will fit the tongue.

You can also attach the back with open or blind dovetails, in which case the sides do not overhang past the back.

Drawer Guides

In its simplest form, a drawer guide is a shelf where the drawer rests. For very small drawers, such as the ones found in the small com-

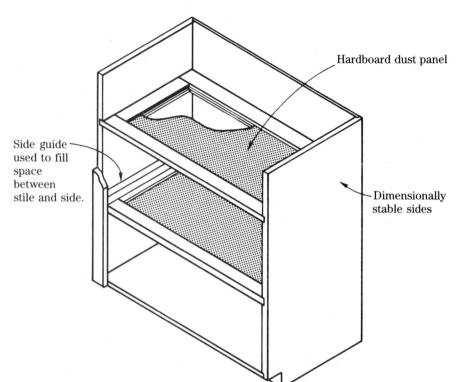

Hardboard dust panel

Side guide used to fill space between stile and side.

Dimensionally stable sides

Illus. 187. You can use this type of frame and dust-panel drawer guide when you use dimensionally stable sides, such as plywood or particle board, in case construction. You can also use it in panel-construction carcasses.

partments of a roll-top desk, the drawer guide is usually just a thin shelf. To save materials, larger drawers use different types of guides.

When the sides of the cabinet are made of panel construction or from a dimensionally stable material such as plywood, the guides can be made of strips put together into open frames. Use mortise-and-tenon, half-lap, or dowel joints to put the frames together. The best-quality construction also incorporates dust panels, which are made of thin material such as ⅛″ hardboard (Illus. 187). The dust panel fits into a groove in the frame. Dust panels not only keep things from falling from one drawer opening into another, but they also help keep the drawer guides square and add rigidity to the entire carcass.

Flush drawers need some type of stop that will prevent them from being pushed too far back into the opening. Small blocks placed at the rear of the frame that will hit the ends of the drawer sides are the best form of stop. To use this method, the drawer needs to be made at least ¾″ smaller than the depth of the opening. A great deal of pressure can be placed on the stop blocks when a drawer is shut, so attach them with glue and screws.

It is customary to let the front of a lipped or overlay drawer stop the drawer; but this is not a good practice because, when a fully loaded drawer is slammed shut, a tremendous stress is placed on the joint between the front and sides. So even though the front will stop these drawers, a stop placed at the back will prolong the life of the drawer.

When the cabinet sides are made of solid wood, a different type of dust-panel construction is necessary to prevent cross-grain shrinkage and swelling from splitting the sides or loosening the joints. Illus. 188 shows the proper way to construct the dust panel for use with solid wood. Instead of using a frame, you only use a ¾"-thick front rail. The dust panel is made of ⅜"-thick solid wood. A ⅜"-thick strip, called a kicker, fills in the lower part of the dado below the dust panel. The kicker should extend past the side far enough for the top of the drawer below to ride against it. You should only glue the kicker in place at the front in an area about 4 inches long. The rest of the kicker is left free to slide in the dado as the sides shrink and swell. You should leave the kicker about ½ inch short of touching the back of the cabinet. If the kicker touches the back, it may push the back off as the sides shrink.

When the sides of the drawer are separated from the sides of the cabinet by a face frame, you need to add side guides to keep the

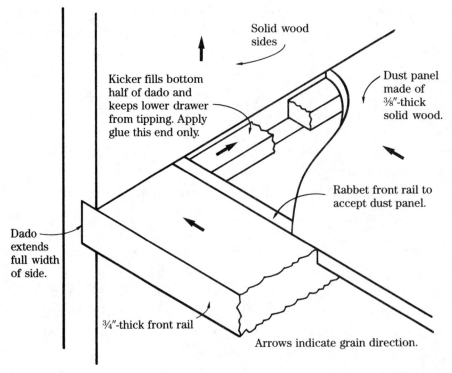

Illus. 188. When you use solid wood sides, you should use this type of dust-panel construction. It allows for dimensional change in the sides.

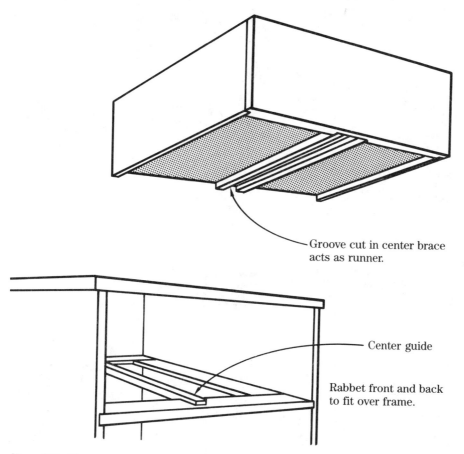

Groove cut in center brace
acts as runner.

Center guide

Rabbet front and back
to fit over frame.

Illus. 189. The center guide is particularly useful for wide drawers because it prevents binding caused by twisting the drawer as it opens.

drawer from twisting when you pull it open (Illus. 187). You can use a center guide instead of side guides (Illus. 189). A hardwood runner with a wide groove is attached to the middle of the bottom of the drawer, and a guide that fits into the groove is attached in the middle of the frame. When the drawers won't be carrying a lot of weight, you can use the center guide alone, without the frame. In this case, the center guide is attached to the front rail and the back of the cabinet.

For wide drawers, the frame type of guide is recommended; but narrower drawers up to about 24 inches wide can be side hung (Illus. 190). Side-hung drawers have a cleat that rides in a groove. You can place the cleat on either the drawer or the cabinet. If you attach the cleat to the cabinet, then you cut a groove into the side of the drawer to fit the cleat. When you attach the cleat to the drawer, you make a dado in the side of the cabinet to fit the cleat.

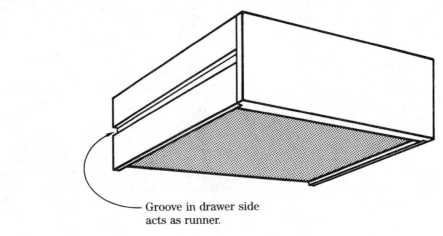

Groove in drawer side
acts as runner.

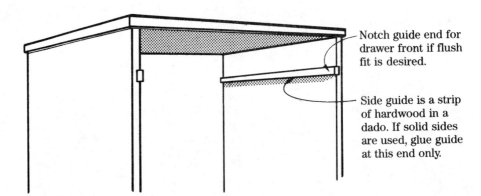

Notch guide end for
drawer front if flush
fit is desired.

Side guide is a strip
of hardwood in a
dado. If solid sides
are used, glue guide
at this end only.

Illus. 190. Side guides are often used for smaller drawers.

Several types of commercial drawer guides are available. The most popular type is similar to the side-hung type just described, but the guides are made of metal and incorporate ball-bearing rollers (Illus. 191). This type is very strong and will support the most weight of any type of drawer guide. It also allows the drawer to be extended to the full length of travel without tipping. The drawer must be smaller than the opening to allow for this type of guide. Usually ½″ clearance is needed on each side of the drawer, but check the instructions that come with the drawer guide for specific measurements. Using this type of guide can simplify the cabinet construction considerably. There is no need for any type of frame or divider between drawers. When you use overlay fronts, you don't even need a rail between the drawers on the front.

The center guide is another type of commercial drawer guide. This type is less expensive than the side-hung type, but it isn't as strong and it requires a front rail between drawers. The guide consists of a steel channel, which fits between the front rail and the back of the cabinet, and a roller, which fits into the channel and attaches to the back of the drawer. The sides of the drawer rest on the front rail; sometimes a roller or plastic glide is supplied to attach to the front rail for the sides to ride on.

There are many types of commercial drawer pulls that are similar to the door pulls described in Chapter 8. Sometimes the drawer pull is incorporated into the design of the drawer front, and a commercial pull is not used. The simplest way is to cut the bottom edge of an overlay front at a 45° angle. This provides a finger hold all along the bottom of the drawer. A slightly better grip is provided if you use a router or shaper to cut a cove along the bottom. You can also use this method with flush drawers if you cut a cove along the top of the rail between drawers. This makes a space that allows you to get your fingers into the cove along the bottom of the drawer.

Illus. 191. Commercial roller guides provide smooth operation and support the open drawer better than other drawer guides.

10
BUILT-IN CABINETS

In kitchens built-in cabinets are a necessity (Illus. 192), but built-in cabinets can save space and add style to any room. You can use an open-shelf unit as an attractive display case or bookcase in the den or living room (Illus. 193). Built-in bathroom vanities hide plumbing under the sink and add storage space as well (Illus. 194). In the bedroom built-ins can help organize a cluttered closet (Illus. 195).

Illus. 192. Built-in kitchen cabinets are a necessity in a modern kitchen. Complete plans for the cabinets shown here are contained in Chapter 11.

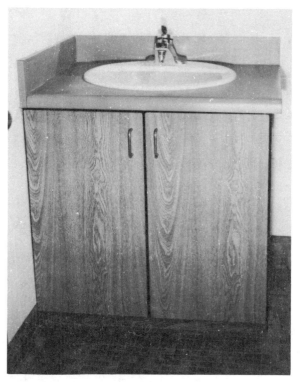

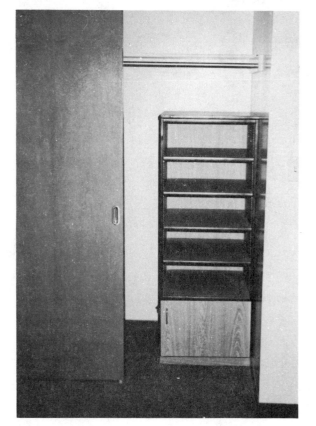

Illus. 193 (top left). An open cabinet can provide an attractive display area.

Illus. 194 (top right). Plans for building this bathroom vanity are contained in the next chapter.

Illus. 195 (left). A built-in cabinet in a closet can help to organize clutter.

Standard Sizes

Over the years some standard dimensions have developed for built-in cabinets. Since a built-in becomes a permanent fixture of the house, it's a good idea to follow the standard dimensions whenever possible.

The standard working counter height is 36″. This height is to the top surface of the counter, so be sure to allow for the thickness of the counter when you build base cabinets. Bathroom vanities are usually 32″ from the floor to the counter top. The standard counter width is 24″ to 26″. Desks and eating areas that will be used with standard chairs should be 29″ to the counter top. Desks for type-writers or computers should be 27″ high. A good height for a TV shelf is about 24 inches, but this is determined more by personal preference.

Wall-hung cabinets are usually 12″ to 14″ wide. Generally, 72″ to

Illus. 196. Refrigerators need proper ventilation to operate efficiently. When building cabinets over a refrigerator, allow at least 6″ between the bottom of the cabinet and the top of the refrigerator. Chapter 11 contains the plans for the cabinet shown here.

80″ is the maximum height for the top shelf. On an overhead cabinet, the distance between the counter top and the bottom should be at least 15″, but 24″ is more practical. Overhead cabinets mounted over a refrigerator are usually at least 72″ above the floor (Illus. 196). The minimum width to allow for a refrigerator or range is 31″, but large units may require wider openings.

Built-in bookcases vary in width from 8″ to 12″. The wider size is preferable because it can handle most sizes of books. If possible, you should use adjustable shelves. If you use fixed shelves, at least one should be spaced wider than 12½″ to accommodate large books. The other shelves can be spaced 10″ apart to accommodate most books. When you place a closed cabinet below open bookshelves, the lower section should be 29″ or 36″ high. If a cabinet incorporates a bench seat, the seat should be 17″ high.

Built-In Construction

Built-ins can be built in place or built in the shop and moved later. The construction practices are similar to those used with free-standing cabinets, but generally involve less complicated joinery. The carcasses are usually made from plywood or particle board, so dimensional stability is not a problem. When face frames are used, they are usually made from solid hardwood. You can make the doors and drawer fronts from either solid lumber or man-made materials.

BUILDING IN PLACE

You can use two different methods for building cabinets in place. One way involves case construction. You build the cabinet basically as a freestanding unit, and then attach it to the walls, just to hold it in place. The other method involves skeleton-frame construction and uses the walls as structural members of the cabinet (Illus. 197). In most cases, the first method is best because you don't have to compensate for out-of-square walls and you have a totally enclosed cabinet that will keep dust, insects, and rodents out better. The second method is less expensive because you don't have to purchase materials to cover areas that are connected to walls.

Joinery in built-in-place cabinets is usually kept very simple. The cabinet gets a lot of its strength from the walls. Butt joints reinforced with nails are frequently used. The stiles and rails in face frames are usually butted or mitred at the corners and attached to the cabinet with finish nails through the face.

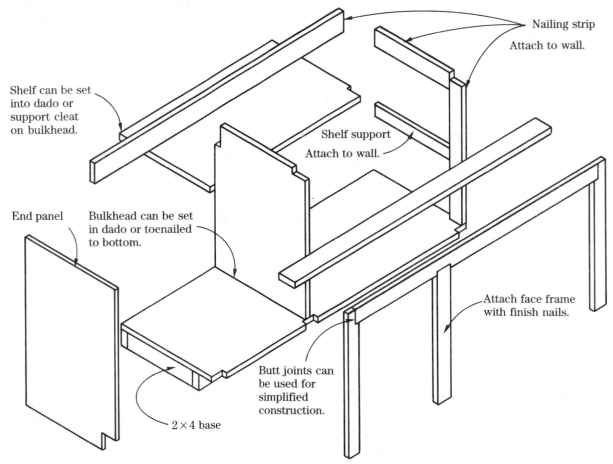

Nailing strip
Attach to wall.

Shelf can be set
into dado or
support cleat
on bulkhead.

Shelf support
Attach to wall.

End panel

Bulkhead can be set
in dado or toenailed
to bottom.

Attach face frame
with finish nails.

Butt joints can
be used for
simplified
construction.

2 × 4 base

Illus. 197. Built-in-place cabinets can use walls for support. You attach the cabinet parts to nailing strips, which are attached to the wall.

PREBUILDING

With prebuilding you spend less time at the actual site and the site stays cleaner. And by building the cabinets in a shop, you have more equipment available than you would have at the site. Prebuilt cabinets can be one piece or modular. When a cabinet is very large, it is difficult to transport and install; when this is the case, you should make the cabinet in smaller sections, called modules, and then assemble the modules in place.

Prebuilt cabinets need to be stronger than built-in-place units because they have to stand the stress of being moved and they can't rely on walls for strength. Case construction is almost always used. Rabbet and dado joints are usually used in the carcass. The face frames should be dowelled; use mortise-and-tenon joints or half-lap joints. The major limiting factor on the size of a prebuilt cabinet is the size of the smallest door opening it must pass through. If the cabinet needs to be larger than the door, you must build it in modules and then assemble it in place.

Modular Construction   Modules can be any size. You should choose an inconspicuous place to join the modules. The best place is the point where the hinge side of two doors meet. For kitchen and bathroom cabinets, the industry has loosely adopted some sizes that you can combine in different arrangements to fit most applications (Illus. 198). A sink or cooking-top module is 36″ wide; a drawer unit is 15″ or 18″ wide; and a single cabinet is 15″ or 18″ wide. Two-door modules can be 24″, 30″, or 36″ wide. Under-the-counter modules are 24″ deep, and overhead modules are 12″ to 14″ deep.

If the cabinets have to fit into an existing alcove, usually you will need to install a filler strip at the corners. To avoid this, you can vary

Illus. 198. These cabinets are too long to be moved in a single piece. Instead, they are built in standard-size modules and assembled in place.

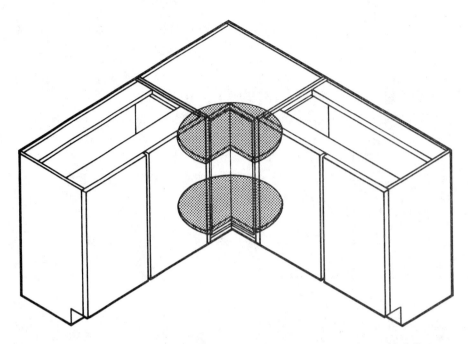

Illus. 199. This shows how you can assemble three under-the-counter modules at a corner. The corner module contains a lazy Susan.

the module sizes to fit the opening. When the cabinets don't have to fit an alcove, the standard module sizes are very convenient.

Each module is a complete cabinet with sides and a back. Under-the-counter cabinets usually don't have a solid top; instead, a 4″-wide strip of plywood joins the sides at the front and back. These strips hold the module together and act as a mounting surface for the actual counter top, which you apply in one piece after installing the modules. The base and toe kick can be integral with each module, or you can build a separate base at the site that will support all of the modules. The separate base makes it easier to accommodate for variations in the floor and to line up the modules. A 2 by 4 on edge is just the right height for a base, so it's convenient to build the base from 2 by 4's. If you install the base before the finished flooring, you can cove the flooring up the base or apply the same moulding used around the floor to the base.

At the upper rear corner of each module include a 4″-wide, ¾″-thick nailing strip. You use the nailing strip to attach the cabinet to the wall, so it should be firmly attached to the cabinet. When you use face frames, they should extend ¼″ past the side of the cabinet. This gives you some room to fit and trim the modules. When cabinets on adjacent walls meet at a corner, you need to use special corner modules (Illus. 199). In base cabinets the module may incorporate a lazy Susan. If you plan on using a lazy Susan, be sure to buy the hardware before starting on the corner module because different manufacturers recommend various construction techniques. Sometimes the corner in overhead cabinets will be blocked out and standard modules will be used.

The next chapter contains a complete set of plans and step-by-step directions for building modular cabinets.

Installation

To install cabinets, you need to know something about the way walls are framed. Since cabinets can carry very heavy loads, they should only be attached to studs. Hollow wall fasteners are usually not adequate for this job.

Wall studs are almost always placed on 16″ centers; this means that once you have found one stud, you can usually find another that is 16″ away on either side of it. Some buildings are built with the studs on 24″ centers, but this is rare. The only exception to the 16″ rule is around openings, such as windows and doors, and at corners. In these cases, you will still find studs 16″ apart, but there may be others that are less than 16″ apart in between. If the wall has been constructed correctly, there will always be a stud at the corner. There is usually a double plate at the top of a wall and a single plate at the bottom. This means that you can find solid backing along the entire wall about 2 inches below the ceiling and about 1 inch above the floor. These measurements take into account the average thickness of the floor and ceiling materials.

The best way to find a stud is with an electronic stud finder. It isn't very expensive; so if you will be doing quite a bit of installation, it's a wise investment. To use the stud finder, simply pass it back and forth over the surface of the wall; when a light flashes, you have found a stud. The magnetic type of stud finder is useful in older buildings that use wood lath because so many nails are present in each stud, but it doesn't work very well in modern buildings because the dry-wall or plasterboard fasteners are farther apart. If you don't have a stud finder, try to find one stud and then find the rest by measuring 16″. You will almost always find a stud alongside a light switch or an electrical outlet. When you have an idea of where a stud may be, drive a nail through the wall in a spot that will later be hidden by the cabinets. If you miss the stud, move the nail ½″ to the side and try again. Keep moving in ½″ increments on both sides of the original hole until you find the stud. Use this stud as a starting point and mark stud positions at 16″ increments on either side of the original one. Most tape measures have an arrow or some other mark at 16″ increments, so it's easy to mark the stud positions.

The easiest way to install wall-hung cabinets is by temporarily nailing a strip (called a ledger strip) to the wall that the bottom-rear edge of the modules can rest on; however, this will leave visible holes in the wall, so it isn't always the best method. It's always a good idea to have someone to help you when you're installing overhead cabinets. Put the first module in position and screw it to the studs. A 4″ nailing strip is wide enough to get three screws in a vertical line on each stud. Put the next cabinet in position. If you have someone to help you hold the module in position, it's best to connect the two modules together before attaching the second one to the wall. Clamp the modules together and then use wood screws to attach the modules to each other. If the modules have face frames, you need to add a ½″ filler strip between the sides of adjoining modules at the rear. Drill pilot holes in the front stiles and screw them together. If you use face-frame screws and drive them with a power screwdriver, you don't need pilot holes. Screw through the sides and into the filler strip at the rear of the module (Illus. 200). Modules without face frames are simply butted together and screws are driven through the side of one module into the other. Finally, you should secure the bottom of the cabinets to the wall by driving screws through the back.

If you are using a separate base for under-the-counter cabinets, start by building the base out of 2 by 4's. Place a cross member where the sides of each module will meet so that there will be solid support for each module. Check the base for level in both length and width. You will probably need to make some adjustments because floors are seldom exactly level. Use cedar shingles wedged between the floor and the base to make minor adjustments; major adjustments may require strips of plywood. When the base is level, nail the back of it to the wall and toenail the front to the floor.

Place the modules in their approximate position; if you plan on using filler strips at the corners, arrange the modules so that the strips come out even. If you use modules with an integral base, you must level each cabinet separately, making sure that the tops all line up. If necessary, place a filler strip where the next module will attach; then clamp the modules together and drive screws through the sides to attach them. When the modules in one section have been assembled, attach them to the wall by screwing through the nailing strip into the studs. After that, attach the modules to the base or floor.

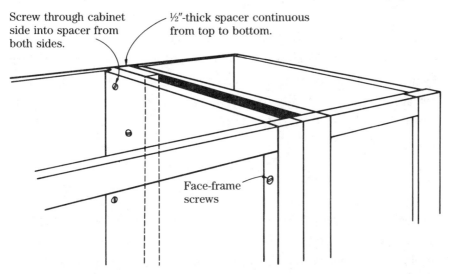

Screw through cabinet side into spacer from both sides.

½″-thick spacer continuous from top to bottom.

Face-frame screws

Illus. 200. Modules with face frames require a filler strip at the rear to compensate for the overhanging face frames. If you use special face-frame screws, it's not necessary to drill pilot holes in the hardwood face frames.

SCRIBING

When stiles or filler strips meet walls, you usually will need to trim them to fit the irregularities of the walls. This process is called scribing.

To scribe a cabinet to a wall, place the cabinet in the correct position and make sure it is level. Push the cabinet as tight as possible against the wall without moving it from a level position. Usually one corner will hit the wall and there will be a gap at the other end. If the gap is less than ⅛″, you only need to make a mark for the cut with a pencil. Lay the pencil against the wall so that the point is on the part to be trimmed and the body of the pencil is flat against the wall. Slide the pencil along the wall to duplicate the contour of the wall on the cabinet.

For larger gaps you can place a piece of thin scrap between the pencil and the wall or you can use a scriber. A scriber is very similar to a drawing compass. It holds a pencil in one leg and has a point on the other. The difference between the two is that the scriber doesn't have any projections on the side of the leg, so it can rest flat against a wall. Start at the widest part of the gap and place the leg with the metal point flat against the wall. Adjust the scriber so that the point of the pencil is just touching the edge of the cabinet or trim piece. Now run the scriber all along the wall to duplicate its contour on the cabinet.

In most cases the wall will be fairly straight but out of plumb; this results in a uniformly tapering cut on the cabinet. Probably the easiest way to make this type of cut is with a block plane. If you are scribing to a very irregular wall, such as one made of brick or stone, the wall contour will be very complex; when this is the case, use a coping saw to trim the part.

DROP CEILING

Overhead cabinets may not always extend to the ceiling. There are several ways to handle the space between the top of the cabinet and the ceiling. The space may simply be left open. If you want to enclose the space, you can build a drop ceiling out of 2-by-4 framing and cover it with dry wall or plasterboard. This method is commonly used in new construction and when extensive remodeling is being done.

A somewhat less complex method involves building a 1-by-2 framework between the cabinet and the ceiling and covering it with ¼″ plywood that matches the cabinet. Use a moulding to conceal the joint between the cabinets and the ¼″ plywood. When the space to be enclosed is not too tall, you can simply attach a ¾″-thick filler strip to the top of the cabinet, as has been done on the cabinets in Illus. 198 (see Chapter 11 for more details).

COUNTER TOPS

You can cover counter tops with a variety of materials, but the two most popular are plastic laminates and ceramic tile.

You apply ceramic tile after assembling the cabinets, which makes it easy to attach the counter tops. The top should be made from ¾″-thick plywood or particle board. Apply several beads of panel adhesive to the mounting strips in the cabinet and put the top in place. Since you apply the tile later, you can simply attach the top with screws driven down from the top. You can cover the front edge with special edge tiles, or you can apply a hardwood strip to the front of the counter, as has been done on the cabinets in Illus. 192.

You can build plastic laminate counter tops in a similar way. The overhanging front lip is usually thickened by attaching a ¾"-thick strip under the top. Fill any holes or voids in the top before applying the plastic laminate. If you use a backsplash of plastic laminate, apply it before installing the counter top. The easiest way to install a plastic laminate backsplash is by making it several inches oversized and gluing it to the wall before installing any of the cabinets. You can use a special moulding where the counter joins the backsplash that has a slot to accept the laminate, or you can scribe the top to fit closely and later cover the joint with a small bead of caulking. Make any cutouts in the plywood top before installing the laminate, but wait to make the cutouts in the plastic laminate until after you've installed it. A router with a laminate-trimming bit will follow the cutout in the plywood; drill an entrance hole in the waste area to get the bit in position. For complete details on applying plastic laminates, see Chapter 1.

Preformed plastic laminate counters are also available. This type of counter has the plastic laminate already bonded to a particle board core. The laminate has been heat-bent into a shape that provides a backsplash and self-edge in a single seamless piece. The bathroom vanity in Illus. 194 and the kitchen cabinets in Illus. 197 both use preformed counter tops. This type of counter is usually order-cut to length. When the counter has a corner in it, the joint is usually factory-cut. Before attaching the counter to the cabinets, temporarily position it to see if scribing is necessary. The backsplash incorporates a scribing strip in its construction, so you can scribe it to fit tightly against the wall (Illus. 201).

Since the plastic laminate is already applied to the top, all fasteners must be installed from inside the cabinets. Use panel adhesive on the mounting strips and make sure that the screws won't break the surface of the laminate. Corner joints come from the factory prepared to take a special type of fastener that clamps them tightly together (Illus. 202). When an end of the counter will show, end-cap kits are provided by the factory. They include a precut cap and filler strips. Glue and nail the filler strip along the underside of the counter and between the backsplash and the wall so that there is solid backing for the end cap. Apply the cap with contact cement (Illus. 203). Since the end cap is precut to the approximate outline of the counter, only a small amount of trimming with a file is usually necessary. If you need to do a lot of trimming, you can use a router with a laminate-trimming bit.

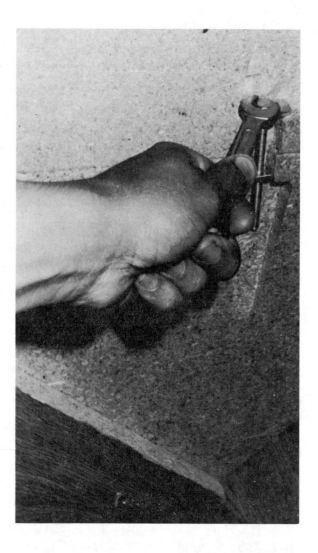

Illus. 201 (top left). Use a scriber to mark the backsplash for trimming so that it will fit closely against the wall.

Illus. 202 (top right). You can order preformed counter tops with factory-cut mitres. They come with special clamps that fit in routed recesses under the counter. Tightening the clamps with a wrench pulls the joint together.

Illus. 203 (right). Precut end caps are available for use with preformed counter tops. You must install filler strips under the edge of the counter to provide solid backing for the end cap.

11
CABINET CONSTRUCTION

This chapter contains a complete set of plans for an entire system of modular cabinets. Using this set of plans, you can build several styles of cabinets. Illustrations 204 through 206 show three possible styles. This system's versatility is due to the fact that full overlay doors and drawer fronts are used. This means that the style of the cabinet can be changed simply by altering the doors and drawer fronts. Construction is simplified because no face frames are used. A special type of fully concealed hinge permits this type of construction.

To make the plans as versatile as possible, only the dimensions that are the same for all module sizes are printed on the drawings. The various bills of materials give specific dimensions for each part. This system contains modules that you can use for kitchens, bathrooms, and other applications. The modules are the following standard widths: 15″, 18″, 24″, 30″, and 36″. Under-the-counter modules are 36″ high for kitchens and 32″ high for bathrooms. Overhead cabinets are 35″ high (30″ for styles two and three) for most applications and 25″ high (20″ for styles two and three) for over refrigerators, range hoods, etc.

The bills of materials and the step-by-step directions refer to the parts by the letters shown on the exploded-view plans.

These modules are designed to be built from particle board or plywood. If you use particle board, use the plastic laminate-covered variety for all parts that show, or cover the particle board with plastic laminate, following the directions given in the last section of

Chapter 1. Doors and drawer fronts for style three are made from solid lumber.

Use the built-in planer in the Appendix to help you lay out the design and decide on the modules that will be necessary. Using the appropriate bill of materials, make a list of all the parts that you will need. Cut out all of the parts at once, and cut all the joints requiring a particular setup at the same time.

Illus. 204. Style one: These cabinets have slab doors accented with dark plastic T moulding and ¼" spacing between doors. The space between the cabinets and the ceiling is covered with a trim strip made from the same material as the doors.

Illus. 205. Style two: Slab doors are accented with a hardwood-edge moulding. The cabinets in this photo are covered with almond-colored plastic laminate and the edging is oak with a natural finish. A matching-oak trim is used around the edge of the ceramic tile counter top and under the overhead cabinets. This kitchen has an illuminated false ceiling; if a standard-height ceiling is used, the dimensions shown in the bill of materials will allow for a space between the ceiling and the top of the cabinets. An oak moulding is used as a cornice across the top of the cabinets.

Illus. 206. Style three: Panel doors give this style a traditional look. The doors in the photo were made using a matched set of router bits to raise the panel and cut the sticking and coped stub-tenon joints. A matching piece of moulding acts as a cornice across the top. The cabinets do not extend to the ceiling; the area in between can be used for display, as shown here.

Plans

Here is a list of the plans that appear on the following pages:

Illus. 207. Front and cross section (installed view).

Illus. 208. Carcass joint layout.

Illus. 209. Drawer joint layout.

Illus. 210. Style one.

Illus. 211. Style two.

Illus. 212. Style-two alternatives.

Illus. 213. Style three.

Illus. 214. Style-three door construction.

Illus. 215. Under-the-counter single door (exploded view).

Illus. 216. Under-the-counter double door (exploded view).

Illus. 217. Under-the-counter drawer unit (exploded view).

Illus. 218. Drawer (exploded view).

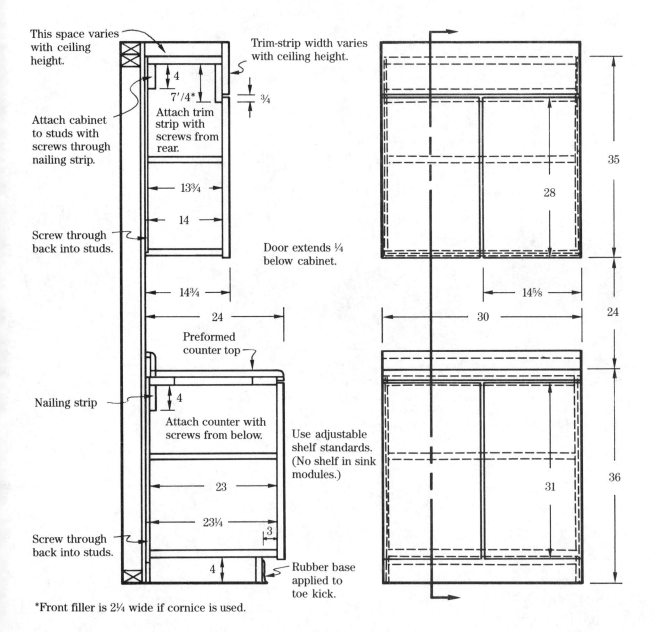

*Front filler is 2¼ wide if cornice is used.

Illus 207. Front and cross section (installed view).

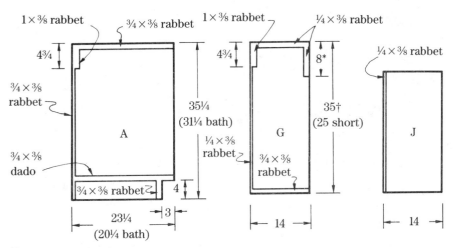

*3 if cornice is used.
†For style #2 and #3—30 (long) and 20 (short).

Illus. 208. Carcass joint layout.

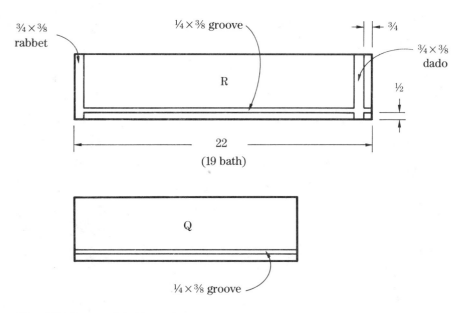

Illus. 209. Drawer joint layout.

Trim strip fills space between cabinets and ceiling.

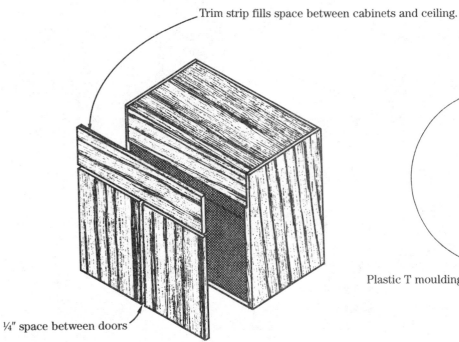

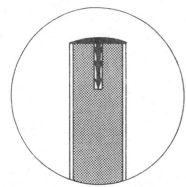

Plastic T moulding used on exposed edges.

¼″ space between doors

Illus. 210. Style one.

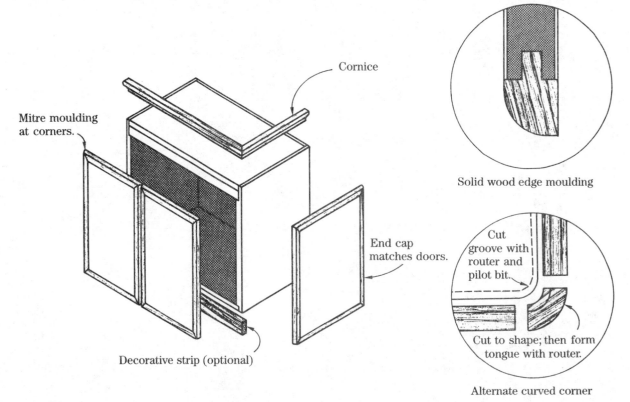

Cornice

Mitre moulding at corners.

Solid wood edge moulding

End cap matches doors.

Cut groove with router and pilot bit.

Cut to shape; then form tongue with router.

Decorative strip (optional)

Alternate curved corner

Illus. 211. Style two.

Use finger-pull moulding as cornice.

Finger-pull moulding
applied to bottom of
doors (apply to top of
under-the-counter doors).

Omit cornice. Extend doors to top.

Finger-pull moulding
applied to edge of door.

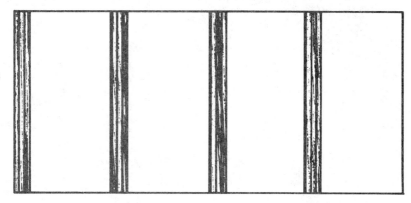

Use all single-door modules hinged on same side.

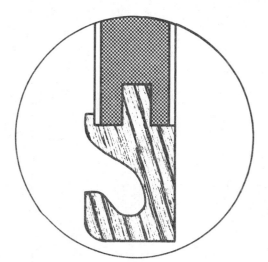

Commercial finger-pull moulding

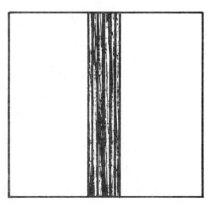

Finger-pull mouldings meet in middle.

Illus. 212. Style-two alternatives.

Cornice

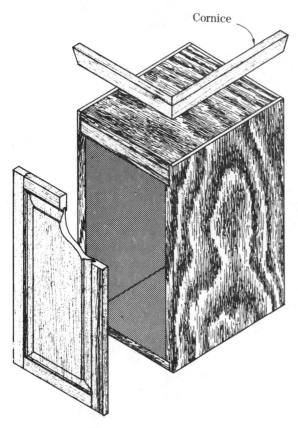

Illus. 213. Style three.

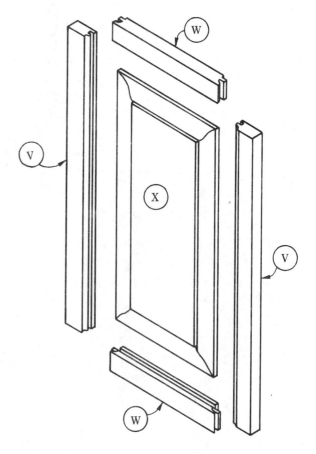

Illus. 214. Style-three door construction.

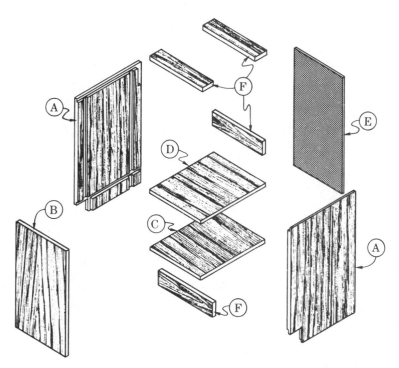

Illus. 215. Under-the-counter single door (exploded view).

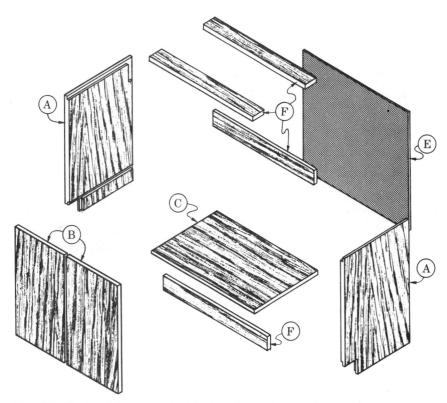

Illus. 216. Under-the-counter double door (exploded view).

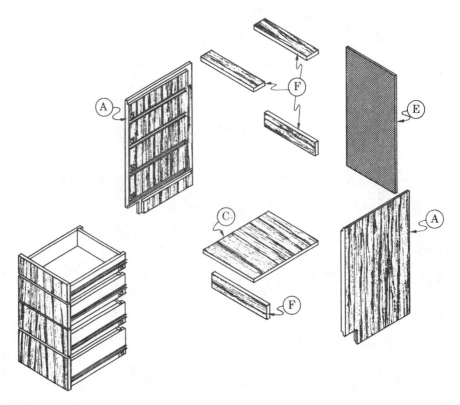

Illus. 217. Under-the-counter drawer unit (exploded view).

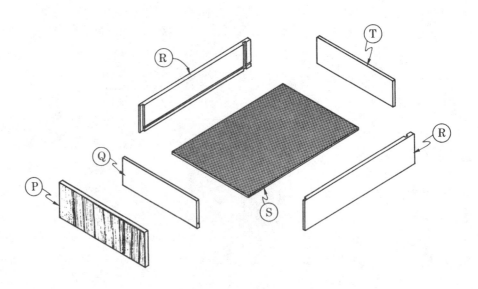

Illus. 218. Drawer (exploded view).

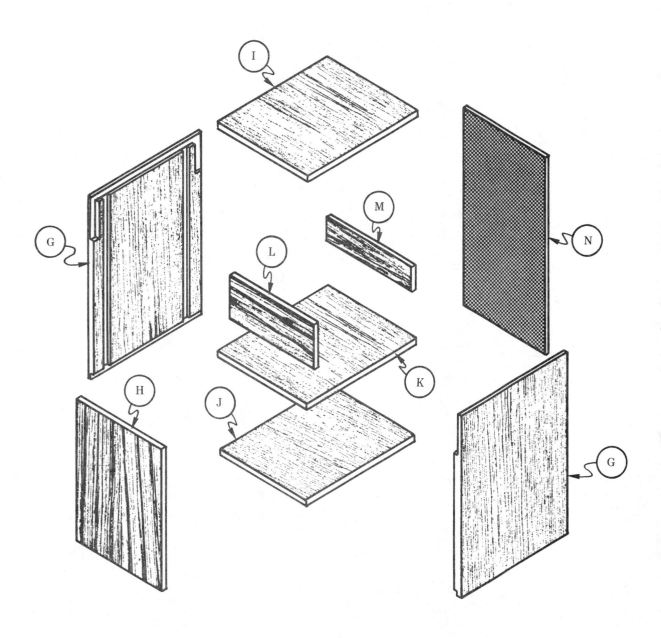

Illus. 219. Overhead cabinet (exploded view).

Illus. 220. Under-the-counter corner module (exploded view).

Note: Door is shown open 45° for clarity.

Illus. 221. Under-the-counter diagonal corner module (exploded view).

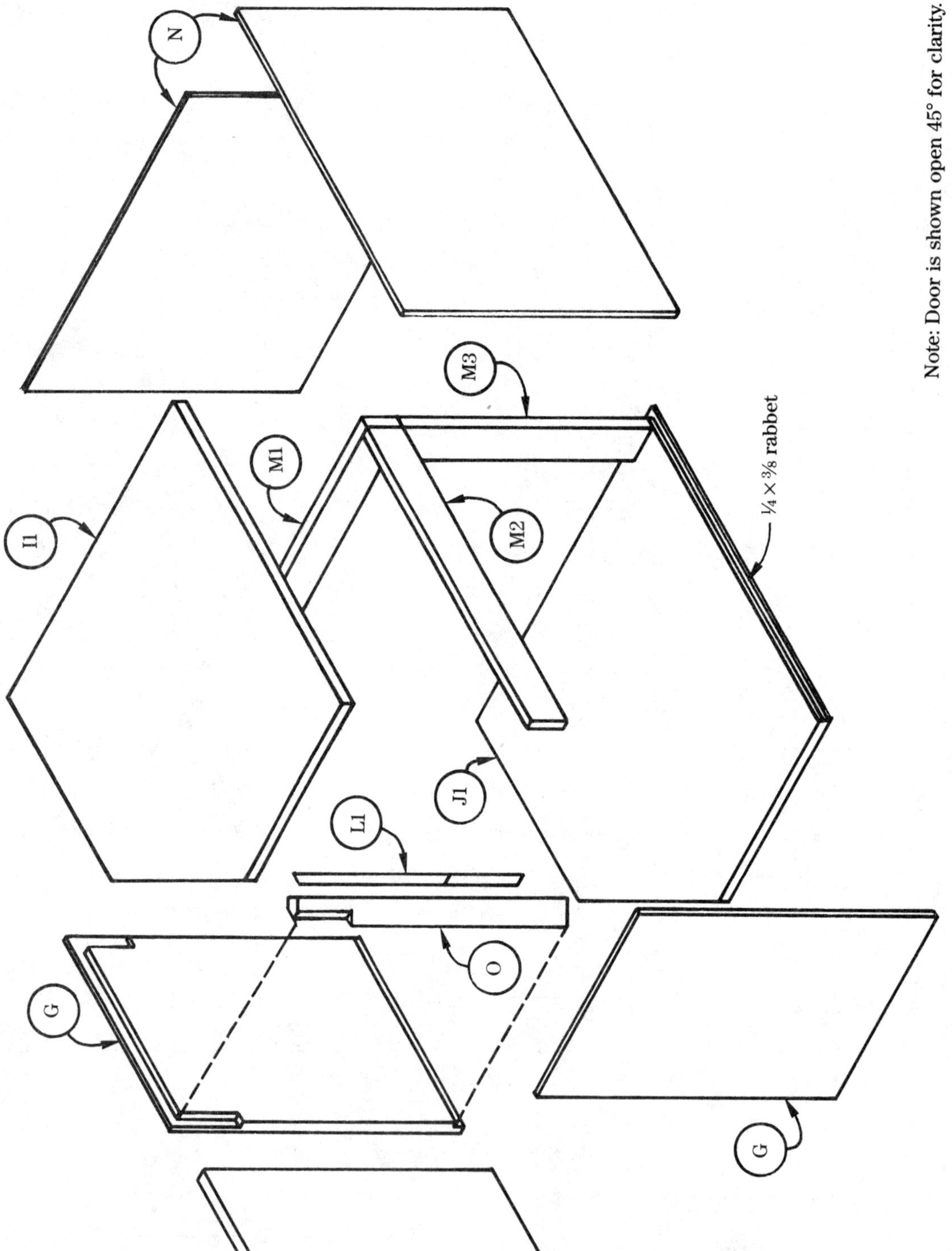
N
I1
M1
M2
M3
1/4 × 3/8 rabbet
J1
L1
O
G
G
H
Note: Door is shown open 45° for clarity.

Illus. 222. Overhead corner module (exploded view).

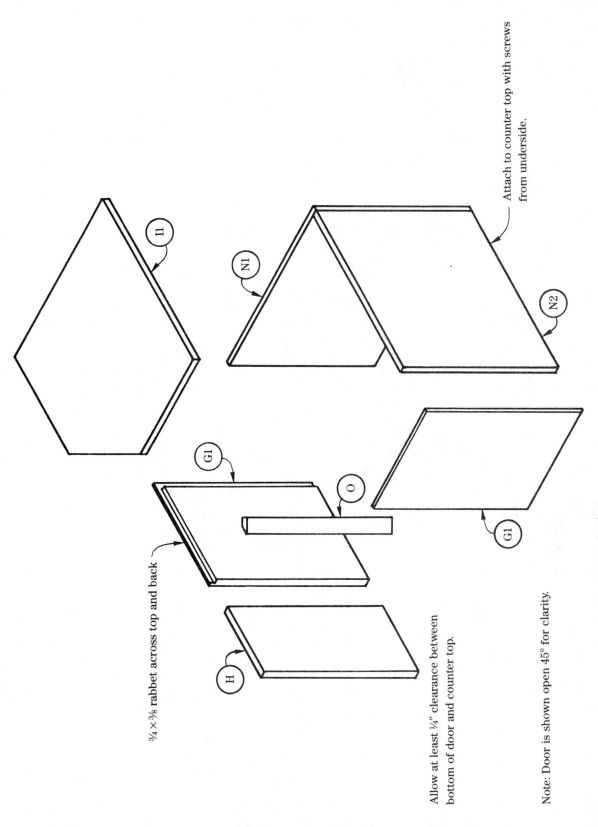

Illus. 223. Corner appliance garage (exploded view).

Attach to counter top with screws from underside.

¾ × ⅜ rabbet across top and back

Allow at least ¼" clearance between bottom of door and counter top.

Note: Door is shown open 45° for clarity.

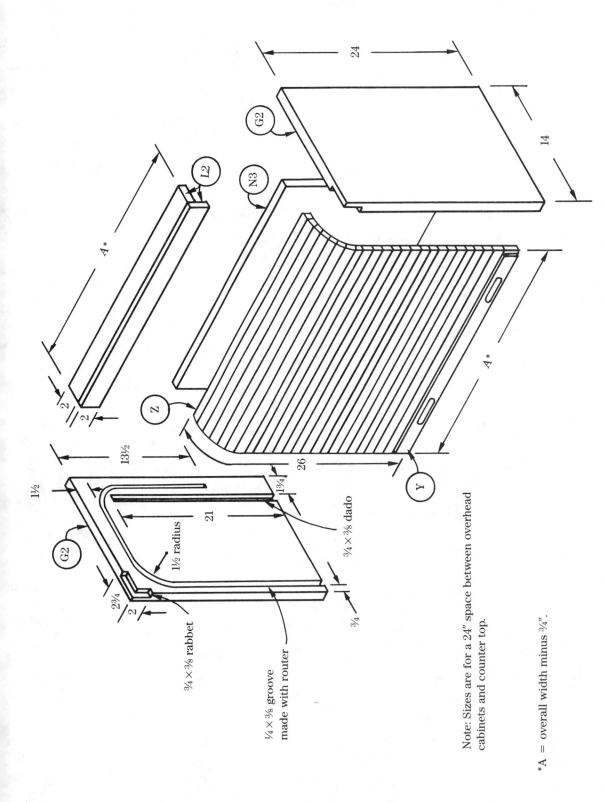

24

14

G2

L2

N3

A*

2

2

Z

13½

1½

G2

2¾

2

¾ × ⅜ rabbet

1½ radius

21

1¾

¾ × ⅜ dado

¼ × ⅜ groove
made with router

¾

26

A*

Y

Note: Sizes are for a 24" space between overhead
cabinets and counter top.

*A = overall width minus ¾".

Illus. 224. Roll-top appliance garage (exploded view).

Step-by-Step Directions

CARCASS

1. Cut out the parts. A table saw will make cutting out the parts faster, especially if it has a fence extension so that you can set the fence to make all of the cuts. If you don't have access to a table saw, you can use a portable circular saw. Clamp a board to the work to act as a guide for the saw (Illus. 225).

Illus. 225. You can use a portable circular saw to cut out the parts of the cabinets. Use a board clamped to the work to guide the saw.

2. Make rabbets. The joint-layout plan shows the location of the rabbets on parts A, G, and J. You can use a table saw to make the rabbets, but a router is easier to handle on these large parts and easier to use for making the stopped rabbets. Use an auxiliary fence to guide the router (Illus. 226). You can use a ¾″ router bit to make all of the rabbets and dadoes. First set the fence so that only ¼″ of the bit is exposed, and then set the router depth to ⅜″. Use this setting to cut the rabbets at the back of parts A, G, and J. Parts A and J are "handed"; there is a left-hand and right-hand side for each module. Mark the top and back edge of these parts so that you will make the rabbets in the correct location.

Next change the fence setting so that the entire ¾″-bit diameter is exposed; leave the depth setting at ⅜″. Use this setting to cut the rabbets at the top of A and at the top and bottom of G. This setting is also used to make the stopped rabbet on the front edge of G.

To make the stopped rabbet at the back-top corner of parts A and G, set the fence so that it is 1″ away from the far side of the bit. Leave the depth setting at ⅜″. This cut combined with the ¼″-wide rabbet already made will make a 1″-wide rabbet at this point.

The rabbet for the toe kick is cut as a dado before the side is notched back.

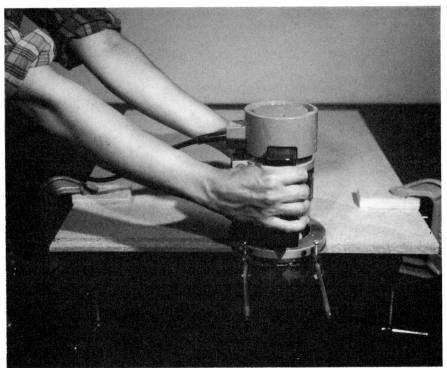

Illus. 226. Use a fence attached to the router for guiding the rabbet cuts.

3. Make dadoes. Use a router guide similar to the one described in Chapter 4 to guide the router. Use a ¾″ bit set to a ⅜″ depth of cut. Clamp the guide in place and cut the dado across the bottom of part A (Illus. 227). Reposition the guide and cut a stopped dado for the toe kick.

You can use any type of adjustable shelf standard with this system. The cabinets in the illustrations use the metal-standard type (see Chapter 7). If you use this type, cut the dadoes for the standards at this time.

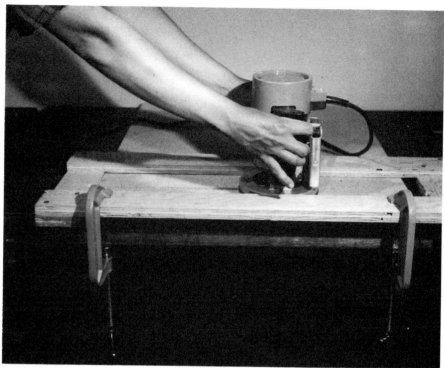

Illus. 227. The router guide described in Chapter 4 makes it easy to cut the dadoes with a router.

4. Notch for toe space. Use a handsaw to cut the notch for the toe space in part A (Illus. 228). Saw along the front edge of the short dado and along the bottom edge of the long dado. This leaves a rabbet for the toe kick and the front overhang of the bottom.

5. Cut edging kerfs. You can use any of the edging methods described in Chapter 1 with this set of plans. The cabinets in the illustrations use plastic T molding. If you use this type of edge treatment, cut the kerfs at this point in the procedure.

6. Assemble. Assemble the carcasses using glue and nails (Illus. 229). Use box nails on parts that won't show. Determine which side panels (parts A and G) will show. Use finish nails set below the surface for assembling these parts. Clamps will help in aligning the parts, but you can assemble the carcasses without them.

To assemble the under-the-counter modules, start by applying glue to the bottom dado in one side (part A). Insert the bottom (part C) into the dado so that it is flush with the front. The bottom should stop at the rear rabbet to allow the back to overhang the bottom. Turn the two parts over so that the free end of the bottom is resting on the floor. Support the top of the side with a short saw horse or anything that is approximately the correct height. Drive 6d nails through the side and into the bottom. It will be easier to hit the bottom with the nails if you measure the distance from the bottom edge of the side to the middle of the dado and draw a line on the outside of part A at that measurement. Space the nails about 4 inches apart all along the dado. Next apply glue to the top rabbet and install the two counter-mounting strips (part F). The front strip should be flush with the front of the side. The rear strip should be flush with the back of the ¼″ × ⅜″ rabbet for the back; this means that it will extend ¾″ into the 1″-wide stopped rabbet. Use three 6d nails driven through the side to attach each strip.

At this point, turn the carcass over so that the side is resting on the floor. If this is a side that will show, use a piece of carpet on the floor to protect the side. Apply glue to the bottom dado and the top rabbet of the other side and set it in place. Nail this side in the manner described for the first side.

Now install the toe kick and the nailing strip (part F). After nailing these parts in place, turn the carcass over so that it is resting on the front edges and the rabbet for the back is on top. Check the

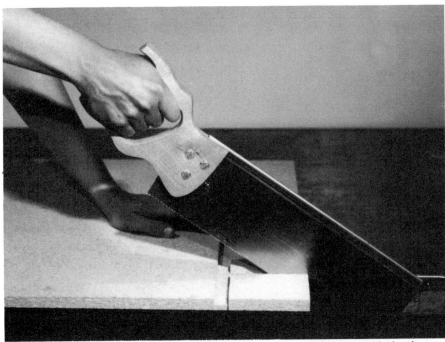

Illus. 228. After cutting the dadoes, use a handsaw to notch back the side for the toe kick. Cut along the front edge of the vertical dado and along the bottom of the horizontal dado. This will leave a rabbet for the toe kick and the overhanging part of the bottom.

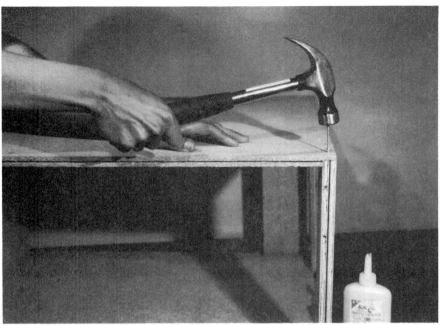

Illus. 229. Assemble the parts using glue and nails. Assembly will be easier if you position the parts so that you are always nailing against a firm surface.

carcass for square by measuring the diagonals, and correct any that are out of square before applying the back (see Chapter 6). Attach the back with 3d box nails spaced about 3″ apart. Drive the nails through the back into the lip of the rabbet along the sides; slightly angling the nails towards the outside of the cabinet will help prevent them from breaking through the inside. At the top, nail the back to the rear-counter mounting strip (part F). At the bottom, nail the back to the rear edge of the bottom (part C). The back should be flush with the top of the carcass and extend pass the bottom.

Overhead modules are assembled in a similar fashion. Place the top (part I) and the bottom (part J) into their rabbets in one side (part G). You should place part J so that the rabbet at its rear lines up with the rabbet in the rear of the side (part G). Part I should be flush with the front of the side and stop in line with the rear ¼″ × ⅜″ rabbet for the back. After attaching both sides, install the nailing strip (part M) and the front filler strip (part L). Finally, square the carcass and attach the back. The back fits into the rabbet in part J and overhangs the top (part I).

DRAWERS

1. Cut out the parts. You can use plywood, particle board, or solid lumber. The drawers in the illustrations are made from vinyl-covered particle board and the edges are covered with plastic T moulding. When using particle board, use ¾"-thick sides for added strength; if you are using solid lumber, you can use ½"-thick sides, but you will have to modify the dimensions given in the bill of materials.

2. Cut joints. For small parts, such as drawer components, the easiest way to cut the joints is with a table saw or a router mounted in a router table, although you can use a router the same way as described for carcasses. Refer to the drawer joint layout plan (Illus. 209) for the location of the rabbets and dadoes.

3. Assemble. Apply glue to the dado at the rear of one side (part R) and insert the back (part T). The back should be flush with the top of the side and stop at the top of the groove along the bottom edge of part R. Nail the back in place with 6d box nails through the side.

Glue and nail the front into its rabbet on the front edge of part Q. Use 6d finish nails driven through the side into part Q. Make sure that the groove in part Q lines up with the one in part R. Attach the other side in a similar manner.

Slide the bottom (part S) into the grooves from the rear of the drawer. Square the drawer and nail the bottom in place along the rear by nailing through the bottom into part T. Use 6d box nails.

4. Install guides. The drawers are designed for a commercial side guide that requires ½" clearance on each side of the drawer. If you use a different type of guide, you may need to change the drawer dimensions. Refer to the drawer-guide directions for exact procedures for installing the guides.

DOORS AND DRAWER FRONTS

Style One   This style, shown in Illus. 204, is the simplest to make. It has slab doors and drawer fronts. You can use hardwood-veneered plywood or plastic laminate-covered particle board. And you can use any edge treatment discussed in Chapter 1. For hardwood plywood, veneer tape is recommended; for particle board, plastic T moulding is recommended. The dimensions listed in the bill of materials are for plastic T moulding. If you use other edge treatments, you should modify the dimensions. Notice that as part of the design, there is a ¼" gap between doors; if you want the doors to meet closer, you need to add to the dimensions given in the bill of materials.

Grain direction and figure matching are optional and depend on personal taste. The cabinets in Illus. 204 have the grain running vertically. The doors are not figure-matched, but the drawers are.

Style Two   Style two is very similar to style one, but the appearance is changed by adding a ¾″-wide hardwood-edging strip around each door or drawer front (Illus. 205). The main part of the door or drawer front is made from a solid-color piece of plastic laminate-covered particle board. The size should be smaller than listed in the bill of materials to allow for the edging strips. Cut a ¼″ × ¼″ groove in the middle of all four edges. Use commercial hardwood-edge moulding that has a ¼″ × ¼″ tongue or make your own moulding. The simplest form of this style has square corners and the moulding is mitred. The round corners shown in Illus. 205 require that the corners of the door or drawer front be rounded; then a router with a special bit, which has a ball-bearing pilot that will follow curves, is used to extend the groove around the corner. Special curved-corner mouldings are used at the corners, and the straight moulding butts the ends of the corner moulding.

Apply glue to the moulding and insert it into the groove. Clamps are the best way to hold the moulding in place as the glue dries, but a few finish nails can be driven through the sides of the moulding into the particle board. Drill pilot holes for the nails where they will be inconspicuous and set the nail heads. Fill the holes with colored putty to match the moulding finish. A web clamp is very useful for installing the round-corner moulding. It is a special type of clamp that is made from fabric webbing. Wrap it around all four edges, and tighten it to clamp all four corners at once.

Another variation on this style uses a commercial edge moulding that has a built-in finger pull. You apply this moulding the same way, but only to one edge of each door or drawer front. The rest of the edges are covered with plastic T moulding or plastic laminate self-edge.

You build end caps (part U or V) the same way as doors. They are applied to the exposed ends of modules after installation. Use screws driven from inside the cabinet into the backs of the end caps to hold them in place.

Style Three   This style is more complicated than the other two, but the traditional styling allows this modular system to be used in traditionally designed buildings. The door fronts are made using panel construction techniques (see Chapters 6 and 7). The doors in Illus. 206 were made using a special set of matched router bits that cut the edge on the raised panel and that cut the sticking and coped joints. You can purchase these types of bits from several of the mail-order woodworking-supply companies if you can't find them locally. Any of the other methods for making panel doors discussed in Chapters 6 and 8 can be used. The router-bit set will produce a coped stub-tenon joint that is strong enough for most applications. If you used another method for making the joints, you can get more strength by using haunched tenons. The size of part W, listed in the bill of materials, allows enough length for a haunched tenon.

There are two options for drawer fronts with this style: You can simply use solid boards with a shaped edge, or you can cut a simulated, raised panel. You need to make the simulated, raised panel with a special bit in a router. Make a template from 1/4" hardboard to fit each drawer size or use a commercial guide made for this purpose.

You aren't limited to the three styles shown; almost any type of door or drawer front can be used with this system. For a country look, make cleated doors. If you don't want to go to the trouble of making genuine panel doors, you can use applied mouldings with the slab doors to create a traditional look. Even glazed doors can be used with this system.

CORNER MODULES

When two cabinets meet at a corner, a special module is required. The simplest type uses a modified two-door module (Illus. 216). Illus. 230 shows how the modules are placed in the corner. If you don't need a filler strip, you can butt the cabinets directly against each other. To modify the standard double-door module, attach the inactive door solidly to the carcass instead of hinging it. In some cases, it's better to have the active door open on the opposite side. To do this, it has to be hinged where the two doors meet. Install a 2"-wide filler behind the edge of the inactive door where the hinge can be attached. You can also use this method with overhead cabinets (Illus. 231).

A major advantage with this type of corner module is that you can adjust it to fit tightly in an alcove. A disadvantage is that the space in the corner is wasted and the part of the shelf behind the inactive door is hard to reach.

The type of corner module shown in Illus. 220 eliminates the disadvantages of the first type, but it can't be adjusted to the size of an alcove as easily. This type can be used with a lazy Susan, making it easy to reach all the items stored in the unit.

The sides (part A) are the same as those used in the other

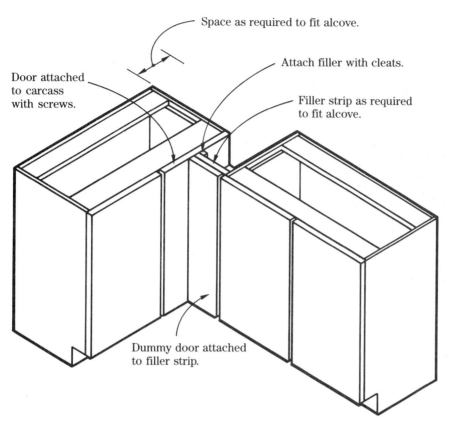

Space as required to fit alcove.

Attach filler with cleats.

Door attached to carcass with screws.

Filler strip as required to fit alcove.

Dummy door attached to filler strip.

Illus. 230. You can use a modified two-door module as a corner module. The door that falls behind the filler strip is called the inactive door. It is attached to the carcass with screws instead of hinges. If the spacing is not critical, you can omit the filler strip and dummy door and simply butt the second cabinet against the inactive door of the first cabinet.

modules. The bottom (part C1) and the front-counter mounting strip (part F4) have the front corner cut out so that the front of the module will line up with both banks of cabinets. A nailing strip (part F3) is used to reinforce the joint where the two backs (part E) meet. The size given in the bill of materials for part E is for the longest side; since a butt joint is used at the rear corner, one of the backs must be trimmed ¼". The long toe kick (part F5) extends the full width of the module and the short toe kick (part F6) butts into it. Assembly is basically the same as for a standard module. The doors are hinged to the sides (part A) and meet in the center; there shouldn't be any overlap where the doors meet or else they won't work independently.

Another type of corner module is shown in Illus. 221 (exploded view) and Illus. 205 (photo). In this module a single door is used; it is set diagonally across the corner. This type offers a large interior that works well with a lazy Susan, but it won't work with the standard corner mitre used on preformed counters. The counter top must follow the diagonal across the corner. This module is built in much the same way as the one in Illus. 220, except that some parts towards the front of the module must be cut at a 45° angle. The

Illus. 231. This photo shows how the same corner treatment in Illus. 230 can be used with overhead cabinets. The cabinet on the left is the module with the inactive door, and the one on the right has a small filler strip and dummy door. Notice that the active door is hinged from the inactive door in this instance. The small amount of space between the end of the inactive door and the dummy door would make it awkward to get into the cabinet if the active door was hinged from the side. You must install a hinge-mounting strip behind the edge of the inactive door to hinge the active door in this direction.

counter-mounting strip (part F8) is cut at a 45° angle on the ends to fit into the rabbet along the top of part A. The bottom (part C2) has the front corner cut off at a 45° angle. The toe kick (part F7) is cut at a 45° angle on both ends. You must use a special door-mounting strip (part O) for the door to function correctly. It is cut at a 45° angle along one edge and attached to the side from which the door will be hinged. This provides a mounting surface for the hinge that is square with the door.

You can also use this type of corner module for overhead cabinets.

Its construction is shown in Illus. 222. The front filler strip (part L1) is cut at a 45° angle on both ends and installed in the rabbet at the top of the side (part G). When installing these corner modules, it may be necessary to add a spacer between the corner module and the adjacent cabinet to get sufficient door clearance.

INSTALLATION

After you have assembled all the carcasses and made all the doors and drawers, you're ready to install the cabinets. Install the overhead modules first. If the walls will be painted after the cabinets are installed, then the best way to line up the cabinets is to nail a ledger strip to the wall that the rear of the cabinet can rest on during installation. Standard height for the ledger strip is 60″ from the floor. The short cabinets that go over refrigerators should be mounted 70″ from the floor. Build a brace from 2 by 4's this same height to place under the front edge of the module during installation.

To install the cabinets, place the rear edge on the ledger strip and put the brace under the module; install 3″-long screws through the nailing strip into wall studs (see Chapter 10). Place the next module on the ledger strip and clamp it to the first with C-clamps. Attach it to the wall studs and then fasten the two modules together by installing 1¼″ screws through the side of one cabinet into the side of the other. Install screws through the back along the bottom to keep the lower portion of the cabinet against the wall. When all of the overhead modules are attached to the wall, remove the ledger strip and fill the nail holes in the wall.

Next, install the under-the-counter modules. Begin by placing all of the modules in their proper positions and then use tapered shims to level the cabinets and clamp them together with C-clamps (Illus. 232). When all of the modules are level and in proper alignment, attach them to each other with 1¼″ screws through the sides. Then attach the modules to the wall studs with 3″ screws through the nailing strip and along the bottom of the back (Illus. 233). If you are using plastic T moulding on the edges, install it at this point (Illus. 234).

Next, install the doors. The type of hinge used requires a 1⅜″-diameter flat-bottomed recess in the back of the door (Illus. 235). Dealers that sell the hinges usually sell a special drill bit to make the recess. First attach the hinges to the doors and then attach the mounting plates to the sides of the modules. Style-one doors are spaced ¼″ apart. They should be spaced ⅛″ from the outside of each

Illus. 232 (left). Use cedar shingles or tapered wedges to shim the bottom of the modules so that they are all even at the top and level. After shimming, tighten the C-clamp to hold the modules together while installing screws in the sides to attach them to each other. Illus. 233 (right). Attach the module to the wall with 3"-long dry-wall screws, which are driven through the nailing strip into wall studs.

module so that the combined effect is a ¼″ space. Measure for the door spacing from the edge of the board since the plastic T moulding will make the actual space between doors smaller. The hinges have three independent adjustments to square the door on the cabinet; raise or lower the door and adjust the clearance between doors. Once you have installed all of the doors, use the adjustments to line them up.

Place the drawers in their runners and then attach the drawer fronts (Illus. 236). Use 1¼″ screws to attach the drawer fronts. Align each front with the preceding one before attaching them. The sizes

Illus. 234 (left). Use a rubber mallet to tap the T moulding into the kerf. Illus. 235 (right). This specialized hinge makes the simplified construction of these cabinets possible. It pushes the door away from the side of the cabinet as it opens, providing clearance for the full overlay design of the doors. Its adjustment capabilities make it easy to line up the doors after installation. A special 35-mm drill bit is recommended for making the recess in the door.

listed in the bill of materials for the drawer fronts allow for an overhanging counter top and ¼″ gaps between drawers. Styles two and three may require tighter spacing; you can make all of the drawer fronts larger or simply make the top or bottom one larger to compensate for the difference.

Illus. 236. You need to attach the drawer fronts after the cabinets are installed and the runners are in place. This allows the fronts to be lined up with each other and the adjacent doors, and compensates for minor imperfections in runner spacing. Use four 1¼″ dry-wall screws, driven from inside the drawers, to attach the fronts. After attaching the fronts, drill the holes for drawer pulls. You will need extra-long screws for the drawer pulls because they must pass through the combined 1½″ thickness of the front.

After the doors are in place, install the trim strip or cornice at the top. Style-one cabinets are designed to reach to the ceiling. Any gap between the cabinets and the ceiling is covered by the trim strip. The width of the trim strip depends on the ceiling height; for an 8′ ceiling, the strip will be approximately 8″. Scribe the strip so that it fits the ceiling and has an even reveal along the top edge of the doors (Illus. 237). Attach the trim from behind with 1¼″ screws through the front filler of the modules.

Styles two and three are designed to have an open space between the top of the cabinet and the ceiling. To finish the top edge of the

Illus. 237. You need to use a trim strip with style-one modules to hide the space between the cabinets and the ceiling. A trim strip is made from the same material as the doors. Use plastic T moulding along its lower edge. Scribe the top edge to fit the irregularities of the ceiling. To attach the trim strip, drive 1¼" dry-wall screws through the front filler inside the cabinet into the back of the trim strip.

cabinets, apply a piece of decorative moulding as a cornice. After the cabinets are in place, you can attach on optional ¾" × 3" hardwood strip to the underside of the front edge if you want the cabinets to appear exactly as shown in Illus. 205.

COUNTER TOP

If you are using a preformed plastic laminate counter, apply a bead of panel adhesive along the counter-mounting strips and set the counter in place. Attach the counter with screws from below through the counter-mounting strips (part F). If the counter has a corner, order the mitres precut and clamp them together with the special clamps provided (see Chapter 10). Cover the exposed ends with precut end caps (see Chapter 10).

To prepare the top for ceramic tile, attach ¾" plywood to the top with panel adhesive and screws through the mounting strips (part F). You can cover the front edge with ceramic tile or apply a hardwood strip.

There are several ways you can cover the toe kick. Carpet or vinyl flooring can be coved up the walls and over the toe kick. If you have used wood moulding on the walls, you can apply it to the toe kick, or you can apply rubber base to the toe kick as shown in Illus. 238.

Illus. 238. You should cover the toe kick with the same type of moulding as you used around the rest of the room. In this case, rubber base is applied over the toe kick.

APPLIANCE GARAGES

An appliance garage is a cabinet placed on the counter to hide small kitchen appliances when they are not in use. An appliance garage is attached directly to the counter top and has no bottom so that the appliances can slide over the counter top into the garage. When you use plastic laminate for the counter top, you should install the appliance garage after the laminate is in place; if you use ceramic tile, install the garage before the tile and cut the tile to fit around the sides of the garage.

Corner Appliance Garage   The appliance garage shown in Illus. 223 and Illus. 239 is very similar to the overhead-corner module in Illus. 222. The sides (part G1) have a ¾″ × ⅜″ rabbet along the top and back. The two back pieces (parts N1 and N2) are made from ¾″-thick material to give strength to the carcass. After assembly, slide the appliance garage between the counter top and the bottom of the overhead cabinets. Attach the sides to the counter top with screws driven from the underside of the counter top. Attach the top of the garage to the underside of the overhead cabinets with screws through the top.

Illus. 239. This corner appliance garage hides small kitchen appliances and yet keeps them at counter level for easy use.

Roll-Top Appliance Garage   The tambour door is ideally suited for use on an appliance garage because it rolls completely out of the way to allow easy access to the appliances. The roll-top appliance garage, shown in Illus. 240 (photo) and in Illus. 223 (exploded view), can be made in any width up to 36″.

Begin by making the sides (part G2). Cut a template for the tambour groove from ¼″ hardboard. The template should be 11¾″ wide and 22⅛″ high. Round the two top corners to a 1½″ radius. Clamp the template to the inside surface of the side (part G2). Space the template 1⅛″ from each side and place the bottom of the template flush with the bottom of the side. Mount a template-following collar and a ¼″ bit in a router. Make a mark on the rear edge of the side 13½″ down from the top. This mark represents the end of the tambour groove. Set the router to make a ⅜″-deep cut—be sure to take into account the ¼″ thickness of the template. Position the router so that the template-following collar is against the template at the bottom-front corner. Start the router and follow the template around to the mark at the rear. Repeat this process on the other side. Remember that the sides are handed; so when they are placed together like the open covers of a book, the rear edges will be touching.

Next, cut the stopped rabbets at the top-front corner. To complete the sides, make the stopped dado at the rear.

The width of the tambour is ¾″ less than the overall width of the appliance garage. The pull strip is ¾″ thick and 1″ wide. Cut a ¼″ × ¼″ rabbet on the front and back edges of both ends. This will leave a ¼″ tongue on the end of the pull strip that will fit into the tambour groove. Rout finger pulls into the front of the pull strip. Next, cut thirty-six ¼″ × ¾″ strips to make the tambour. Refer to Chapter 8 for complete details on tambour construction. The final finished height of the tambour, including the pull strip, should be 26″.

Assemble the unit by gluing the back into the dado and installing the two strips (part L2) in the rabbets in the front corners of the sides. Slide the tambour into the groove from the opening at the bottom-front corner.

Attach the appliance garage to the counter top with screws through the counter top into the sides. Drive screws through the bottom of the overhead cabinets into the sides and front strip (part L2).

Illus. 240. The tambour door on this roll-top appliance garage rolls completely out of the way to reveal a usable work space.

Modular Cabinets

BILL OF MATERIALS
(All Dimensions Actual)

Style: 1
Type: Under-the-Counter Single Door
Size: 15"
Refer to: Illus. 207, 208, 210, and 215

Part	Description	Material	Size	No. Req'd
A	sides	¾ PLP	35¼ × 23¼	2
B	door	¾ PLP	31 × 14¾	1
C	bottom	¾ PLP	23 × 14¼	1
D	shelf	¾ PLP	23 × 13½	varies
E	back	¼ VCP	32 × 14¼	1
F	strips	¾ PLY	4 × 14¼	4

Material Key:

PLP = plastic laminate-covered particle board
VCP = vinyl-covered particle board
PLY = fir plywood

Notes:

Sides are handed. Make one left side and one right side for each module.

If counter top has an overhanging front lip, subtract lip measurement from door height. Door sizes are for use with plastic-T-moulding edging. If other edge treatment is used, modify door sizes.

Shelf sizes are for adjustable shelves, using flush-mounted metal standards. Other brackets may require more clearance. Fixed shelves should use dado joints; length will be same as part C. No shelves are used in sink modules.

If toe kick is not to be covered with base moulding, substitute PLP for PLY.

Modular Cabinets

BILL OF MATERIALS
(All Dimensions Actual)

Style: 1
Type: Under-the-Counter Single Door
Size: 18″
Refer to: Illus. 207, 208, 210, and 215

Part	Description	Material	Size	No. Req'd
A	sides	¾ PLP	35¼ × 23¼	2
B	door	¾ PLP	31 × 17¾	1
C	bottom	¾ PLP	23 × 17¼	1
D	shelf	¾ PLP	23 × 16½	varies
E	back	¼ VCP	32 × 17¼	1
F	strips	¾ PLY	4 × 17¼	4

Material Key:

PLP = plastic laminate-covered particle board
VCP = vinyl-covered particle board
PLY = fir plywood

Notes:

Sides are handed. Make one left side and one right side for each module.

If counter top has an overhanging front lip, subtract lip measurement from door height. Door sizes are for use with plastic-T-moulding edging. If other edge treatment is used, modify door sizes.

Shelf sizes are for adjustable shelves, using flush-mounted metal standards. Other brackets may require more clearance. Fixed shelves should use dado joints; length will be same as part C. No shelves are used in sink modules.

If toe kick is not to be covered with base moulding, substitute PLP for PLY.

Modular Cabinets

BILL OF MATERIALS
(All Dimensions Actual)

Style: 1
Type: Under-the-Counter Double Door
Size: 24″
Refer to: Illus. 207, 208, 210, and 216

Part	Description	Material	Size	No. Req'd
A	sides	¾ PLP	35¼ × 23¼	2
B	door	¾ PLP	31 × 11¾	2
C	bottom	¾ PLP	23 × 23¼	1
D	shelf	¾ PLP	23 × 22½	varies
E	back	¼ VCP	32 × 23¼	1
F	strips	¾ PLY	4 × 23¼	4

Material Key:

PLP = plastic laminate-covered particle board
VCP = vinyl-covered particle board
PLY = fir plywood

Notes:

Sides are handed. Make one left side and one right side for each module.

If counter top has an overhanging front lip, subtract lip measurement from door height. Door sizes are for use with plastic-T-moulding edging. If other edge treatment is used, modify door sizes.

Shelf sizes are for adjustable shelves, using flush-mounted metal standards. Other brackets may require more clearance. Fixed shelves should use dado joints; length will be same as part C. No shelves are used in sink modules.

If toe kick is not to be covered with base moulding, substitute PLP for PLY.

Modular Cabinets

BILL OF MATERIALS
(All Dimensions Actual)

Style: 1
Type: Under-the-Counter Double Door
Size: 30″
Refer to: Illus. 207, 208, 210, and 216

Part	Description	Material	Size	No. Req'd
A	sides	¾ PLP	35¼ × 23¼	2
B	door	¾ PLP	31 × 14¾	2
C	bottom	¾ PLP	23 × 29¼	1
D	shelf	¾ PLP	23 × 28½	varies
E	back	¼ VCP	32 × 29¼	1
F	strips	¾ PLY	4 × 29¼	4

Material Key:

PLP = plastic laminate-covered particle board
VCP = vinyl-covered particle board
PLY = fir plywood

Notes:

Sides are handed. Make one left side and one right side for each module.

If counter top has an overhanging front lip, subtract lip measurement from door height. Door sizes are for use with plastic-T-moulding edging. If other edge treatment is used, modify door sizes.

Shelf sizes are for adjustable shelves, using flush-mounted metal standards. Other brackets may require more clearance. Fixed shelves should use dado joints; length will be same as part C. No shelves are used in sink modules.

If toe kick is not to be covered with base moulding, substitute PLP for PLY.

Modular Cabinets

BILL OF MATERIALS
(All Dimensions Actual)

Style: 1
Type: Under-the-Counter Double Door
Size: 36″
Refer to: Illus. 207, 208, 210, and 216

Part	Description	Material	Size	No. Req'd
A	sides	¾ PLP	35¼ × 23¼	2
B	door	¾ PLP	31 × 17¾	2
C	bottom	¾ PLP	23 × 35¼	1
D	shelf	¾ PLP	23 × 34½	varies
E	back	¼ VCP	32 × 35¼	1
F	strips	¾ PLY	4 × 35¼	4

Material Key:

PLP = plastic laminate-covered particle board
VCP = vinyl-covered particle board
PLY = fir plywood

Notes:

Sides are handed. Make one left side and one right side for each module.

If counter top has an overhanging front lip, subtract lip measurement from door height. Door sizes are for use with plastic-T-moulding edging. If other edge treatment is used, modify door sizes.

Shelf sizes are for adjustable shelves, using flush-mounted metal standards. Other brackets may require more clearance. Fixed shelves should use dado joints; length will be same as part C. No shelves are used in sink modules.

If toe kick is not to be covered with base moulding, substitute PLP for PLY.

Modular Cabinets

BILL OF MATERIALS
(All Dimensions Actual)

Style: 1
Type: Under-the-Counter Drawer Module
Size: 15″
Refer to: Illus. 207, 208, 210, and 217

Part	Description	Material	Size	No. Req'd
A	sides	¾ PB	35¼ × 23¼	2
C	bottom	¾ PB	23 × 14¼	1
E	back	¼ OSB	32 × 14¼	1
F	strips	¾ PLY	4 × 14¼	4

Material Key:
PLP = plastic laminate-covered particle board
PLY = fir plywood
PB = particle board
OSB = oriented strand board

Notes:
Sides are handed. Make one left side and one right side for each module.

If sides will show, substitute PLP for PB.

If toe kick is not to be covered with base moulding, substitute PLP for PLY.

Modular Cabinets

BILL OF MATERIALS
(All Dimensions Actual)

Style: 1
Type: Under-the-Counter Drawer Module
Size: 18″
Refer to: Illus. 207, 208, 210, and 217

Part	Description	Material	Size	No. Req'd
A	sides	¾ PB	35¼ × 23¼	2
C	bottom	¾ PB	23 × 17¼	1
E	back	¼ OSB	32 × 17¼	1
F	strips	¾ PLY	4 × 17¼	4

Material Key:

PLP = plastic laminate-covered particle board
PLY = fir plywood
PB = particle board
OSB = oriented strand board

Notes:

Sides are handed. Make one left side and one right side for each module.

If sides will show, substitute PLP for PB.

If toe kick is not to be covered with base moulding, substitute PLP for PLY.

Modular Cabinets

BILL OF MATERIALS
(All Dimensions Actual)

Style: 1
Type: Bathroom Vanity Single Door
Size: 15"
Refer to: Illus. 207, 208, 210, and 215

Part	Description	Material	Size	No. Req'd
A	sides	¾ PLP	31¼ × 20¼	2
B	door	¾ PLP	27 × 14¾	1
C	bottom	¾ PLP	20 × 14¼	1
D	shelf	¾ PLP	20 × 13½	varies
E	back	¼ VCP	28 × 14¼	1
F	strips	¾ PLY	4 × 14¼	4

Material Key:

PLP = plastic laminate-covered particle board
VCP = vinyl-covered particle board
PLY = fir plywood

Notes:

Sides are handed. Make one left side and one right side for each module.

If counter top has an overhanging front lip, subtract lip measurement from door height. Door sizes are for use with plastic-T-moulding edging. If other edge treatment is used, modify door sizes.

Shelf sizes are for adjustable shelves, using flush-mounted metal standards. Other brackets may require more clearance. Fixed shelves should use dado joints; length will be same as part C. No shelves are used in sink modules.

If toe kick is not to be covered with base moulding, substitute PLP for PLY.

Modular Cabinets

BILL OF MATERIALS
(All Dimensions Actual)

Style: 1
Type: Bathroom Vanity Single Door
Size: 18″
Refer to: Illus. 207, 208, 210, and 215

Part	Description	Material	Size	No. Req'd
A	sides	¾ PLP	31¼ × 20¼	2
B	door	¾ PLP	27 × 17¾	1
C	bottom	¾ PLP	20 × 17¼	1
D	shelf	¾ PLP	20 × 16½	varies
E	back	¼ VCP	28 × 17¼	1
F	strips	¾ PLY	4 × 17¼	4

Material Key:

PLP = plastic laminate-covered particle board
VCP = vinyl-covered particle board
PLY = fir plywood

Notes:

Sides are handed. Make one left side and one right side for each module.

If counter top has an overhanging front lip, subtract lip measurement from door height. Door sizes are for use with plastic-T-moulding edging. If other edge treatment is used, modify door sizes.

Shelf sizes are for adjustable shelves, using flush-mounted metal standards. Other brackets may require more clearance. Fixed shelves should use dado joints; length will be same as part C. No shelves are used in sink modules.

If toe kick is not to be covered with base moulding, substitute PLP for PLY.

Modular Cabinets

BILL OF MATERIALS
(All Dimensions Actual)

Style: 1
Type: Bathroom Vanity Double Door
Size: 24″
Refer to: Illus. 207, 208, 210, and 216

Part	Description	Material	Size	No. Req'd
A	sides	¾ PLP	31¼ × 20¼	2
B	door	¾ PLP	27 × 11¾	2
C	bottom	¾ PLP	20 × 23¼	1
D	shelf	¾ PLP	20 × 22½	varies
E	back	¼ VCP	28 × 23¼	1
F	strips	¾ PLY	4 × 23¼	4

Material Key:

PLP = plastic laminate-covered particle board
VCP = vinyl-covered particle board
PLY = fir plywood

Notes:

Sides are handed. Make one left side and one right side for each module.

If counter top has an overhanging front lip, subtract lip measurement from door height. Door sizes are for use with plastic-T-moulding edging. If other edge treatment is used, modify door sizes.

Shelf sizes are for adjustable shelves, using flush-mounted metal standards. Other brackets may require more clearance. Fixed shelves should use dado joints; length will be same as part C. No shelves are used in sink modules.

If toe kick is not to be covered with base moulding, substitute PLP for PLY.

Modular Cabinets

BILL OF MATERIALS
(All Dimensions Actual)

Style: 1
Type: Bathroom Vanity Double Door
Size: 30″
Refer to: Illus. 207, 208, 210, and 216

Part	Description	Material	Size	No. Req'd
A	sides	¾ PLP	31¼ × 20¼	2
B	door	¾ PLP	27 × 14¾	2
C	bottom	¾ PLP	20 × 29¼	1
D	shelf	¾ PLP	20 × 28½	varies
E	back	¼ VCP	28 × 29¼	1
F	strips	¾ PLY	4 × 29¼	4

Material Key:
PLP = plastic laminate-covered particle board
VCP = vinyl-covered particle board
PLY = fir plywood

Notes:
Sides are handed. Make one left side and one right side for each module.

If counter top has an overhanging front lip, subtract lip measurement from door height. Door sizes are for use with plastic-T-moulding edging. If other edge treatment is used, modify door sizes.

Shelf sizes are for adjustable shelves, using flush-mounted metal standards. Other brackets may require more clearance. Fixed shelves should use dado joints; length will be same as part C. No shelves are used in sink modules.

If toe kick is not to be covered with base moulding, substitute PLP for PLY.

Modular Cabinets

BILL OF MATERIALS
(All Dimensions Actual)

Style: 1
Type: Bathroom Vanity Double Door
Size: 36″
Refer to: Illus. 207, 208, 210, and 216

Part	Description	Material	Size	No. Req'd
A	sides	¾ PLP	31¼ × 20¼	2
B	door	¾ PLP	27 × 17¾	2
C	bottom	¾ PLP	20 × 35¼	1
D	shelf	¾ PLP	20 × 34½	varies
E	back	¼ VCP	28 × 35¼	1
F	strips	¾ PLY	4 × 35¼	4

Material Key:

PLP = plastic laminate-covered particle board
VCP = vinyl-covered particle board
PLY = fir plywood

Notes:

Sides are handed. Make one left side and one right side for each module.

If counter top has an overhanging front lip, subtract lip measurement from door height. Door sizes are for use with plastic-T-moulding edging. If other edge treatment is used, modify door sizes.

Shelf sizes are for adjustable shelves, using flush-mounted metal standards. Other brackets may require more clearance. Fixed shelves should use dado joints; length will be same as part C. No shelves are used in sink modules.

If toe kick is not to be covered with base moulding, substitute PLP for PLY.

Modular Cabinets

BILL OF MATERIALS
(All Dimensions Actual)

Style: 1
Type: Bathroom Vanity Drawer Module
Size: 15"
Refer to: Illus. 207, 208, 210, and 217

Part	Description	Material	Size	No. Req'd
A	sides	¾ PB	31¼ × 20¼	2
C	bottom	¾ PB	20 × 14¼	1
E	back	¼ OSB	28 × 14¼	1
F	strips	¾ PLY	4 × 14¼	4

Material Key:

PLP = plastic laminate-covered particle board
PLY = fir plywood
PB = particle board
OSB = oriented strand board

Notes:

Sides are handed. Make one left side and one right side for each module.

If sides will show, substitute PLP for PB.

If toe kick is not to be covered with base moulding, substitute PLP for PLY.

Modular Cabinets

BILL OF MATERIALS
(All Dimensions Actual)

Style: 1
Type: Bathroom Vanity Drawer Module
Size: 18″
Refer to: Illus. 207, 208, 210, and 217

Part	Description	Material	Size	No. Req'd
A	sides	¾ PB	31¼ × 20¼	2
C	bottom	¾ PB	20 × 17¼	1
E	back	¼ OSB	28 × 17¼	1
F	strips	¾ PLY	4 × 17¼	4

Material Key:

PLP = plastic laminate-cover particle board
PLY = fir plywood
PB   = particle board
OSB = oriented strand board

Notes:

Sides are handed. Make one left side and one right side for each module.

If sides will show, substitute PLP for PB.

If toe kick is not to be covered with base moulding, substitute PLP for PLY.

Modular Cabinets

BILL OF MATERIALS
(All Dimensions Actual)

Style: 1
Type: Overhead Long Module
Size: 15″
Refer to: Illus. 207, 208, 210, and 219

Part	Description	Material	Size	No. Req'd
G	sides	¾ PLP	35 × 14	2
H	door	¾ PLP	28 × 14¾	1
I	top	¾ PLP	13¾ × 14¼	1
J	bottom	¾ PLP	14 × 14¼	1
K	shelf	¾ PLP	13¾ × 13½	varies
L	front filler	¾ PLP	7¼ × 14¼	1
M	nailing strip	¾ PLP	4 × 14¼	1
N	back	¼ VCP	34⅝ × 14¼	1

Material Key:

PLP = plastic laminate-covered particle board
VCP = vinyl-covered particle board

Notes:

Sides are handed. Make one left side and one right side for each module.

Shelf sizes are for adjustable shelves, using flush-mounted metal standards. Other brackets may require more clearance. Fixed shelves should use dado joints; length will be same as part J.

Door sizes are for use with plastic-T-moulding edging. If other edge treatment is used, modify door sizes.

Modular Cabinets

BILL OF MATERIALS
(All Dimensions Actual)

Style: 1
Type: Overhead Long Module
Size: 18″
Refer to: Illus. 207, 208, 210, and 219

Part	Description	Material	Size	No. Req'd
G	sides	¾ PLP	35 × 14	2
H	door	¾ PLP	28 × 17¾	1
I	top	¾ PLP	13¾ × 17¼	1
J	bottom	¾ PLP	14 × 17¼	1
K	shelf	¾ PLP	13¾ × 16½	varies
L	front filler	¾ PLP	7¼ × 17¼	1
M	nailing strip	¾ PLP	4 × 17¼	1
N	back	¼ VCP	34⅝ × 17¼	1

Material Key:

PLP = plastic laminate-covered particle board
VCP = vinyl-covered particle board

Notes:

Sides are handed. Make one left side and one right side for each module.

Shelf sizes are for adjustable shelves, using flush-mounted metal standards. Other brackets may require more clearance. Fixed shelves should use dado joints; length will be same as part J.

Door sizes are for use with plastic-T-moulding edging. If other edge treatment is used, modify door sizes.

Modular Cabinets

BILL OF MATERIALS
(All Dimensions Actual)

Style: 1
Type: Overhead Long Module
Size: 24″
Refer to: Illus. 207, 208, 210, and 219

Part	Description	Material	Size	No. Req'd
G	sides	¾ PLP	35 × 14	2
H	door	¾ PLP	28 × 11¾	2
I	top	¾ PLP	13¾ × 23¼	1
J	bottom	¾ PLP	14 × 23¼	1
K	shelf	¾ PLP	13¾ × 22½	varies
L	front filler	¾ PLP	7¼ × 23¼	1
M	nailing strip	¾ PLP	4 × 23¼	1
N	back	¼ VCP	34⅝ × 23¼	1

Material Key:

PLP = plastic laminate-covered particle board
VCP = vinyl-covered particle board

Notes:

Sides are handed. Make one left side and one right side for each module.

Shelf sizes are for adjustable shelves, using flush-mounted metal standards. Other brackets may require more clearance. Fixed shelves should use dado joints; length will be same as part J.

Door sizes are for use with plastic-T-moulding edging. If other edge treatment is used, modify door sizes.

Modular Cabinets

BILL OF MATERIALS
(All Dimensions Actual)

Style: 1
Type: Overhead Long Module
Size: 30″
Refer to: Illus. 207, 208, 210, and 219

Part	Description	Material	Size	No. Req'd
G	sides	¾ PLP	35 × 14	2
H	door	¾ PLP	28 × 14¾	2
I	top	¾ PLP	13¾ × 29¼	1
J	bottom	¾ PLP	14 × 29¼	1
K	shelf	¾ PLP	13¾ × 28½	varies
L	front filler	¾ PLP	7¼ × 29¼	1
M	nailing strip	¾ PLP	4 × 29¼	1
N	back	¼ VCP	34⅝ × 29¼	1

Material Key:

PLP = plastic laminate-covered particle board
VCP = vinyl-covered particle board

Notes:

Sides are handed. Make one left side and one right side for each module.

Shelf sizes are for adjustable shelves, using flush-mounted metal standards. Other brackets may require more clearance. Fixed shelves should use dado joints; length will be same as part J.

Door sizes are for use with plastic-T-moulding edging. If other edge treatment is used, modify door sizes.

Modular Cabinets

BILL OF MATERIALS
(All Dimensions Actual)

Style: 1
Type: Overhead Long Module
Size: 36″
Refer to: Illus. 207, 208, 210, and 219

Part	Description	Material	Size	No. Req'd
G	sides	¾ PLP	35 × 14	2
H	door	¾ PLP	28 × 17¾	2
I	top	¾ PLP	13¾ × 35¼	1
J	bottom	¾ PLP	14 × 35¼	1
K	shelf	¾ PLP	13¾ × 34½	varies
L	front filler	¾ PLP	7¼ × 35¼	1
M	nailing strip	¾ PLP	4 × 35¼	1
N	back	¼ VCP	34⅝ × 35¼	1

Material Key:

PLP = plastic laminate-covered particle board
VCP = vinyl-covered particle board

Notes:

Sides are handed. Make one left side and one right side for each module.

Shelf sizes are for adjustable shelves, using flush-mounted metal standards. Other brackets may require more clearance. Fixed shelves should use dado joints; length will be same as part J.

Door sizes are for use with plastic-T-moulding edging. If other edge treatment is used, modify door sizes.

Modular Cabinets

BILL OF MATERIALS
(All Dimensions Actual)

Style: 1
Type: Overhead Short Module
Size: 15″
Refer to: Illus. 207, 208, 210, and 219

Part	Description	Material	Size	No. Req'd
G	sides	¾ PLP	25 × 14	2
H	door	¾ PLP	18 × 14¾	1
I	top	¾ PLP	13¾ × 14¼	1
J	bottom	¾ PLP	14 × 14¼	1
K	shelf	¾ PLP	13¾ × 13½	varies
L	front filler	¾ PLP	7¼ × 14¼	1
M	nailing strip	¾ PLP	4 × 14¼	1
N	back	¼ VCP	24⅝ × 14¼	1

Material Key:
PLP = plastic laminate-covered particle board
VCP = vinyl-covered particle board

Notes:
Sides are handed. Make one left side and one right side for each module.

Shelf sizes are for adjustable shelves, using flush-mounted metal standards. Other brackets may require more clearance. Fixed shelves should use dado joints; length will be same as part J.

Door sizes are for use with plastic-T-moulding edging. If other edge treatment is used, modify door sizes.

Modular Cabinets

BILL OF MATERIALS
(All Dimensions Actual)

Style: 1
Type: Overhead Short Module
Size: 18″
Refer to: Illus. 207, 208, 210, and 219

Part	Description	Material	Size	No. Req'd
G	sides	¾ PLP	25 × 14	2
H	door	¾ PLP	18 × 17¾	1
I	top	¾ PLP	13¾ × 17¼	1
J	bottom	¾ PLP	14 × 17¼	1
K	shelf	¾ PLP	13¾ × 16½	varies
L	front filler	¾ PLP	7¼ × 17¼	1
M	nailing strip	¾ PLP	4 × 17¼	1
N	back	¼ VCP	24⅝ × 17¼	1

Material Key:

PLP = plastic laminate-covered particle board
VCP = vinyl-covered particle board

Notes:

Sides are handed. Make one left side and one right side for each module.

Shelf sizes are for adjustable shelves, using flush-mounted metal standards. Other brackets may require more clearance. Fixed shelves should use dado joints; length will be same as part J.

Door sizes are for use with plastic-T-moulding edging. If other edge treatment is used, modify door sizes.

Modular Cabinets

BILL OF MATERIALS
(All Dimensions Actual)

Style: 1
Type: Overhead Short Module
Size: 24″
Refer to: Illus. 207, 208, 210, and 219

Part	Description	Material	Size	No. Req'd
G	sides	¾ PLP	25 × 14	2
H	door	¾ PLP	18 × 11¾	2
I	top	¾ PLP	13¾ × 23¼	1
J	bottom	¾ PLP	14 × 23¼	1
K	shelf	¾ PLP	13¾ × 22½	varies
L	front filler	¾ PLP	7¼ × 23¼	1
M	nailing strip	¾ PLP	4 × 23¼	1
N	back	¼ VCP	24⅝ × 23¼	1

Material Key:
PLP = plastic laminate-covered particle board
VCP = vinyl-covered particle board

Notes:
Sides are handed. Make one left side and one right side for each module.

Shelf sizes are for adjustable shelves, using flush-mounted metal standards. Other brackets may require more clearance. Fixed shelves should use dado joints; length will be same as part J.

Door sizes are for use with plastic-T-moulding edging. If other edge treatment is used, modify door sizes.

Modular Cabinets

BILL OF MATERIALS
(All Dimensions Actual)

Style: 1
Type: Overhead Short Module
Size: 30″
Refer to: Illus. 207, 208, 210, and 219

Part	Description	Material	Size	No. Req'd
G	sides	¾ PLP	25 × 14	2
H	door	¾ PLP	18 × 14¾	2
I	top	¾ PLP	13¾ × 29¼	1
J	bottom	¾ PLP	14 × 29¼	1
K	shelf	¾ PLP	13¾ × 28½	varies
L	front filler	¾ PLP	7¼ × 29¼	1
M	nailing strip	¾ PLP	4 × 29¼	1
N	back	¼ VCP	24⅝ × 29¼	1

Material Key:

PLP = plastic laminate-covered particle board
VCP = vinyl-covered particle board

Notes:

Sides are handed. Make one left side and one right side for each module.

Shelf sizes are for adjustable shelves, using flush-mounted metal standards. Other brackets may require more clearance. Fixed shelves should use dado joints; length will be same as part J.

Door sizes are for use with plastic-T-moulding edging. If other edge treatment is used, modify door sizes.

Modular Cabinets

BILL OF MATERIALS
(All Dimensions Actual)

Style: 1
Type: Overhead Short Module
Size: 36″
Refer to: Illus. 207, 208, 210, and 219

Part	Description	Material	Size	No. Req'd
G	sides	¾ PLP	25 × 14	2
H	door	¾ PLP	18 × 17¾	2
I	top	¾ PLP	13¾ × 35¼	1
J	bottom	¾ PLP	14 × 35¼	1
K	shelf	¾ PLP	13¾ × 34½	varies
L	front filler	¾ PLP	7¼ × 35¼	1
M	nailing strip	¾ PLP	4 × 35¼	1
N	back	¼ VCP	24⅝ × 35¼	1

Material Key:

PLP = plastic laminate-covered particle board
VCP = vinyl-covered particle board

Notes:

Sides are handed. Make one left side and one right side for each module.

Shelf sizes are for adjustable shelves, using flush-mounted metal standards. Other brackets may require more clearance. Fixed shelves should use dado joints; length will be same as part J.

Door sizes are for use with plastic-T-moulding edging. If other edge treatment is used, modify door sizes.

Modular Cabinets

BILL OF MATERIALS
(All Dimensions Actual)

Style: 2
Type: Under-the-Counter Single Door
Size: 15″
Refer to: Illus. 207, 208, 211, and 215

Part	Description	Material	Size	No. Req'd
A	sides	¾ PLP	35¼ × 23¼	2
B	door	¾ PLP	31 × 15	1
C	bottom	¾ PLP	23 × 14¼	1
D	shelf	¾ PLP	23 × 13½	varies
E	back	¼ VCP	32 × 14¼	1
F	strips	¾ PLY	4 × 14¼	4
U	side panel	¾ PLP	31 × 23¼	varies

Material Key:

PLP = plastic laminate-covered particle board
VCP = vinyl-covered particle board
PLY = fir plywood

Notes:
Sides are handed. Make one left side and one right side for each module.

Door sizes are finished-size with mouldings applied; subtract moulding widths to get cutting size.

If counter top has an overhanging front lip, subtract lip measurement from door height.

Shelf sizes are for adjustable shelves, using flush-mounted metal standards. Other brackets may require more clearance. Fixed shelves should use dado joints; length will be same as part C. No shelves are used in sink modules.

If toe kick is not to be covered with base moulding, substitute PLP for PLY.

Modular Cabinets

BILL OF MATERIALS
(All Dimensions Actual)

Style: 2
Type: Under-the-Counter Single Door
Size: 18″
Refer to: Illus. 207, 208, 211, and 215

Part	Description	Material	Size	No. Req'd
A	sides	¾ PLP	35¼ × 23¼	2
B	door	¾ PLP	31 × 18	1
C	bottom	¾ PLP	23 × 17¼	1
D	shelf	¾ PLP	23 × 16½	varies
E	back	¼ VCP	32 × 17¼	1
F	strips	¾ PLY	4 × 17¼	4
U	side panel	¾ PLP	31 × 23¼	varies

Material Key:

PLP = plastic laminate-covered particle board
VCP = vinyl-covered particle board
PLY = fir plywood

Notes:

Sides are handed. Make one left side and one right side for each module.

Door sizes are finished-size with mouldings applied; subtract moulding widths to get cutting size.

If counter top has an overhanging front lip, subtract lip measurement from door height.

Shelf sizes are for adjustable shelves, using flush-mounted metal standards. Other brackets may require more clearance. Fixed shelves should use dado joints; length will be same as part C. No shelves are used in sink modules.

If toe kick is not to be covered with base moulding, substitute PLP for PLY.

Modular Cabinets

BILL OF MATERIALS
(All Dimensions Actual)

Style: 2
Type: Under-the-Counter Double Door
Size: 24″
Refer to: Illus. 207, 208, 211, and 216

Part	Description	Material	Size	No. Req'd
A	sides	¾ PLP	35¼ × 23¼	2
B	door	¾ PLP	31 × 12	2
C	bottom	¾ PLP	23 × 23¼	1
D	shelf	¾ PLP	23 × 22½	varies
E	back	¼ VCP	32 × 23¼	1
F	strips	¾ PLY	4 × 23¼	4
U	side panel	¾ PLP	31 × 23¼	varies

Material Key:

PLP = plastic laminate-covered particle board
VCP = vinyl-covered particle board
PLY = fir plywood

Notes:

Sides are handed. Make one left side and one right side for each module.

Door sizes are finished-size with mouldings applied; subtract moulding widths to get cutting size.

If counter top has an overhanging front lip, subtract lip measurement from door height.

Shelf sizes are for adjustable shelves, using flush-mounted metal standards. Other brackets may require more clearance. Fixed shelves should use dado joints; length will be same as part C. No shelves are used in sink modules.

If toe kick is not to be covered with base moulding, substitute PLP for PLY.

Modular Cabinets

BILL OF MATERIALS
(All Dimensions Actual)

Style: 2
Type: Under-the-Counter Double Door
Size: 30″
Refer to: Illus. 207, 208, 211, and 216

Part	Description	Material	Size	No. Req'd
A	sides	¾ PLP	35¼ × 23¼	2
B	door	¾ PLP	31 × 15	2
C	bottom	¾ PLP	23 × 29¼	1
D	shelf	¾ PLP	23 × 28½	varies
E	back	¼ VCP	32 × 29¼	1
F	strips	¾ PLY	4 × 29¼	4
U	side panel	¾ PLP	31 × 23¼	varies

Material Key:
PLP = plastic laminate-covered particle board
VCP = vinyl-covered particle board
PLY = fir plywood

Notes:
Sides are handed. Make one left side and one right side for each module.

Door sizes are finished-size with mouldings applied; subtract moulding widths to get cutting size.

If counter top has an overhanging front lip, subtract lip measurement from door height.

Shelf sizes are for adjustable shelves, using flush-mounted metal standards. Other brackets may require more clearance. Fixed shelves should use dado joints; length will be same as part C. No shelves are used in sink modules.

If toe kick is not to be covered with base moulding, substitute PLP for PLY.

Modular Cabinets

BILL OF MATERIALS
(All Dimensions Actual)

Style: 2
Type: Under-the-Counter Double Door
Size: 36″
Refer to: Illus. 207, 208, 211, and 216

Part	Description	Material	Size	No. Req'd
A	sides	¾ PLP	35¼ × 23¼	2
B	door	¾ PLP	31 × 18	2
C	bottom	¾ PLP	23 × 35¼	1
D	shelf	¾ PLP	23 × 34½	varies
E	back	¼ VCP	32 × 35¼	1
F	strips	¾ PLY	4 × 35¼	4
U	side panel	¾ PLP	31 × 23¼	varies

Material Key:

PLP = plastic laminate-covered particle board
VCP = vinyl-covered particle board
PLY = fir plywood

Notes:

Sides are handed. Make one left side and one right side for each module.

Door sizes are finished-size with mouldings applied; subtract moulding widths to get cutting size.

If counter top has an overhanging front lip, subtract lip measurement from door height.

Shelf sizes are for adjustable shelves, using flush-mounted metal standards. Other brackets may require more clearance. Fixed shelves should use dado joints; length will be same as part C. No shelves are used in sink modules.

If toe kick is not to be covered with base moulding, substitute PLP for PLY.

Modular Cabinets

BILL OF MATERIALS
(All Dimensions Actual)

Style: 2
Type: Under-the-Counter Drawer Module
Size: 15″
Refer to: Illus. 207, 208, 211, and 217

Part	Description	Material	Size	No. Req'd
A	sides	¾ PB	35¼ × 23¼	2
C	bottom	¾ PB	23 × 14¼	1
E	back	¼ OSB	32 × 14¼	1
F	strips	¾ PLY	4 × 14¼	4
U	side panel	¾ PLP	31 × 23¼	varies

Material Key:

PLP = plastic laminate-covered particle board
PLY = fir plywood
PB = particle board
OSB = oriented strand board

Notes:

Sides are handed. Make one left side and one right side for each module.

If toe kick is not to be covered with base moulding, substitute PLP for PLY.

Modular Cabinets

BILL OF MATERIALS
(All Dimensions Actual)

Style: 2
Type: Under-the-Counter Drawer Module
Size: 18″
Refer to: Illus. 207, 208, 211, and 217

Part	Description	Material	Size	No. Req'd
A	sides	¾ PB	35¼ × 23¼	2
C	bottom	¾ PB	23 × 17¼	1
E	back	¼ OSB	32 × 17¼	1
F	strips	¾ PLY	4 × 17¼	4
U	side panel	¾ PLP	31 × 23¼	varies

Material Key:

PLP = plastic laminate-covered particle board
PLY = fir plywood
PB = particle board
OSB = oriented strand board

Notes:

Sides are handed. Make one left side and one right side for each module.

If toe kick is not to be covered with base moulding, substitute PLP for PLY.

Modular Cabinets

BILL OF MATERIALS
(All Dimensions Actual)

Style: 2
Type: Bathroom Vanity Single Door
Size: 15″
Refer to: Illus. 207, 208, 211, and 215

Part	Description	Material	Size	No. Req'd
A	sides	¾ PLP	31¼ × 20¼	2
B	door	¾ PLP	27 × 15	1
C	bottom	¾ PLP	20 × 14¼	1
D	shelf	¾ PLP	20 × 13½	varies
E	back	¼ VCP	28 × 14¼	1
F	strips	¾ PLY	4 × 14¼	4
U	side panel	¾ PLP	27 × 20¼	varies

Material Key:

PLP = plastic laminate-covered particle board
VCP = vinyl-covered particle board
PLY = fir plywood

Notes:

Sides are handed. Make one left side and one right side for each module.

Door sizes are finished-size with mouldings applied; subtract moulding widths to get cutting size.

If counter top has an overhanging front lip, subtract lip measurement from door height.

Shelf sizes are for adjustable shelves using flush-mounted metal standards. Other brackets may require more clearance. Fixed shelves should use dado joints; length will be same as part C. No shelves are used in sink modules.

If toe kick is not to be covered with base moulding, substitute PLP for PLY.

Modular Cabinets

BILL OF MATERIALS
(All Dimensions Actual)

Style: 2
Type: Bathroom Vanity Single Door
Size: 18″
Refer to: Illus. 207, 208, 211, and 215

Part	Description	Material	Size	No. Req'd
A	sides	¾ PLP	31¼ × 20¼	2
B	door	¾ PLP	27 × 18	1
C	bottom	¾ PLP	20 × 17¼	1
D	shelf	¾ PLP	20 × 16½	varies
E	back	¼ VCP	28 × 17¼	1
F	strips	¾ PLY	4 × 17¼	4
U	side panel	¾ PLP	27 × 20¼	varies

Material Key:
PLP = plastic laminate-covered particle board
VCP = vinyl-covered particle board
PLY = fir plywood

Notes:
Sides are handed. Make one left side and one right side for each module.

Door sizes are finished-size with mouldings applied; subtract moulding widths to get cutting size.

If counter top has an overhanging front lip, subtract lip measurement from door height.

Shelf sizes are for adjustable shelves, using flush-mounted metal standards. Other brackets may require more clearance. Fixed shelves should use dado joints; length will be same as part C. No shelves are used in sink modules.

If toe kick is not to be covered with base moulding, substitute PLP for PLY.

Modular Cabinets

BILL OF MATERIALS
(All Dimensions Actual)

Style: 2
Type: Bathroom Vanity Double Door
Size: 24″
Refer to: Illus. 207, 208, 211, and 216

Part	Description	Material	Size	No. Req'd
A	sides	¾ PLP	31¼ × 20¼	2
B	door	¾ PLP	27 × 12	2
C	bottom	¾ PLP	20 × 23¼	1
D	shelf	¾ PLP	20 × 22½	varies
E	back	¼ VCP	28 × 23¼	1
F	strips	¾ PLY	4 × 23¼	4
U	side panel	¾ PLP	27 × 20¼	varies

Material Key:
PLP = plastic laminate-covered particle board
VCP = vinyl-covered particle board
PLY = fir plywood

Notes:
Sides are handed. Make one left side and one right side for each module.

Door sizes are finished-size with mouldings applied; subtract moulding widths to get cutting size.

If counter top has an overhanging front lip, subtract lip measurement from door height.

Shelf sizes are for adjustable shelves, using flush-mounted metal standards. Other brackets may require more clearance. Fixed shelves should use dado joints; length will be same as part C. No shelves are used in sink modules.

If toe kick is not to be covered with base moulding, substitute PLP for PLY.

Modular Cabinets

BILL OF MATERIALS
(All Dimensions Actual)

Style: 2
Type: Bathroom Vanity Double Door
Size: 30″
Refer to: Illus. 207, 208, 211, and 216

Part	Description	Material	Size	No. Req'd
A	sides	¾ PLP	31¼ × 20¼	2
B	door	¾ PLP	27 × 15	2
C	bottom	¾ PLP	20 × 29¼	1
D	shelf	¾ PLP	20 × 28½	varies
E	back	¼ VCP	28 × 29¼	1
F	strips	¾ PLY	4 × 29¼	4
U	side panel	¾ PLP	27 × 20¼	varies

Material Key:

PLP = plastic laminate-covered particle board
VCP = vinyl-covered particle board
PLY = fir plywood

Notes:

Sides are handed. Make one left side and one right side for each module.

Door sizes are finished-size with mouldings applied; subtract moulding widths to get cutting size.

If counter top has an overhanging front lip, subtract lip measurement from door height.

Shelf sizes are for adjustable shelves, using flush-mounted metal standards. Other brackets may require more clearance. Fixed shelves should use dado joints; length will be same as part C. No shelves are used in sink modules.

If toe kick is not to be covered with base moulding, substitute PLP for PLY.

Modular Cabinets

BILL OF MATERIALS
(All Dimensions Actual)

Style: 2
Type: Bathroom Vanity Double Door
Size: 36″
Refer to: Illus. 207, 208, 211, and 216

Part	Description	Material	Size	No. Req'd
A	sides	¾ PLP	31¼ × 20¼	2
B	door	¾ PLP	27 × 18	2
C	bottom	¾ PLP	20 × 35¼	1
D	shelf	¾ PLP	20 × 34½	varies
E	back	¼ VCP	28 × 35¼	1
F	strips	¾ PLY	4 × 35¼	4
U	side panel	¾ PLP	27 × 20¼	varies

Material Key:

PLP = plastic laminate-covered particle board
VCP = vinyl-covered particle board
PLY = fir plywood

Notes:

Sides are handed. Make one left side and one right side for each module.

Door sizes are finished-size with mouldings applied; subtract moulding widths to get cutting size.

If counter top has an overhanging front lip, subtract lip measurement from door height.

Shelf sizes are for adjustable shelves, using flush-mounted metal standards. Other brackets may require more clearance. Fixed shelves should use dado joints; length will be same as part C. No shelves are used in sink modules.

If toe kick is not to be covered with base moulding, substitute PLP for PLY.

Modular Cabinets

BILL OF MATERIALS
(All Dimensions Actual)

Style: 2
Type: Bathroom Vanity Drawer Module
Size: 15″
Refer to: Illus. 207, 208, 211, and 217

Part	Description	Material	Size	No. Req'd
A	sides	¾ PB	31¼ × 20¼	2
C	bottom	¾ PB	20 × 14¼	1
E	back	¼ OSB	28 × 14¼	1
F	strips	¾ PLY	4 × 14¼	4
U	side panel	¾ PLP	27 × 20¼	varies

Material Key:

PLP = plastic laminate-covered particle board
PLY = fir plywood
PB = particle board
OSB = oriented strand board

Notes:

Sides are handed. Make one left side and one right side for each module.

If toe kick is not to be covered with base moulding, substitute PLP for PLY

Modular Cabinets

BILL OF MATERIALS
(All Dimensions Actual)

Style: 2
Type: Bathroom Vanity Drawer Module
Size: 18″
Refer to: Illus. 207, 208, 211, and 217

Part	Description	Material	Size	No. Req'd
A	sides	¾ PB	31¼ × 20¼	2
C	bottom	¾ PB	20 × 17¼	1
E	back	¼ OSB	28 × 17¼	1
F	strips	¾ PLY	4 × 17¼	4
U	side panel	¾ PLP	27 × 20¼	varies

Material Key:

PLP = plastic laminate-covered particle board
PLY = fir plywood
PB = particle board
OSB = oriented strand board

Notes:

Sides are handed. Make one left side and one right side for each module.

If toe kick is not to be covered with base moulding, substitute PLP for PLY.

Modular Cabinets

BILL OF MATERIALS
(All Dimensions Actual)

Style: 2
Type: Overhead Long Module
Size: 15″
Refer to: Illus. 207, 208, 211, and 219

Part	Description	Material	Size	No. Req'd
G	sides	¾ PLP	30 × 14	2
H	door	¾ PLP	28 × 15	1
I	top	¾ PLP	13¾ × 14¼	1
J	bottom	¾ PLP	14 × 14¼	1
K	shelf	¾ PLP	13¾ × 13½	varies
L	front filler	¾ PLP	2¼ × 14¼	1
M	nailing strip	¾ PLP	4 × 14¼	1
N	back	¼ VCP	29⅝ × 14¼	1
V	end cap	¾ PLP	28 × 14	varies

Material Key:

PLP = plastic laminate-covered particle board
VCP = vinyl-covered particle board

Notes:

Sides are handed. Make one left side and one right side for each module.

Door sizes are finished-size with mouldings applied; subtract moulding widths to get cutting size.

Shelf sizes are for adjustable shelves using flush-mounted metal standards. Other brackets may require more clearance. Fixed shelves should use dado joints; length will be same as part J.

Modular Cabinets

BILL OF MATERIALS
(All Dimensions Actual)

Style: 2
Type: Overhead Long Module
Size: 18″
Refer to: Illus. 207, 208, 211, and 219

Part	Description	Material	Size	No. Req'd
G	sides	¾ PLP	30 × 14	2
H	door	¾ PLP	28 × 18	1
I	top	¾ PLP	13¾ × 17¼	1
J	bottom	¾ PLP	14 × 17¼	1
K	shelf	¾ PLP	13¾ × 16½	varies
L	front filler	¾ PLP	2¼ × 17¼	1
M	nailing strip	¾ PLP	4 × 17¼	1
N	back	¼ VCP	29⅝ × 17¼	1
V	end cap	¾ PLP	28 × 14	varies

Material Key:

PLP = plastic laminate-covered particle board
VCP = vinyl-covered particle board

Notes:

Sides are handed. Make one left side and one right side for each module.

Door sizes are finished-size with mouldings applied; subtract moulding widths to get cutting size.

Shelf sizes are for adjustable shelves, using flush-mounted metal standards. Other brackets may require more clearance. Fixed shelves should use dado joints; length will be same as part J.

Modular Cabinets

BILL OF MATERIALS
(All Dimensions Actual)

Style: 2
Type: Overhead Long Module
Size: 24″
Refer to: Illus. 207, 208, 211, and 219

Part	Description	Material	Size	No. Req'd
G	sides	¾ PLP	30 × 14	2
H	door	¾ PLP	28 × 12	2
I	top	¾ PLP	13¾ × 23¼	1
J	bottom	¾ PLP	14 × 23¼	1
K	shelf	¾ PLP	13¾ × 22½	varies
L	front filler	¾ PLP	2¼ × 23¼	1
M	nailing strip	¾ PLP	4 × 23¼	1
N	back	¼ VCP	29⅝ × 23¼	1
V	end cap	¾ PLP	28 × 14	varies

Material Key:

PLP = plastic laminate-covered particle board
VCP = vinyl-covered particle board

Notes:

Sides are handed. Make one left side and one right side for each module.

Door sizes are finished-size with mouldings applied; subtract moulding widths to get cutting size.

Shelf sizes are for adjustable shelves, using flush-mounted metal standards. Other brackets may require more clearance. Fixed shelves should use dado joints; length will be same as part J.

Modular Cabinets

BILL OF MATERIALS
(All Dimensions Actual)

Style: 2
Type: Overhead Long Module
Size: 30″
Refer to: Illus. 207, 208, 211, and 219

Part	Description	Material	Size	No. Req'd
G	sides	¾ PLP	30 × 14	2
H	door	¾ PLP	28 × 15	2
I	top	¾ PLP	13¾ × 29¼	1
J	bottom	¾ PLP	14 × 29¼	1
K	shelf	¾ PLP	13¾ × 28½	varies
L	front filler	¾ PLP	2¼ × 29¼	1
M	nailing strip	¾ PLP	4 × 29¼	1
N	back	¼ VCP	29⅝ × 29¼	1
V	end cap	¾ PLP	28 × 14	varies

Material Key:
PLP = plastic laminate-covered particle board
VCP = vinyl-covered particle board

Notes:
Sides are handed. Make one left side and one right side for each module.

Door sizes are finished-size with mouldings applied; subtract moulding widths to get cutting size.

Shelf sizes are for adjustable shelves, using flush-mounted metal standards. Other brackets may require more clearance. Fixed shelves should use dado joints; length will be same as part J.

Modular Cabinets

BILL OF MATERIALS
(All Dimensions Actual)

Style: 2
Type: Overhead Long Module
Size: 36″
Refer to: Illus. 207, 208, 211, and 219

Part	Description	Material	Size	No. Req'd
G	sides	¾ PLP	30 × 14	2
H	door	¾ PLP	28 × 18	2
I	top	¾ PLP	13¾ × 35¼	1
J	bottom	¾ PLP	14 × 35¼	1
K	shelf	¾ PLP	13¾ × 34½	varies
L	front filler	¾ PLP	2¼ × 35¼	1
M	nailing strip	¾ PLP	4 × 35¼	1
N	back	¼ VCP	29⅝ × 35¼	1
V	end cap	¾ PLP	28 × 14	varies

Material Key:
PLP = plastic laminate-covered particle board
VCP = vinyl-covered particle board

Notes:
Sides are handed. Make one left side and one right side for each module.

Door sizes are finished-size with mouldings applied; subtract moulding widths to get cutting size.

Shelf sizes are for adjustable shelves, using flush-mounted metal standards. Other brackets may require more clearance. Fixed shelves should use dado joints; length will be same as part J.

Modular Cabinets

BILL OF MATERIALS
(All Dimensions Actual)

Style: 2
Type: Overhead Short Module
Size: 15″
Refer to: Illus. 207, 208, 211, and 219

Part	Description	Material	Size	No. Req'd
G	sides	¾ PLP	20 × 14	2
H	door	¾ PLP	18 × 15	1
I	top	¾ PLP	13¾ × 14¼	1
J	bottom	¾ PLP	14 × 14¼	1
K	shelf	¾ PLP	13¾ × 13½	varies
L	front filler	¾ PLP	2¼ × 14¼	1
M	nailing strip	¾ PLP	4 × 14¼	1
N	back	¼ VCP	19⅝ × 14¼	1
V	end cap	¾ PLP	18 × 14	varies

Material Key:
PLP = plastic laminate-covered particle board
VCP = vinyl-covered particle board

Notes:
Sides are handed. Make one left side and one right side for each module.

Door sizes are finished-size with mouldings applied; subtract moulding widths to get cutting size.

Shelf sizes are for adjustable shelves, using flush-mounted metal standards. Other brackets may require more clearance. Fixed shelves should use dado joints; length will be same as part J.

Modular Cabinets

BILL OF MATERIALS
(All Dimensions Actual)

Style: 2
Type: Overhead Short Module
Size: 18″
Refer to: Illus. 207, 208, 211, and 219

Part	Description	Material	Size	No. Req'd
G	sides	¾ PLP	20 × 14	2
H	door	¾ PLP	18 × 18	1
I	top	¾ PLP	13¾ × 17¼	1
J	bottom	¾ PLP	14 × 17¼	1
K	shelf	¾ PLP	13¾ × 16½	varies
L	front filler	¾ PLP	2¼ × 17¼	1
M	nailing strip	¾ PLP	4 × 17¼	1
N	back	¼ VCP	19⅝ × 17¼	1
V	end cap	¾ PLP	18 × 14	varies

Material Key:

PLP = plastic laminate-covered particle board
VCP = vinyl-covered particle board

Notes:

Sides are handed. Make one left side and one right side for each module.

Door sizes are finished-size with mouldings applied; subtract moulding widths to get cutting size.

Shelf sizes are for adjustable shelves, using flush-mounted metal standards. Other brackets may require more clearance. Fixed shelves should use dado joints; length will be same as part J.

Modular Cabinets

BILL OF MATERIALS
(All Dimensions Actual)

Style: 2
Type: Overhead Short Module
Size: 24″
Refer to: Illus. 207, 208, 211, and 219

Part	Description	Material	Size	No. Req'd
G	sides	¾ PLP	20 × 14	2
H	door	¾ PLP	18 × 12	2
I	top	¾ PLP	13¾ × 23¼	1
J	bottom	¾ PLP	13 × 23¼	1
K	shelf	¾ PLP	13¾ × 22½	varies
L	front filler	¾ PLP	2¼ × 23¼	1
M	nailing strip	¾ PLP	4 × 23¼	1
N	back	¼ VCP	19⅝ × 23¼	1
V	end cap	¾ PLP	18 × 14	varies

Material Key:
PLP = plastic laminate-covered particle board
VCP = vinyl-covered particle board

Notes:
Sides are handed. Make one left side and one right side for each module.

Door sizes are finished-size with mouldings applied; subtract moulding widths to get cutting size.

Shelf sizes are for adjustable shelves, using flush-mounted metal standards. Other brackets may require more clearance. Fixed shelves should use dado joints; length will be same as part J.

Modular Cabinets

BILL OF MATERIALS
(All Dimensions Actual)

Style: 2
Type: Overhead Short Module
Size: 30″
Refer to: Illus. 207, 208, 211, and 219

Part	Description	Material	Size	No. Req'd
G	sides	¾ PLP	20 × 14	2
H	door	¾ PLP	18 × 15	2
I	top	¾ PLP	13¾ × 29¼	1
J	bottom	¾ PLP	14 × 29¼	1
K	shelf	¾ PLP	13¾ × 28½	varies
L	front filler	¾ PLP	2¼ × 29¼	1
M	nailing strip	¾ PLP	4 × 29¼	1
N	back	¼ VCP	19⅝ × 29¼	1
V	end cap	¾ PLP	18 × 14	varies

Material Key:
PLP = plastic laminate-covered particle board
VCP = vinyl-covered particle board

Notes:
Sides are handed. Make one left side and one right side for each module.

Door sizes are finished-size with mouldings applied; subtract moulding widths to get cutting size.

Shelf sizes are for adjustable shelves, using flush-mounted metal standards. Other brackets may require more clearance. Fixed shelves should use dado joints; length will be same as part J.

Modular Cabinets

BILL OF MATERIALS
(All Dimensions Actual)

Style: 2
Type: Overhead Short Module
Size: 36″
Refer to: Illus. 207, 208, 211, and 219

Part	Description	Material	Size	No. Req'd
G	sides	¾ PLP	20 × 14	2
H	door	¾ PLP	18 × 18	2
I	top	¾ PLP	13¾ × 35¼	1
J	bottom	¾ PLP	14 × 35¼	1
K	shelf	¾ PLP	13¾ × 34½	varies
L	front filler	¾ PLP	2¼ × 35¼	1
M	nailing strip	¾ PLP	4 × 35¼	1
N	back	¼ VCP	19⅝ × 35¼	1
V	end cap	¾ PLP	18 × 14	varies

Material Key:

PLP = plastic laminate-covered particle board
VCP = vinyl-covered particle board

Notes:

Sides are handed. Make one left side and one right side for each module.

Door sizes are finished-size with mouldings applied; subtract moulding widths to get cutting size.

Shelf sizes are for adjustable shelves, using flush-mounted metal standards. Other brackets may require more clearance. Fixed shelves should use dado joints; length will be same as part J.

Modular Cabinets

BILL OF MATERIALS
(All Dimensions Actual)

Style: 3
Type: Under-the-Counter Single Door
Size: 15″
Refer to: Illus. 207, 208, 213, and 215

Part	Description	Material	Size	No. Req'd
A	sides	¾ HPW	35¼ × 23¼	2
B	door	panel-finished size	31 × 15	1
C	bottom	¾ HPW	23 × 14¼	1
D	shelf	¾ HPW	23 × 13½	varies
E	back	¼ HPW	32 × 14¼	1
F	strips	¾ PLY	4 × 14¼	4
V	door stiles	¾ SL	2 × 32	2
W	door rails	¾ SL	2 × 14	2
X	door panel	½ SL	28¾ × 11¾	1

Material Key:

PLY = fir plywood
HPW = hardwood plywood
SL = solid lumber

Notes:

Sides are handed. Make one left side and one right side for each module.

If counter top has an overhanging front lip, subtract lip measurement from door height.

Door-stile length includes 1″-trimming allowance for mortices. Door-rail length includes 1½″ tenon on each end.

Shelf sizes are for adjustable shelves, using flush-mounted metal standards. Other brackets may require more clearance. Fixed shelves should use dado joints; length will be same as part C. No shelves are used in sink modules.

If toe kick is not to be covered with base moulding, substitute HPW for PLY.

Modular Cabinets

BILL OF MATERIALS
(All Dimensions Actual)

Style: 3
Type: Under-the-Counter Single Door
Size: 18″
Refer to: Illus. 207, 208, 213, and 215

Part	Description	Material	Size	No. Req'd
A	sides	¾ HPW	35¼ × 23¼	2
B	door	panel-finished size	31 × 18	1
C	bottom	¾ HPW	23 × 17¼	1
D	shelf	¾ HPW	23 × 16½	varies
E	back	¼ HPW	32 × 17¼	1
F	strips	¾ PLY	4 × 17¼	1
V	door stiles	¾ SL	2 × 32	2
W	door rails	¾ SL	2 × 17	2
X	door panel	½ SL	28¾ × 14¾	1

Material Key:

PLY = fir plywood
HPW = hardwood plywood
PB = particle board
SL = solid lumber

Notes:

Sides are handed. Make one left side and one right side for each module.

If counter top has an overhanging front lip, subtract lip measurement from door height.

Door-stile length includes 1″-trimming allowance for mortices. Door-rail length includes 1½″ tenon on each end.

Shelf sizes are for adjustable shelves, using flush-mounted metal standards. Other brackets may require more clearance. Fixed shelves should use dado joints; length will be same as part C. No shelves are used in sink modules.

If toe kick is not to be covered with base moulding, substitute HPW for PLY.

Modular Cabinets

BILL OF MATERIALS
(All Dimensions Actual)

Style: 3
Type: Under-the-Counter Double Door
Size: 24″
Refer to: Illus. 207, 208, 213, and 216

Part	Description	Material	Size	No. Req'd
A	sides	¾ HPW	35¼ × 23¼	2
B	door	panel-finished size	31 × 12	2
C	bottom	¾ HPW	23 × 23¼	1
D	shelf	¾ HPW	23 × 22½	varies
E	back	¼ HPW	32 × 23¼	1
F	strips	¾ PLY	4 × 23¼	4
V	door stiles	¾ SL	2 × 32	2
W	door rails	¾ SL	2 × 11	2
X	door panel	½ SL	28¾ × 8¾	1

Material Key:

PLY = fir plywood
HPW = hardwood plywood
SL   = solid lumber

Notes:

Sides are handed. Make one left side and one right side for each module.

If counter top has an overhanging front lip, subtract lip measurement from door height.

Door-stile length includes 1″-trimming allowance for mortices. Door-rail length includes 1½″ tenon on each end.

Shelf sizes are for adjustable shelves, using flush-mounted metal standards. Other brackets may require more clearance. Fixed shelves should use dado joints; length will be same as part C. No shelves are used in sink modules.

If toe kick is not to be covered with base moulding, substitute HPW for PLY.

Modular Cabinets

BILL OF MATERIALS
(All Dimensions Actual)

Style: 3
Type: Under-the-Counter Double Door
Size: 30″
Refer to: Illus. 207, 208, 213, and 216

Part	Description	Material	Size	No. Req'd
A	sides	¾ HPW	35¼ × 23¼	2
B	door	panel-finished size	31 × 15	2
C	bottom	¾ HPW	23 × 29¼	1
D	shelf	¾ HPW	23 × 28½	varies
E	back	¼ HPW	32 × 29¼	1
F	strips	¾ PLY	4 × 29¼	4
V	door stiles	¾ SL	2 × 32	2
W	door rails	¾ SL	2 × 14	2
X	door panel	½ SL	28¾ × 11¾	1

Material Key:

PLY = fir plywood
HPW = hardwood plywood
SL   = solid lumber

Notes:

Sides are handed. Make one left side and one right side for each module.

If counter top has an overhanging front lip, subtract lip measurement from door height.

Door-stile length includes 1″-trimming allowance for mortices. Door-rail length includes 1½″ tenon on each end.

Shelf sizes are for adjustable shelves, using flush-mounted metal standards. Other brackets may require more clearance. Fixed shelves should use dado joints; length will be same as part C. No shelves are used in sink modules.

If toe kick is not to be covered with base moulding, substitute HPW for PLY.

Modular Cabinets

BILL OF MATERIALS
(All Dimensions Actual)

Style: 3
Type: Under-the-Counter Double Door
Size: 36″
Refer to: Illus. 207, 208, 213, and 216

Part	Description	Material	Size	No. Req'd
A	sides	¾ HPW	35¼ × 23¼	2
B	door	panel-finished size	31 × 18	2
C	bottom	¾ HPW	23 × 35¼	1
D	shelf	¾ HPW	23 × 34½	varies
E	back	¼ HPW	32 × 35¼	1
F	strips	¾ PLY	4 × 35¼	4
V	door stiles	¾ SL	2 × 32	2
W	door rails	¾ SL	2 × 17	2
X	door panel	½ SL	28¾ × 14¾	1

Material Key:

PLY = fir plywood
HPW = hardwood plywood
SL   = solid lumber

Notes:

Sides are handed. Make one left side and one right side for each module.

If counter top has an overhanging front lip, subtract lip measurement from door height.

Door-stile length includes 1″-trimming allowance for mortices. Door-rail length includes 1½″ tenon on each end.

Shelf sizes are for adjustable shelves, using flush-mounted metal standards. Other brackets may require more clearance. Fixed shelves should use dado joints; length will be same as part C. No shelves are used in sink modules.

If toe kick is not to be covered with base moulding, substitute HPW for PLY.

Modular Cabinets

BILL OF MATERIALS
(All Dimensions Actual)

Style: 3
Type: Under-the-Counter Drawer Module
Size: 15″
Refer to: Illus. 207, 208, 213, and 217

Part	Description	Material	Size	No. Req'd
A	sides	¾ PB	35¼ × 23¼	2
C	bottom	¾ PB	23 × 14¼	1
E	back	¼ OSB	32 × 14¼	1
F	strips	¾ PLY	4 × 14¼	4

Material Key:

PLY = fir plywood
HPW = hardwood plywood
PB   = particle board
OSB = oriented strand board

Notes:

Sides are handed. Make one left side and one right side for each module.

If sides will show, substitute HPW for PB.

If toe kick is not to be covered with base moulding, substitute HPW for PLY.

Modular Cabinets

BILL OF MATERIALS
(All Dimensions Actual)

Style: 3
Type: Under-the-Counter Drawer Module
Size: 18″
Refer to: Illus. 207, 208, 213, and 217

Part	Description	Material	Size	No. Req'd
A	sides	¾ PB	35¼ × 23¼	2
C	bottom	¾ PB	23 × 17¼	1
E	back	¼ OSB	32 × 17¼	1
F	strips	¾ PLY	4 × 17¼	4

Material Key:

PLY = fir plywood
HPW = hardwood plywood
PB   = particle board
OSB = oriented strand board

Notes:

Sides are handed. Make one left side and one right side for each module.

If sides will show, substitute HPW for PB.

If toe kick is not to be covered with base moulding, substitute HPW for PLY.

Modular Cabinets

BILL OF MATERIALS
(All Dimensions Actual)

Style: 3
Type: Bathroom Vanity Single Door
Size: 15″
Refer to: Illus. 207, 208, 213, and 215

Part	Description	Material	Size	No. Req'd
A	sides	¾ HPW	31¼ × 20¼	2
B	door	panel-finished size	27 × 15	1
C	bottom	¾ HPW	20 × 14¼	1
D	shelf	¾ HPW	20 × 13½	varies
E	back	¼ HPW	28 × 14¼	1
F	strips	¾ PLY	4 × 14¼	4
V	door stiles	¾ SL	2 × 28	2
W	door rails	¾ SL	2 × 14	2
X	door panel	½ SL	23¾ × 11¾	1

Material Key:

PLY = fir plywood
HPW = hardwood plywood
SL   = solid lumber

Notes:

Sides are handed. Make one left side and one right side for each module.

If counter top has an overhanging front lip, subtract lip measurement from door height.

Door-stile length includes 1″-trimming allowance for mortices. Door-rail length includes 1½″ tenon on each end.

Shelf sizes are for adjustable shelves, using flush-mounted metal standards. Other brackets may require more clearance. Fixed shelves should use dado joints; length will be same as part C. No shelves are used in sink modules.

If toe kick is not to be covered with base moulding, substitute HPW for PLY.

Modular Cabinets

BILL OF MATERIALS
(All Dimensions Actual)

Style: 3
Type: Bathroom Vanity Single Door
Size: 18″
Refer to: Illus. 207, 208, 213, and 215

Part	Description	Material	Size	No. Req'd
A	sides	¾ HPW	31¼ × 20¼	2
B	door	panel-finished size	27 × 18	1
C	bottom	¾ HPW	20 × 17¼	1
D	shelf	¾ HPW	20 × 16½	varies
E	back	¼ HPW	28 × 17¼	1
F	strips	¾ PLY	4 × 17¼	4
V	door stiles	¾ SL	2 × 28	2
W	door rails	¾ SL	2 × 17	2
X	door panel	½ SL	23¾ × 14¾	1

Material Key:

PLY = fir plywood
HPW = hardwood plywood
SL = solid lumber

Notes:

Sides are handed. Make one left side and one right side for each module.

If counter top has an overhanging front lip, subtract lip measurement from door height.

Door-stile length includes 1″-trimming allowance for mortices. Door-rail length includes 1½″ tenon on each end.

Shelf sizes are for adjustable shelves, using flush-mounted metal standards. Other brackets may require more clearance. Fixed shelves should use dado joints; length will be same as part C. No shelves are used in sink modules.

If toe kick is not to be covered with base moulding, substitute HPW for PLY.

Modular Cabinets

BILL OF MATERIALS
(All Dimensions Actual)

Style: 3
Type: Bathroom Vanity Double Door
Size: 24″
Refer to: Illus. 207, 208, 213, and 216

Part	Description	Material	Size	No. Req'd
A	sides	¾ HPW	31¼ × 20¼	2
B	door	panel-finished size	27 × 12	2
C	bottom	¾ HPW	20 × 23¼	1
D	shelf	¾ HPW	20 × 22½	varies
E	back	¼ HPW	28 × 23¼	1
F	strips	¾ PLY	4 × 23¼	4
V	door stiles	¾ SL	2 × 28	2
W	door rails	¾ SL	2 × 11	2
X	door panel	½ SL	23¾ × 8¾	1

Material Key:
PLY = fir plywood
HPW = hardwood plywood
SL   = solid lumber

Notes:
Sides are handed. Make one left side and one right side for each module.

If counter top has an overhanging front lip, subtract lip measurement from door height.

Door-stile length includes 1″-trimming allowance for mortices. Door-rail length includes 1½″ tenon on each end.

Shelf sizes are for adjustable shelves, using flush-mounted metal standards. Other brackets may require more clearance. Fixed shelves should use dado joints; length will be same as part C. No shelves are used in sink modules.

If toe kick is not to be covered with base moulding, substitute HPW for PLY.

Modular Cabinets

BILL OF MATERIALS
(All Dimensions Actual)

Style: 3
Type: Bathroom Vanity Double Door
Size: 30″
Refer to: Illus. 207, 208, 213, and 216

Part	Description	Material	Size	No. Req'd
A	sides	¾ HPW	31¼ × 20¼	2
B	door	panel-finished size	27 × 15	2
C	bottom	¾ HPW	20 × 29¼	1
D	shelf	¾ HPW	20 × 28½	varies
E	back	¼ HPW	28 × 29¼	1
F	strips	¾ PLY	4 × 29¼	4
V	door stiles	¾ SL	2 × 28	2
W	door rails	¾ SL	2 × 14	2
X	door panel	½ SL	23¾ × 11¾	1

Material Key:

PLY = fir plywood
HPW = hardwood plywood
SL   = solid lumber

Notes:

Sides are handed. Make one left side and one right side for each module.

If counter top has an overhanging front lip, subtract lip measurement from door height.

Door-stile length includes 1″-trimming allowance for mortices. Door-rail length includes 1½″ tenon on each end.

Shelf sizes are for adjustable shelves, using flush-mounted metal standards. Other brackets may require more clearance. Fixed shelves should use dado joints; length will be same as part C. No shelves are used in sink modules.

If toe kick is not to be covered with base moulding, substitute HPW for PLY.

Modular Cabinets

BILL OF MATERIALS
(All Dimensions Actual)

Style: 3
Type: Bathroom Vanity Double Door
Size: 36″
Refer to: Illus. 207, 208, 213, and 216

Part	Description	Material	Size	No. Req'd
A	sides	¾ HPW	31¼ × 20¼	2
B	door	panel-finished size	27 × 18	2
C	bottom	¾ HPW	20 × 35¼	1
D	shelf	¾ HPW	20 × 34½	varies
E	back	¼ HPW	28 × 35¼	1
F	strips	¾ PLY	4 × 35¼	4
V	door stiles	¾ SL	2 × 28	2
W	door rails	¾ SL	2 × 17	2
X	door panel	½ SL	23¾ × 14¾	1

Material Key:
PLY = fir plywood
HPW = hardwood plywood
SL   = solid lumber

Notes:
Sides are handed. Make one left side and one right side for each module.

If counter top has an overhanging front lip, subtract lip measurement from door height.

Door-stile length includes 1″-trimming allowance for mortices. Door-rail length includes 1½″ tenon on each end.

Shelf sizes are for adjustable shelves, using flush-mounted metal standards. Other brackets may require more clearance. Fixed shelves should use dado joints; length will be same as part C. No shelves are used in sink modules.

If toe kick is not to be covered with base moulding, substitute HPW for PLY.

Modular Cabinets

BILL OF MATERIALS
(All Dimensions Actual)

Style: 3
Type: Bathroom Vanity Drawer Module
Size: 15″
Refer to: Illus. 207, 208, 213, and 217

Part	Description	Material	Size	No. Req'd
A	sides	¾ PB	31¼ × 20¼	2
C	bottom	¾ PB	20 × 14¼	1
E	back	¼ OSB	28 × 14¼	1
F	strips	¾ PLY	4 × 14¼	4

Material Key:

PLY = fir plywood
HPW = hardwood plywood
PB   = particle board
OSB = oriented strand board

Notes:

Sides are handed. Make one left side and one right side for each module.

If sides will show substitute HPW for PB.

If toe kick is not to be covered with base moulding, substitute HPW for PLY.

Modular Cabinets

BILL OF MATERIALS
(All Dimensions Actual)

Style: 3
Type: Bathroom Vanity Drawer Module
Size: 18″
Refer to: Illus. 207, 208, 213, and 217

Part	Description	Material	Size	No. Req'd
A	sides	¾ PB	31¼ × 20¼	2
C	bottom	¾ PB	20 × 17¼	1
E	back	¼ OSB	28 × 17¼	1
F	strips	¾ PLY	4 × 17¼	4

Material Key:

PLY = fir plywood
HPW = hardwood plywood
PB   = particle board
OSB = oriented strand board

Notes:

Sides are handed. Make one left side and one right side for each module.

If sides will show, substitute HPW for PB.

If toe kick is not to be covered with base moulding, substitute HPW for PLY.

Modular Cabinets

BILL OF MATERIALS
(All Dimensions Actual)

Style: 3
Type: Overhead Long Module
Size: 15″
Refer to: Illus. 207, 208, 213, and 219

Part	Description	Material	Size	No. Req'd
G	sides	¾ HPW	30 × 14	2
H	door	panel-finished size	28 × 15	1
I	top	¾ HPW	13¾ × 14¼	1
J	bottom	¾ HPW	14 × 14¼	1
K	shelf	¾ HPW	13¾ × 13½	varies
L	front filler	¾ SL	2¼ × 14¼	1
M	nailing strip	¾ HPW	4 × 14¼	1
N	back	¼ HPW	29⅝ × 14¼	1
V	door stiles	¾ SL	2 × 29	2
W	door rails	¾ SL	2 × 14	2
X	door panel	½ SL	24¾ × 11¾	1

Material Key:
HPW = hardwood plywood
SL   = solid lumber

Notes:

Sides are handed. Make one left side and one right side for each module.

Door-stile length includes 1″-trimming allowance for mortises. Door-rail length includes 1½″ tenon on each end.

Shelf sizes are for adjustable shelves, using flush-mounted metal standards. Other brackets may require more clearance. Fixed shelves should use dado joints; length will be same as part J.

Modular Cabinets

BILL OF MATERIALS
(All Dimensions Actual)

Style: 3
Type: Overhead Long Module
Size: 18″
Refer to: Illus. 207, 208, 213, and 219

Part	Description	Material	Size	No. Req'd
G	sides	¾ HPW	30 × 14	2
H	door	panel-finished size	28 × 18	1
I	top	¾ HPW	13¾ × 17¼	1
J	bottom	¾ HPW	14 × 17¼	1
K	shelf	¾ HPW	13¾ × 16½	varies
L	front filler	¾ SL	2¼ × 17¼	1
M	nailing strip	¾ HPW	4 × 17¼	1
N	back	¼ HPW	29⅝ × 17¼	1
V	door stiles	¾ SL	2 × 29	2
W	door rails	¾ SL	2 × 17	2
X	door panel	½ SL	24¾ × 14¾	1

Material Key:

HPW = hardwood plywood
SL   = solid lumber

Notes:

Sides are handed. Make one left side and one right side for each module.

Door-stile length includes 1″-trimming allowance for mortises. Door-rail length includes 1½″ tenon on each end.

Shelf sizes are for adjustable shelves, using flush-mounted metal standards. Other brackets may require more clearance. Fixed shelves should use dado joints; length will be same as part J.

Modular Cabinets

BILL OF MATERIALS
(All Dimensions Actual)

Style: 3
Type: Overhead Long Module
Size: 24″
Refer to: Illus. 207, 208, 213, and 219

Part	Description	Material	Size	No. Req'd
G	sides	¾ HPW	30 × 14	2
H	door	panel-finished size	28 × 12	2
I	top	¾ HPW	13¾ × 23¼	1
J	bottom	¾ HPW	14 × 23¼	1
K	shelf	¾ HPW	13¾ × 22½	varies
L	front filler	¾ SL	2¼ × 23¼	1
M	nailing strip	¾ HPW	4 × 23¼	1
N	back	¼ HPW	29⅝ × 23¼	1
V	door stiles	¾ SL	2 × 29	2
W	door rails	¾ SL	2 × 11	2
X	door panel	½ SL	24¾ × 8¾	1

Material Key:

HPW = hardwood plywood
SL   = solid lumber

Notes:

Sides are handed. Make one left side and one right side for each module.

Door-stile length includes 1″-trimming allowance for mortises. Door-rail length includes 1½″ tenon on each end.

Shelf sizes are for adjustable shelves, using flush-mounted metal standards. Other brackets may require more clearance. Fixed shelves should use dado joints; length will be same as part J.

Modular Cabinets

BILL OF MATERIALS
(All Dimensions Actual)

Style: 3
Type: Overhead Long Module
Size: 30″
Refer to: Illus. 207, 208, 213, and 219

Part	Description	Material	Size	No. Req'd
G	sides	¾ HPW	30 × 14	2
H	door	panel-finished size	28 × 15	2
I	top	¾ HPW	13¾ × 29¼	1
J	bottom	¾ HPW	14 × 29¼	1
K	shelf	¾ HPW	13¾ × 28½	varies
L	front filler	¾ SL	2¼ × 29¼	1
M	nailing strip	¾ HPW	4 × 29¼	1
N	back	¼ HPW	29⅝ × 29¼	1
V	door stiles	¾ SL	2 × 29	2
W	door rails	¾ SL	2 × 14	2
X	door panel	½ SL	24¾ × 11¾	1

Material Key:

HPW = hardwood plywood
SL = solid lumber

Notes:

Sides are handed. Make one left side and one right side for each module.

Door-stile length includes 1″-trimming allowance for mortises. Door-rail length includes 1½″ tenon on each end.

Shelf sizes are for adjustable shelves, using flush-mounted metal standards. Other brackets may require more clearance. Fixed shelves should use dado joints; length will be same as part J.

Modular Cabinets

BILL OF MATERIALS
(All Dimensions Actual)

Style: 3
Type: Overhead Long Module
Size: 36″
Refer to: Illus. 207, 208, 213, and 219

Part	Description	Material	Size	No. Req'd
G	sides	¾ HPW	30 × 14	2
H	door	panel-finished size	28 × 18	2
I	top	¾ HPW	13¾ × 35¼	1
J	bottom	¾ HPW	14 × 35¼	1
K	shelf	¾ HPW	13¾ × 34½	varies
L	front filler	¾ SL	2¼ × 35¼	1
M	nailing strip	¾ HPW	4 × 35¼	1
N	back	¼ HPW	29⅝ × 35¼	1
V	door stiles	¾ SL	2 × 29	2
W	door rails	¾ SL	2 × 17	2
X	door panel	½ SL	24¾ × 14¾	1

Material Key:

HPW = hardwood plywood
SL   = solid lumber

Notes:

Sides are handed. Make one left side and one right side for each module.

Door-stile length includes 1″-trimming allowance for mortises. Door-rail length includes 1½″ tenon on each end.

Shelf sizes are for adjustable shelves, using flush-mounted metal standards. Other brackets may require more clearance. Fixed shelves should use dado joints; length will be same as part J.

Modular Cabinets

BILL OF MATERIALS
(All Dimensions Actual)

Style: 3
Type: Overhead Short Module
Size: 15″
Refer to: Illus. 207, 208, 213, and 219

Part	Description	Material	Size	No. Req'd
G	sides	¾ HPW	20 × 14	2
H	door	panel-finished size	18 × 15	1
I	top	¾ HPW	13¾ × 14¼	1
J	bottom	¾ HPW	14 × 14¼	1
K	shelf	¾ HPW	13¾ × 13½	varies
L	front filler	¾ SL	2¼ × 14¼	1
M	nailing strip	¾ HPW	4 × 14¼	1
N	back	¼ HPW	19⅝ × 14¼	1
V	door stiles	¾ SL	2 × 19	2
W	door rails	¾ SL	2 × 14	2
X	door panel	½ SL	14¾ × 11¾	1

Material Key:

HPW = hardwood plywood
SL   = solid lumber

Notes:

Sides are handed. Make one left side and one right side for each module.

Door-stile length includes 1″-trimming allowance for mortises. Door-rail length includes 1½″ tenon on each end.

Shelf sizes are for adjustable shelves, using flush-mounted metal standards. Other brackets may require more clearance. Fixed shelves should use dado joints; length will be same as part J.

Modular Cabinets

BILL OF MATERIALS
(All Dimensions Actual)

Style: 3
Type: Overhead Short Module
Size: 18″
Refer to: Illus. 207, 208, 213, and 219

Part	Description	Material	Size	No. Req'd
G	sides	¾ HPW	20 × 14	2
H	door	panel-finished size	18 × 18	1
I	top	¾ HPW	13¾ × 17¼	1
J	bottom	¾ HPW	14 × 17¼	1
K	shelf	¾ HPW	13¾ × 16½	varies
L	front filler	¾ SL	2¼ × 17¼	1
M	nailing strip	¾ HPW	4 × 17¼	1
N	back	¼ HPW	19⅝ × 17¼	1
V	door stiles	¾ SL	2 × 19	2
W	door rails	¾ SL	2 × 17	2
X	door panel	½ SL	14¾ × 14¾	1

Material Key:

HPW = hardwood plywood
SL = solid lumber

Notes:

Sides are handed. Make one left side and one right side for each module.

Door-stile length includes 1″-trimming allowance for mortises. Door-rail length includes 1½″ tenon on each end.

Shelf sizes are for adjustable shelves, using flush-mounted metal standards. Other brackets may require more clearance. Fixed shelves should use dado joints; length will be same as part J.

Modular Cabinets

BILL OF MATERIALS
(All Dimensions Actual)

Style: 3
Type: Overhead Short Module
Size: 24″
Refer to: Illus. 207, 208, 213, and 219

Part	Description	Material	Size	No. Req'd
G	sides	¾ HPW	20 × 14	2
H	door	panel-finished size	18 × 12	2
I	top	¾ HPW	13¾ × 23¼	1
J	bottom	¾ HPW	14 × 23¼	1
K	shelf	¾ HPW	13¾ × 22½	varies
L	front filler	¾ SL	2¼ × 23¼	1
M	nailing strip	¾ HPW	4 × 23¼	1
N	back	¼ HPW	19⅝ × 23¼	1
V	door stiles	¾ SL	2 × 19	2
W	door rails	¾ SL	2 × 11	2
X	door panel	½ SL	14¾ × 8¾	1

Material Key:

HPW = hardwood plywood
SL   = solid lumber

Notes:

Sides are handed. Make one left side and one right side for each module.

Door-stile length includes 1″-trimming allowance for mortises. Door-rail length includes 1½″ tenon on each end.

Shelf sizes are for adjustable shelves, using flush-mounted metal standards. Other brackets may require more clearance. Fixed shelves should use dado joints; length will be same as part J.

Modular Cabinets

BILL OF MATERIALS
(All Dimensions Actual)

Style: 3
Type: Overhead Short Module
Size: 30″
Refer to: Illus. 207, 208, 213, and 219

Part	Description	Material	Size	No. Req'd
G	sides	¾ HPW	20 × 14	2
H	door	panel-finished size	18 × 15	2
I	top	¾ HPW	13¾ × 29¼	1
J	bottom	¾ HPW	14 × 29¼	1
K	shelf	¾ HPW	13¾ × 28½	varies
L	front filler	¾ SL	2¼ × 29¼	1
M	nailing strip	¾ HPW	4 × 29¼	1
N	back	¼ HPW	19⅝ × 29¼	1
V	door stiles	¾ SL	2 × 19	2
W	door rails	¾ SL	2 × 14	2
X	door panel	½ SL	14¾ × 11¾	1

Material Key:

HPW = hardwood plywood
SL = solid lumber

Notes:

Sides are handed. Make one left side and one right side for each module.

Door-stile length includes 1″-trimming allowance for mortises. Door-rail length includes 1½″ tenon on each end.

Shelf sizes are for adjustable shelves, using flush-mounted metal standards. Other brackets may require more clearance. Fixed shelves should use dado joints; length will be same as part J.

Modular Cabinets

BILL OF MATERIALS
(All Dimensions Actual)

Style: 3
Type: Overhead Short Module
Size: 36″
Refer to: Illus. 207, 208, 213, and 219

Part	Description	Material	Size	No. Req'd
G	sides	¾ HPW	20 × 14	2
H	door	panel-finished size	18 × 18	2
I	top	¾ HPW	13¾ × 35¼	1
J	bottom	¾ HPW	14 × 35¼	1
K	shelf	¾ HPW	13¾ × 34½	varies
L	front filler	¾ SL	2¼ × 35¼	1
M	nailing strip	¾ HPW	4 × 35¼	1
N	back	¼ HPW	19⅝ × 35¼	1
V	door stiles	¾ SL	2 × 19	2
W	door rails	¾ SL	2 × 17	2
X	door panel	½ SL	14¾ × 14¾	1

Material Key:

HPW = hardwood plywood
SL   = solid lumber

Notes:

Sides are handed. Make one left side and one right side for each module.

Door-stile length includes 1″-trimming allowance for mortises. Door-rail length includes 1½″ tenon on each end.

Shelf sizes are for adjustable shelves, using flush-mounted metal standards. Other brackets may require more clearance. Fixed shelves should use dado joints; length will be same as part J.

Modular Cabinets

BILL OF MATERIALS
(All Dimensions Actual)

Style: All
Type: 4″ Top Drawer, Full Size
Size: 15″
Refer to: Illus. 209, 217, and 218

Part	Description	Material	Size	No. Req'd
P	false front	¾ *	6 × 15	1
Q	front	¾ VCP	4 × 11¾	1
R	side	¾ VCP	4 × 22	2
S	bottom	¼ VCP	21⅜ × 11¾	1
T	back	¾ VCP	3¼ × 11¾	1

*Material to match doors.

Material Key:
VCP = vinyl-covered particle board

Notes:
Sides are handed. Make one left side and one right side for each drawer.

Sizes are for use with metal side guides requiring ½″ clearance.

Adjust size of part P to provide proper clearance between drawers.

Full-size modules require one 4″ drawer, two 6″ drawers, and one 8″ drawer. Bathroom vanities require two 6″ drawers and one 8″ drawer.

Modular Cabinets

BILL OF MATERIALS
(All Dimensions Actual)

Style: All
Type: 6″ Middle Drawer, Full Size
Size: 15″
Refer to: Illus. 209, 217, and 218

Part	Description	Material	Size	No. Req'd
P	false front	¾ *	7 × 15	1
Q	front	¾ VCP	6 × 11¾	1
R	side	¾ VCP	6 × 22	2
S	bottom	¼ VCP	21⅜ × 11¾	1
T	back	¾ VCP	5¼ × 11¾	1

*Material to match doors

Material Key:
VCP = vinyl-covered particle board

Notes:
Sides are handed. Make one left side and one right side for each drawer.

Sizes are for use with metal side guides requiring ½″ clearance.

Adjust size of part P to provide proper clearance between drawers.

Full-size modules require one 4″ drawer, two 6″ drawers, and one 8″ drawer. Bathroom vanities require two 6″ drawers and one 8″ drawer.

Modular Cabinets

BILL OF MATERIALS
(All Dimensions Actual)

Style: All
Type: 8″ Bottom Drawer, Full Size
Size: 15″
Refer to: Illus. 209, 217, and 218

Part	Description	Material	Size	No. Req'd
P	false front	¾ *	10 × 15	1
Q	front	¾ VCP	8 × 11¾	1
R	side	¾ VCP	8 × 22	2
S	bottom	¼ VCP	21⅜ × 11¾	1
T	back	¾ VCP	7¼ × 11¾	1

*Material to match doors.

Material Key:
VCP = vinyl-covered particle board

Notes:
Sides are handed. Make one left side and one right side for each drawer.

Sizes are for use with metal side guides requiring ½″ clearance.

Adjust size of part P to provide proper clearance between drawers.

Full-size modules require one 4″ drawer, two 6″ drawers, and one 8″ drawer. Bathroom vanities require two 6″ drawers and one 8″ drawer.

Modular Cabinets

BILL OF MATERIALS
(All Dimensions Actual)

Style: All
Type: 4″ Top Drawer, Full Size
Size: 18″
Refer to: Illus. 209, 217, and 218

Part	Description	Material	Size	No. Req'd
P	false front	¾ *	5 × 18	1
Q	front	¾ VCP	4 × 14¾	1
R	side	¾ VCP	4 × 22	2
S	bottom	¼ VCP	21⅜ × 14¾	1
T	back	¾ VCP	3¼ × 14¾	1

*Material to match doors.

Material Key:
VCP = vinyl-covered particle board

Notes:
Sides are handed. Make one left side and one right side for each drawer.

Sizes are for use with metal side guides requiring ½″ clearance.

Adjust size of part P to provide proper clearance between drawers.

Full-size modules require one 4″ drawer, two 6″ drawers, and one 8″ drawer. Bathroom vanities require two 6″ drawers and one 8″ drawer.

Modular Cabinets

BILL OF MATERIALS
(All Dimensions Actual)

Style: All
Type: 6″ Middle Drawer, Full Size
Size: 18″
Refer to: Illus. 209, 217, and 218

Part	Description	Material	Size	No. Req'd
P	false front	¾ *	7 × 18	1
Q	front	¾ VCP	6 × 14¾	1
R	side	¾ VCP	6 × 22	2
S	bottom	¼ VCP	21⅜ × 14¾	1
T	back	¾ VCP	5¼ × 14¾	1

*Material to match doors.

Material Key:
VCP = vinyl-covered particle board

Notes:
Sides are handed. Make one left side and one right side for each drawer.

Sizes are for use with metal side guides requiring ½″ clearance.

Adjust size of part P to provide proper clearance between drawers.

Full-size modules require one 4″ drawer, two 6″ drawers, and one 8″ drawer. Bathroom vanities require two 6″ drawers and one 8″ drawer.

Modular Cabinets

BILL OF MATERIALS
(All Dimensions Actual)

Style: All
Type: 8″ Bottom Drawer, Full Size
Size: 18″
Refer to: Illus. 209, 217, and 218

Part	Description	Material	Size	No. Req'd
P	false front	¾ *	10 × 18	1
Q	front	¾ VCP	8 × 14¾	1
R	side	¾ VCP	8 × 22	2
S	bottom	¼ VCP	21⅜ × 14¾	1
T	back	¾ VCP	7¼ × 14¾	1

*Material to match doors.

Material Key:
VCP = vinyl-covered particle board

Notes:
Sides are handed. Make one left side and one right side for each drawer.

Sizes are for use with metal side guides requiring ½″ clearance.

Adjust size of part P to provide proper clearance between drawers.

Full-size modules require one 4″ drawer, two 6″ drawers, and one 8″ drawer. Bathroom vanities require two 6″ drawers and one 8″ drawer.

Modular Cabinets

BILL OF MATERIALS
(All Dimensions Actual)

Style: All
Type: 6″ Middle Drawer, Vanity Size
Size: 15″
Refer to: Illus. 209, 217, and 218

Part	Description	Material	Size	No. Req'd
P	false front	¾ *	7 × 15	1
Q	front	¾ VCP	6 × 11¾	1
R	side	¾ VCP	6 × 19	2
S	bottom	¼ VCP	18⅜ × 11¾	1
T	back	¾ VCP	5¼ × 11¾	1

*Material to match doors.

Material Key:
VCP = vinyl-covered particle board

Notes:
Sides are handed. Make one left side and one right side for each drawer.

Sizes are for use with metal side guides requiring ½″ clearance.

Adjust size of part P to provide proper clearance between drawers.

Full-size modules require one 4″ drawer, two 6″ drawers, and one 8″ drawer. Bathroom vanities require two 6″ drawers and one 8″ drawer.

Modular Cabinets

BILL OF MATERIALS
(All Dimensions Actual)

Style: All
Type: 8″ Bottom Drawer, Vanity Size
Size: 15″
Refer to: Illus. 209, 217, and 218

Part	Description	Material	Size	No. Req'd
P	false front	¾ *	10 × 15	1
Q	front	¾ VCP	8 × 11¾	1
R	side	¾ VCP	8 × 19	2
S	bottom	¼ VCP	18⅜ × 11¾	1
T	back	¾ VCP	7¼ × 11¾	1

*Material to match doors.

Material Key:

VCP = vinyl-covered particle board

Notes:

Sides are handed. Make one left side and one right side for each drawer.

Sizes are for use with metal side guides requiring ½″ clearance.

Adjust size of part P to provide proper clearance between drawers.

Full-size modules require one 4″ drawer, two 6″ drawers, and one 8″ drawer. Bathroom vanities require two 6″ drawers and one 8″ drawer.

Modular Cabinets

BILL OF MATERIALS
(All Dimensions Actual)

Style: All
Type: 6″ Middle Drawer, Vanity Size
Size: 18″
Refer to: Illus. 209, 217, and 218

Part	Description	Material	Size	No. Req'd
P	false front	¾ *	7 × 18	1
Q	front	¾ VCP	6 × 14¾	1
R	side	¾ VCP	6 × 19	2
S	bottom	¼ VCP	18⅜ × 14¾	1
T	back	¾ VCP	5¼ × 14¾	1

*Material to match doors.

Material Key:

VCP = vinyl-covered particle board

Notes:

Sides are handed. Make one left side and one right side for each drawer.

Sizes are for use with metal side guides requiring ½″ clearance.

Adjust size of part P to provide proper clearance between drawers.

Full-size modules require one 4″ drawer, two 6″ drawers, and one 8″ drawer. Bathroom vanities require two 6″ drawers and one 8″ drawer.

Modular Cabinets

BILL OF MATERIALS
(All Dimensions Actual)

Style: All
Type: 8″ Bottom Drawer, Vanity Size
Size: 18″
Refer to: Illus. 209, 217, and 218

Part	Description	Material	Size	No. Req'd
P	false front	¾ *	10 × 18	1
Q	front	¾ VCP	8 × 14¾	1
R	side	¾ VCP	8 × 19	2
S	bottom	¼ VCP	18⅜ × 14¾	1
T	back	¾ VCP	7¼ × 14¾	1

*Material to match doors.

Material Key:
VCP = vinyl-covered particle board

Notes:
Sides are handed. Make one left side and one right side for each drawer.

Sizes are for use with metal side guides requiring ½″ clearance.

Adjust size of part P to provide proper clearance between drawers.

Full-size modules require one 4″ drawer, two 6″ drawers, and one 8″ drawer. Bathroom vanities require two 6″ drawers and one 8″ drawer.

Modular Cabinets

BILL OF MATERIALS
(All Dimensions Actual)

Style: All
Type: Two-Door Base Corner Module
Size: 36″
Refer to: Illus. 220

Part	Description	Material	Size	No. Req'd
A	sides	¾ *	35¼ × 23¼	2
B	doors	¾ #	31 × 12	2
C1	bottom	¾ *	35⅜ × 35⅜	1
E	back	¼ *	32 × 35⅝	2
F1	strip	¾ PLY	4 × 35⅜	3
F2	strip	¾ PLY	4 × 34⅝	2
F3	strip	¾ PLY	4 × 25¾	1
F4	strip	¾ PLY	16⅜ × 35⅜	1
F5	strip	¾ PLY	4 × 34⅝	1
F6	strip	¾ PLY	4 × 14⅜	1

*Material to match style. PLP for styles 1 and 2; HPW for style 3. Backs for styles 1 or 2 are VCP.
#Door materials to match style. PLP for styles 1 and 2. For style 3 use SL. Refer to bill of materials for 24″ under-the-counter double doors for sizes of style-3 door parts.

Material Key:

PLP = plastic laminate-covered particle board
VCP = vinyl-covered particle board
PLY = fir plywood
HPW = hardwood plywood
SL = solid lumber

Notes:

Sides are handed. Make one left side and one right side.

To lay out notch in front corner of C1, measure 23″ from rear, along edges that attach to sides. Use notch in C1 to lay out F4.

Door sizes are full size; if counter top has overhanging lip or if plastic T moulding is used, adjust door size.

If toe kick is not to be covered with base moulding, substitute PLP or HPW for PLY on F5 and F6.

Modular Cabinets

BILL OF MATERIALS
(All Dimensions Actual)

Style: All
Type: Two-Door Base Corner Module (Bathroom)
Size: 33″
Refer to: Illus. 220

Part	Description	Material	Size	No. Req'd
A	sides	¾ *	31¼ × 20¼	2
B	doors	¾ #	27 × 12	2
C1	bottom	¾ *	32⅜ × 32⅜	1
E	back	¼ *	28 × 32⅝	2
F1	strip	¾ PLY	4 × 32⅜	3
F2	strip	¾ PLY	4 × 31⅝	2
F3	strip	¾ PLY	4 × 21¾	1
F4	strip	¾ PLY	16⅜ × 32⅜	1
F5	strip	¾ PLY	4 × 31⅝	1
F6	strip	¾ PLY	4 × 14⅜	1

*Material to match style. PLP for styles 1 and 2; HPW for style 3. Backs for styles 1 or 2 are VCP.

#Door materials to match style. PLP for styles 1 and 2. For style 3 use SL. Refer to bill of materials for 24″ bathroom-vanity double doors for sizes of style-3 door parts.

Material Key:

PLP = plastic laminate-covered particle board
VCP = vinyl-covered particle board
PLY = fir plywood
HPW = hardwood plywood
SL   = solid lumber

Notes:

Sides are handed. Make one left and one right side.

To lay out notch in front corner of C1, measure 20″ from rear, along edges that attach to sides. Use notch in C1 to lay out F4.

Door sizes are full size; if counter top has overhanging lip or if plastic T moulding is used, adjust door size.

If toe kick is not to be covered with base moulding, substitute PLP or HPW for PLY on F5 and F6.

Modular Cabinets

BILL OF MATERIALS
(All Dimensions Actual)

Style: All   **Size:** 36″
Type: Single-Door Base Corner Module   **Refer to:** Illus. 221

Part	Description	Material	Size	No. Req'd
A	sides	¾ *	35¼ × 23¼	2
B	doors	¾ #	31 × 18	1
C1	bottom	¾ *	35⅜ × 35⅜	1
E	back	¼ *	32 × 35⅝	2
F1	strip	¾ PLY	4 × 35⅜	3
F2	strip	¾ PLY	4 × 34⅝	2
F3	strip	¾ PLY	4 × 25¾	1
F5	strip	¾ PLY	4 × 34⅝	1
F6	strip	¾ PLY	4 × 14⅜	1
F7	strip	¾ PLY	4 × 22¼	1
F8	strip	¾ PLY	4 × 25⅜	1
F9	strip	¾ PLY	4 × 31⅜	1
O	door-mounting strip	¾ SL	3 × 29¾	1

*Material to match style. PLP for styles 1 and 2; HPW for style 3. Backs for styles 1 or 2 are VCP.

#Door materials to match style. PLP for styles 1 and 2. For style 3 use SL. Refer to bill of materials for 36″ under-the-counter double doors for sizes of style-3 door parts.

Material Key:

PLP = plastic laminate-covered particle board
VCP = vinyl-covered particle board
PLY = fir plywood
HPW = hardwood plywood
SL = solid lumber

Notes:

Sides are handed. Make one left side and one right side.

To layout angle on front corner of C1, measure 23″ from rear, along edges that attach to sides.

Door sizes are full size; if counter top has overhanging lip or if plastic T moulding is used, adjust door size.

If toe kick is not to be covered with base moulding, substitute PLP or HPW for PLY on F7.

When installing the corner module, it may be necessary to add a spacer between the sides of the corner module and the side of the adjacent cabinet to get sufficient door clearance.

Modular Cabinets

BILL OF MATERIALS
(All Dimensions Actual)

Style: All   **Refer to:** Illus. 221

Type: Single-Door Base Corner Module (Bathroom)   **Size:** 33″

Part	Description	Material	Size	No. Req'd
A	sides	¾ *	31¼ × 20¼	2
B	doors	¾ #	27 × 18	1
C1	bottom	¾ *	32⅜ × 32⅜	1
E	back	¼ *	28 × 32⅝	2
F1	strip	¾ PLY	4 × 32⅜	3
F2	strip	¾ PLY	4 × 31⅝	2
F3	strip	¾ PLY	4 × 21¾	1
F5	strip	¾ PLY	4 × 31⅝	1
F6	strip	¾ PLY	4 × 14⅜	1
F7	strip	¾ PLY	4 × 22¼	1
F8	strip	¾ PLY	4 × 25⅜	1
F9	strip	¾ PLY	4 × 28⅜	1
O	door-mounting strip	¾ SL	3 × 25¾	1

*Material to match style. PLP for styles 1 and 2; HPW for style 3. Backs for styles 1 or 2 are VCP.

#Door materials to match style. PLP for styles 1 and 2. For style 3 use SL. Refer to bill of materials for 36″ bathroom-vanity double doors for sizes of style-3 door parts.

Material Key:

PLP = plastic laminate-covered particle board

VCP = vinyl-covered particle board

PLY = fir plywood

HPW = hardwood plywood

SL   = solid lumber

Notes:

Sides are handed. Make one left side and one right side.

To lay out angle on front corner of C1, measure 20″ from rear, along edges that attach to sides.

Door sizes are full size; if counter top has overhanging lip or if plastic T moulding is used, adjust door size.

If toe kick is not to be covered with base moulding, substitute PLP or HPW for PLY on F7.

When installing this corner module, it may be necessary to add a spacer between the sides of the corner module and the side of the adjacent cabinet to get sufficient door clearance.

Modular Cabinets

BILL OF MATERIALS
(All Dimensions Actual)

Style: 1
Type: Single-Door Overhead Long Corner Module
Size: 26¾″
Refer to: Illus. 222

Part	Description	Material	Size	No. Req'd
G	sides	¾ PLP	35 × 14	2
H	door	¾ PLP	28 × 18	1
I1	top	¾ PLP	26⅛ × 26⅛	1
J1	bottom	¾ PLP	26⅜ × 26⅜	1
L1	front filler	¾ PLP	7¼ × 19	1
M1	strip	¾ PLY	4 × 26⅛	1
M2	strip	¾ PLY	4 × 25⅜	1
M3	strip	¾ PLY	4 × 29½	1
N	back	¼ VCP	34⅝ × 26⅜	2
O	door-mounting strip	¾ SL	3 × 33½	1

Material Key:
PLP = plastic laminate-covered particle board
VCP = vinyl-covered particle board
PLY = fir plywood
SL   = solid lumber

Notes:
Sides are handed. Make one left side and one right side.

To lay out angle on front corner of J1, measure 14″ from rear, along edges that attach to sides. Use J1 to lay out I1.

Door sizes are full size.

When installing this corner module, it may be necessary to add a spacer between the sides of the corner module and the side of the adjacent cabinet to get sufficient door clearance.

Modular Cabinets

BILL OF MATERIALS
(All Dimensions Actual)

Style: 1
Type: Single-Door Overhead Short Corner Module
Size: 26¾″
Refer to: Illus. 222

Part	Description	Material	Size	No. Req'd
G	sides	¾ PLP	25 × 14	2
H	door	¾ PLP	18 × 18	1
I1	top	¾ PLP	26⅛ × 26⅛	1
J1	bottom	¾ PLP	26⅜ × 26⅜	1
L1	front filler	¾ PLP	7¼ × 19	1
M1	strip	¾ PLY	4 × 26⅛	1
M2	strip	¾ PLY	4 × 25⅜	1
M3	strip	¾ PLY	4 × 19½	1
N	back	¼ VCP	24⅝ × 26⅜	2
O	door-mounting strip	¾ SL	3 × 23½	1

Material Key:
PLP = plastic laminate-covered particle board
VCP = vinyl-covered particle board
PLY = fir plywood
SL = solid lumber

Notes:
Sides are handed. Make one left side and one right side.

To lay out angle on front corner of J1, measure 14″ from rear, along edges that attach to sides. Use J1 to lay out I1.

Door sizes are full size.

When installing this corner module, it may be necessary to add a spacer between the sides of the corner module and the side of the adjacent cabinet to get sufficient door clearance.

Modular Cabinets

BILL OF MATERIALS
(All Dimensions Actual)

Style: 2 & 3
Type: Single-Door Overhead Long Corner Module
Size: 26¾"
Refer to: Illus. 222

Part	Description	Material	Size	No. Req'd
G	sides	¾ *	30 × 14	2
H	door	¾ #	28 × 18	1
I1	top	¾ *	26⅛ × 26⅛	1
J1	bottom	¾ *	26⅜ × 26⅜	1
L1	front filler	¾ *	2¼ × 19	1
M1	strip	¾ PLY	4 × 26⅛	1
M2	strip	¾ PLY	4 × 25⅜	1
M3	strip	¾ PLY	4 × 24½	1
N	back	¼ *	29⅝ × 26⅜	2
O	door-mounting strip	¾ SL	3 × 28½	1

*Material to match style. PLP for style 2; HPW for style 3. Backs for style 3 are HPW.
#Door materials to match style. PLP for style 2. For style 3 use SL. Refer to bill of materials for 18″ overhead long module for sizes of style-3 door parts.

Material Key:

PLP = plastic laminate-covered particle board
PLY = fir plywood
HPW = hardwood plywood
SL = solid lumber

Notes:

Sides are handed. Make one left side and one right side.

To lay out angle on front corner of J1, measure 14″ from rear, along edges that attach to sides. Use J1 to lay out I1.

Door sizes are full size.

When installing this corner module, it may be necessary to add a spacer between the sides of the corner module and the side of the adjacent cabinet to get sufficient door clearance.

Modular Cabinets

BILL OF MATERIALS
(All Dimensions Actual)

Style: 2 & 3
Type: Single-Door Overhead Short Corner Module
Size: 26¾″
Refer to: Illus. 222

Part	Description	Material	Size	No. Req'd
G	sides	¾ *	20 × 14	2
H	door	¾ #	18 × 18	1
I1	top	¾ *	26⅛ × 26⅛	1
J1	bottom	¾ *	26⅜ × 26⅜	1
L1	front filler	¾ *	2¼ × 19	1
M1	strip	¾ PLY	4 × 26⅛	1
M2	strip	¾ PLY	4 × 25⅜	1
M3	strip	¾ PLY	4 × 14½	1
N	back	¼ *	19⅝ × 26⅜	2
O	door-mounting strip	¾ SL	3 × 18½	1

*Material to match style. PLP for style 2; HPW for style 3. Backs for style 3 are HPW.
#Door materials to match style. PLP for style 2. For style 3 use SL. Refer to bill of materials for 18″ overhead short module for sizes of style-3 door parts.

Material Key:

PLP = plastic laminate-covered particle board
VCP = vinyl-covered particle board
PLY = fir plywood
HPW = hardwood plywood
SL = solid lumber

Notes:

Sides are handed. Make one left side and one right side.

To lay out angle on front corner of J1, measure 14″ from rear, along edges that attach to sides. Use J1 to lay out I1.

Door sizes are full size.

When installing this corner module, it may be necessary to add a spacer between the sides of the corner module and the side of the adjacent cabinet to get sufficient door clearance.

Modular Cabinets

BILL OF MATERIALS
(All Dimensions Actual)

Style: All
Type: Corner Appliance Garage
Size: 26¾″
Refer to: Illus. 223

Part	Description	Material	Size	No. Req'd
G1	sides	¾ *	24 × 14	2
H	door	¾ #	23¾ × 18	1
I1	top	¾ *	26 × 26	1
N1	back	¾ *	24 × 26⅜	1
N2	back	¾ *	24 × 25⅝	1
O	door-mounting strip	¾ SL	3 × 23¼	1

*Material to match style. PLP for style 1 and 2; HPW for style 3.
#Door materials to match style. PLP for style 2. For style 3 use SL. Refer to bill of materials for 18″ overhead long module for sizes of style-3 door parts. Change length of part V to 24¾″. Change length of part X to 20½″.

Material Key:

PLP = plastic laminate-covered particle board
HPW = hardwood plywood
SL = solid lumber

Notes:

Sides are handed. Make one left side and one right side.

To lay out angle on front corner of I1, measure 13¼″ from rear, along edges that attach to sides.

Door sizes are full size.

Sizes are to fit 24″ spacing between counter top and overhead cabinets.

Modular Cabinets

BILL OF MATERIALS
(All Dimensions Actual)

Style: All
Type: Roll-Top Appliance Garage
Size: All
Refer to: Illus. 224

Part	Description	Material	Size	No. Req'd
G2	sides	¾ *	24 × 14	2
L2	strips	¾ SL	2 × A	2
N3	back	¾ *	21 × A	1
Y	pull strip	¾ SL	1 × A	1
Z	tambour strips	¼ SL	¾ × A	36

*Material to match style. PLP for style 1 and 2; HPW for style 3.
A = overall width minus ¾"

Material Key:

PLP = plastic laminate-covered particle board
HPW = hardwood plywood
SL = solid lumber

Notes:

Sides are handed. Make one left side and one right side.

Sizes are to fit 24" spacing between counter top and overhead cabinets.

APPENDIX: BUILT-IN PLANNER

This planner is designed to help you visualize how a completed built-in cabinet installation will look and to give you the opportunity to try various layouts on paper. It is specifically designed for use with the modular cabinet system described in Chapter 11, but it will be helpful in the planning of any built-in cabinet installation.

You can use the planner to produce three types of plans: a front elevation that depicts one wall (Illus. 241), an oblique projection that adds a three-dimensional quality to one wall (Illus. 242), or a modified oblique view that depicts up to three walls in a single view (Illus. 243).

The first step in planning the installation is to decide on the basic layout. If you are designing a kitchen, it would be a good idea to consult a book on kitchen design for information on traffic flow, work areas, and appliance layout. To determine the basic layout for any modular cabinet system, accurately measure the area that is available for the cabinets. Make a rough sketch, showing the dimensions and indicating the possible positions for appliances. Once you have this information, you can begin to put the planner to use.

Using the Planner

The planner consists of a layout grid (Illus. 250) and a set of scale drawings of the various sizes of cabinet modules described in Chapter 11 (Illus. 244–247). There is also a set of drawings of a few common appliances (Illus. 248 and 249).

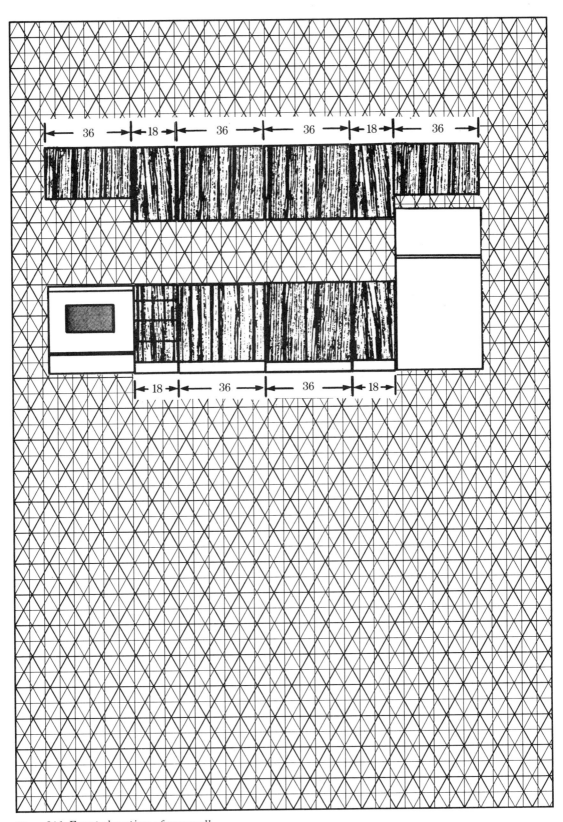

Illus. 241. Front elevation of one wall.

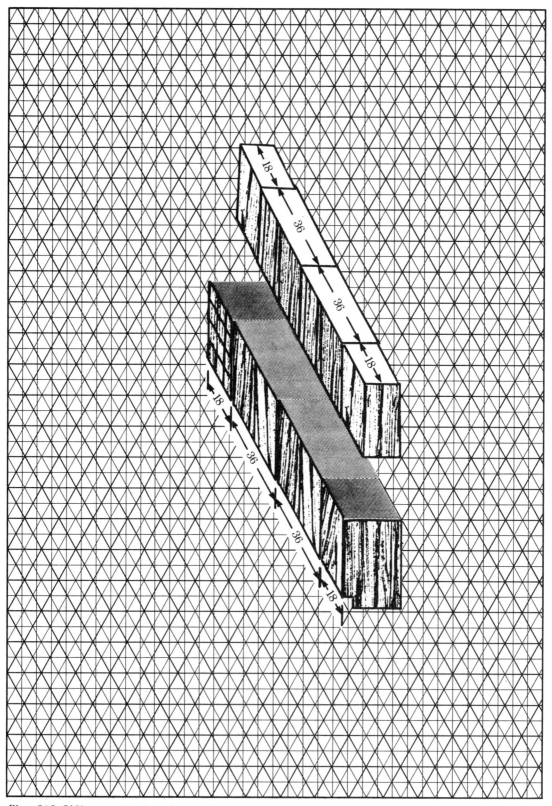

Illus. 242. Oblique projection of one wall.

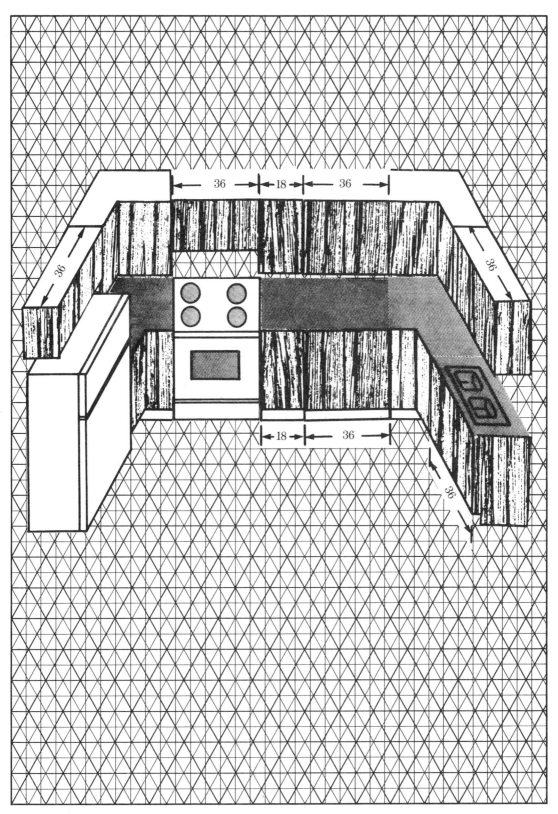

Illus. 243. Complete three-wall view.

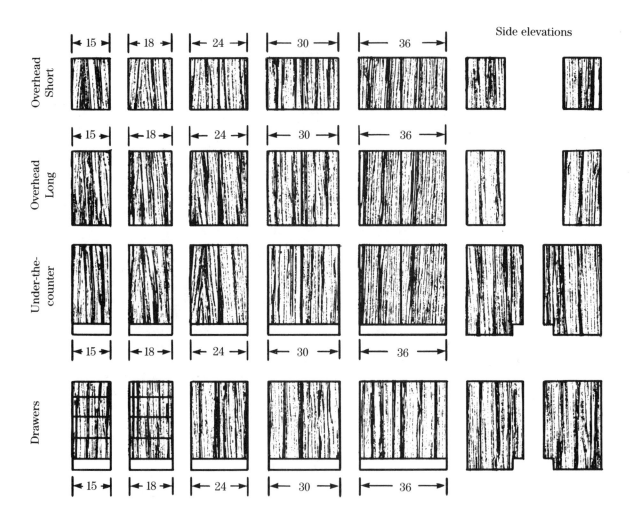

Illus. 244. Front elevations.

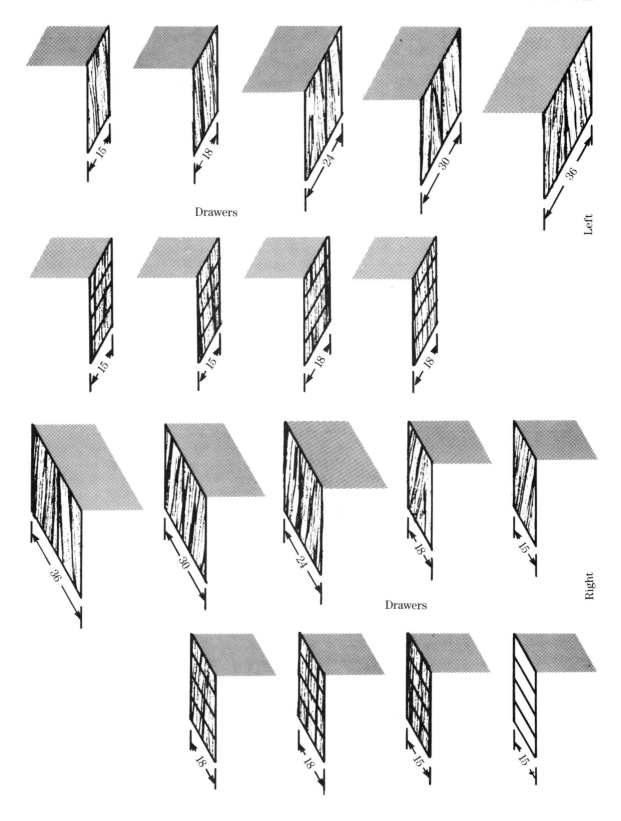

Illus. 245. Under-the-counter modules (oblique).

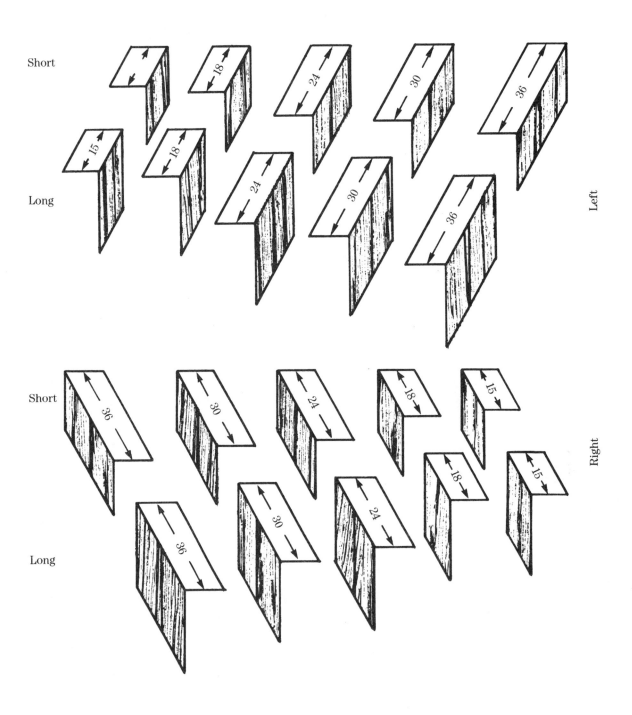

Illus. 246. Overhead modules (oblique).

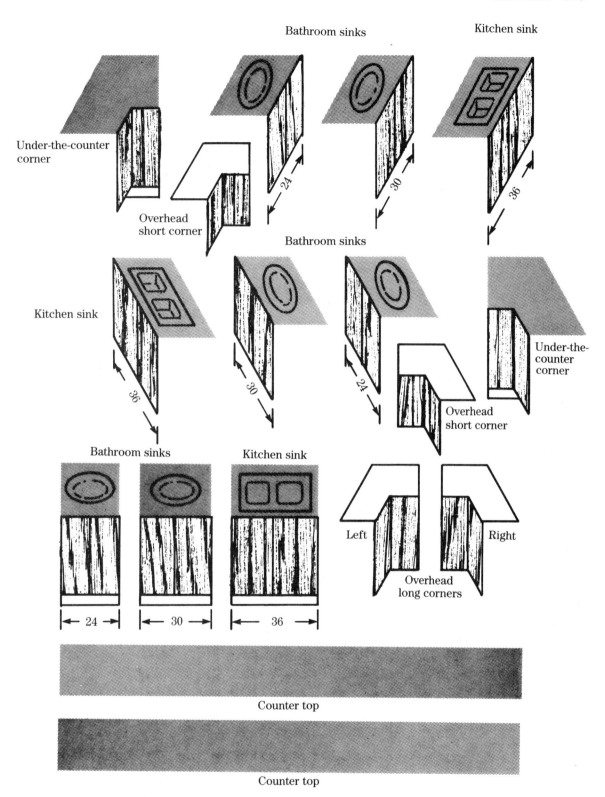

Illus. 247. Sink and corner modules (oblique).

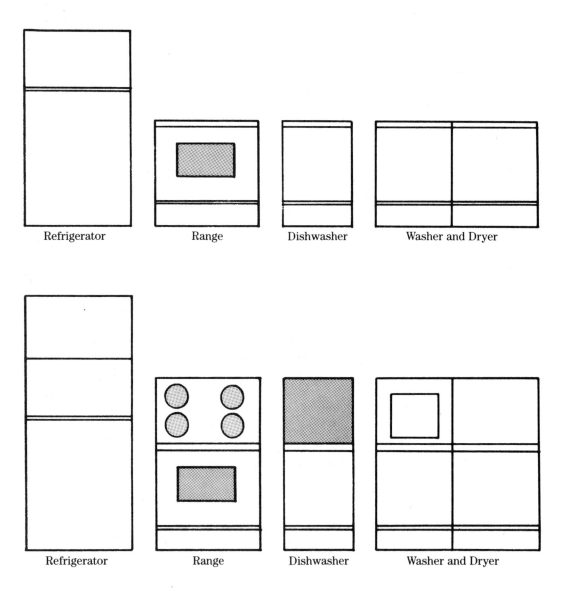

Illus. 248. Appliances (front elevation).

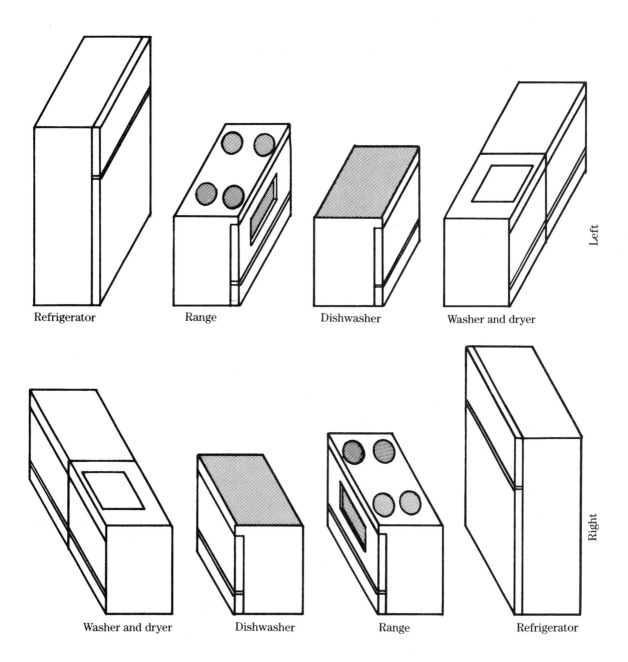

Refrigerator   Range   Dishwasher   Washer and dryer

Left

Washer and dryer   Dishwasher   Range   Refrigerator

Right

Illus. 249. Appliances (oblique).

Illus. 250. Built-in planner layout grid.

The first step in using the planner is to make a front elevation of each wall. Since you will probably need more copies of the cabinet modules than the amount included in this book, it's a good idea to make several photocopies of the pages you will need; also make as many copies of the layout grid as you will need to complete the set of plans. The layout grid is large enough to handle most average-sized installations; but if you are planning a very large installation, you may need to tape two copies of the layout grid together.

Use the measurements you indicated on your rough sketch to draw an outline of the first wall on the layout grid. The layout grid is divided into small squares; each square equals 6″. At this point, use only the vertical and horizontal lines and ignore the diagonal lines. There is a scale at the bottom of the page. Cut it out and use it to measure the outline of the wall. This scale operates in the same way as the architect's scale described in Chapter 2.

Next, cut out the front elevations of the appliances that you intend to place on that wall. Lay them on the layout grid and try them in various locations until you are satisfied. With the appliances in position, you can now determine the size of the cabinet modules that you can use. The purpose of the appliance drawings is to indicate the usual clearance allowed in a cabinet installation for a particular appliance. If you plan on using especially large appliances, such as a side-by-side refrigerator/freezer, be sure to check on the actual size of the appliance. If you are using smaller appliances, it is usually a good idea to allow the normal clearance anyway so that you can change to full-size appliances at a later date.

Use the scale provided to measure the distance between the appliances; then look over the different-sized modules shown on the front elevation illustration and decide on a combination that will fit. You may want to move an appliance one way or another to make the modules come out even. Now cut out the modules you have chosen and lay them on the layout grid. At this point you can look at your design and decide if it is right; you may want to move things around until you are more satisfied. If the cabinets must fit tightly between two walls, it is unlikely that the standard-module sizes will come out even. Chapter 11 describes how to use filler strips or corner modules to adjust the size. On the planner, try to arrange the modules so that the size of the filler strips is as small as possible; then cut the picture of a larger-size module to the appropriate size and place it where the filler should go.

When you are satisfied with the layout, you can make it permanent by gluing the cutouts to the layout grid. A glue stick or rubber cement works well. Illus. 241 shows what a completed front elevation looks like. If the installation consists of more than one wall, make a front elevation for each wall.

After making the front elevations, you can use the planner to add a three-dimensional quality that will give you a better idea of how the completed installation will look. If only one wall is involved, you can make an oblique projection of a single wall, as shown in Illus. 242. This is not the usual type of oblique projection that's described in Chapter 2, but it gives you the impression of standing off to the side of the cabinets looking down the length of the room.

To make this view, decide whether you want it to be on the right or left side of the page. The cutouts on the oblique illustrations are labelled *left* and *right*. Cut out the same-size appliances and cabinet modules from the oblique illustrations that you used in the front elevation. Arrange them on the layout grid the same way you did for the front elevation—only this time, align them with the diagonal lines. Cut out the sides from the front elevation illustration to fill in the ends of the cabinets.

This planner is especially useful for installations that involve more than one wall. In most types of drawings, you can't see the front surface of three walls in a single view; but this planner uses a modified type of oblique drawing that is similar to a perspective drawing. The drawings are not true perspective drawings since all of the modules appear the same size instead of getting smaller as the distance from the viewpoint increases. This means that the completed drawing won't have the depth of a perspective drawing, but it will still give you a fairly good idea of what the completed room will look like. This is a major advantage because it is much easier to change a feature you don't like while it is on paper than it is to change it after the cabinets are installed.

Illus. 243 shows a complete plan, including all three walls of the installation. To make a plan like this one, start with the longest wall. Make a front elevation of this wall the same way as described earlier, except use the appliances and sink modules that include a top view. Next, cut out a strip of counter top and place it along the top of the under-the-counter cabinets. Where the cabinets join at a corner, use one of the special corner cutouts. One point to keep in mind when designing cabinets that meet at a corner is that the under-the-counter cabinets extend out from the wall farther than the overhead cabinets. This can affect the way the fronts of the upper and lower cabinets line up. If you want the doors on the upper cabinets to line up with the doors on the lower cabinets, you will have to add an additional cabinet or spacer at the ends of the overhead cabinets to compensate for the difference in the projection from the wall between the upper and lower cabinets.

After the corners are in place, use the oblique cutouts to make the other two walls in the same manner as described earlier for an oblique drawing of a single wall. Use the cutouts labelled *left* on the left side of the page and those labelled *right* on the right side of the page.

If you are satisfied with the layout you have produced, the final step is to make a full-size story stick. For small installations, the story stick can be a long scrap of plywood. For larger installations, place masking tape on the floor of the room parallel to the walls that will receive the cabinets, or place the masking tape on the floor of your shop. Make marks on the stick or tape that indicate the exact length of one wall. Refer to the front elevation for that wall and make marks for the exact sizes of each module or appliance. When you have marked all of the modules on the story stick, you can measure directly from the end of the last module to the wall mark to get the exact size of the filler or nonstandard-sized module needed to fit the available space. The story stick also lets you double-check your layout at full scale so that you can see exactly how far a walk it will be from the sink to the refrigerator.

If everything works out on the story stick, make a list of all of the modules you need and then go to Chapter 11 for instructions on building them.

METRIC EQUIVALENTS
INCHES TO MILLIMETRES AND CENTIMETRES

MM—millimetres   *CM—centimetres*

Inches	MM	CM	Inches	CM	Inches	CM	Inches	MM	CM	Inches	CM	Inches	CM
1/8	3	0.3	9	22.9	30	76.2	2	51	5.1	20	50.8	41	104.1
1/4	6	0.6	10	25.4	31	78.7	2½	64	6.4	21	53.3	42	106.7
3/8	10	1.0	11	27.9	32	81.3	3	76	7.6	22	55.9	43	109.2
½	13	1.3	12	30.5	33	83.8	3½	89	8.9	23	58.4	44	111.8
5/8	16	1.6	13	33.0	34	86.4	4	102	10.2	24	61.0	45	114.3
3/4	19	1.9	14	35.6	35	88.9	4½	114	11.4	25	63.5	46	116.8
7/8	22	2.2	15	38.1	36	91.4	5	127	12.7	26	66.0	47	119.4
1	25	2.5	16	40.6	37	94.0	6	152	15.2	27	68.6	48	121.9
1¼	32	3.2	17	43.2	38	96.5	7	178	17.8	28	71.1	49	124.5
1½	38	3.8	18	45.7	39	99.1	8	203	20.3	29	73.7	50	127.0
1¾	44	4.4	19	48.3	40	101.6							

ABOUT THE AUTHOR

Sam Allen began building custom cabinets for friends and relatives while he was still in high school. In his senior year, he was chosen to represent his school in a statewide industrial arts competition. He earned money for college by building cabinets for a local unfinished-furniture store.

After graduating from Brigham Young University with a Bachelor of Science degree in Industrial Education, he worked as a carpenter and cabinetmaker, gaining experience in both custom and mass-production cabinetmaking techniques.

His appreciation of hand-tool techniques and antique reproductions began with his study of the cabinets and furniture produced by the early settlers of his native state, Utah. The dry climate of Utah tends to exaggerate problems caused by wood movement; this has led Mr. Allen to extensively study and experiment with techniques that will minimize these problems.

Mr. Allen is a widely published free-lance writer. He is the author of the book, *Wood Finisher's Handbook*, and he has had numerous articles in magazines, such as *Popular Mechanics*, *The Woodworker's Journal*, *Fine Woodworking*, and *Popular Woodworker*.

INDEX